MASSACHUSETTS
Real Estate
PRACTICE & LAW

Anita C. Hill, CRB, CBR, CAI, QSC, ASR

SEVENTH EDITION

Dearborn™
Real Estate Education

President: Roy Lipner
Vice President of Product Development & Publishing: Evan M. Butterfield
Managing Editor: Kate DeVivo
Senior Development Editor: Tony Peregrin
Director of Production: Daniel Frey
Senior Managing Editor, Production: Jack Kiburz
Creative Director: Lucy Jenkins
Typesetter: Caitlin Ostrow

Published by Dearborn™ Real Estate Education
30 South Wacker Drive
Chicago, Illinois 60606-7481
312-836-4400
www.dearbornRE.com

Printed in the United States of America

07   08   09   10   9   8   7   6   5   4   3   2

Library of Congress Cataloging-in-Publication Data

Hill, Anita C.
   Massachusetts real estate : practice & law / Anita C. Hill. — 7th ed.
     p. cm.
   Includes index.
   ISBN-13: 978-1-4195-9683-4
   ISBN-10: 1-4195-9683-7
   1.   Real estate business—Law and legislation—Massachusetts. 2.   Vendors and purchasers—Massachusetts. 3.   Real property—Massachusetts. 4.   Real estate business—Massachusetts.   I. Title.
   KF2042.R4 G34 2007 Massachusetts 2
   346.74404'37—dc22
                                              2007005944

Contents

Preface

Massachusetts Real Estate: Practice & Law is a key component of Dearborn™ Real Estate Education's complete real estate principles learning system. This system offers students and educators a complete turnkey package for prelicense real estate courses, continuing education, and professional enrichment. As the demographics and structure of the real estate industry change, Dearborn™ Real Estate Education is helping students, instructors, and practitioners adapt to this new industry environment by providing more accessible and versatile educational tools.

The purpose of *Massachusetts Real Estate: Practice & Law* is to highlight the *unique* aspects of the real estate business as it is practiced in Massachusetts. Questions that may be used for both testing and comprehension of the material follow each chapter. These questions are prepared in a format similar to the Massachusetts Real Estate License Examination. The Answer Key for the questions is included at the end of the book. After completing each chapter you should be certain that you can answer each question correctly before proceeding to the next chapter.

Both Massachusetts specific and general real estate law and practice are included in the licensing examination. Students need to be thoroughly familiar with the material contained in this book *and* any of the following principles books or software:

- Modern Real Estate Practice
- Mastering Real Estate Principles
- Real Estate Fundamentals
- National Real Estate Principles

■ HOW TO USE THIS BOOK

The conversion table on the next page provides a quick and easy reference for using *Massachusetts Real Estate: Practice & Law* in conjunction with various principles books. For instance, *Massachusetts Real Estate: Practice & Law* Chapter 2, "Seller and Buyer Representation Agreements," may be read in conjunction with Chapter 6 in *Modern Real Estate Practice*, 17th Edition; Chapter 7 and Chapter 8 in *Real Estate Fundamentals*, 7th Edition; Chapter 15 in *Mastering Real Estate Principles*, 4th Edition; and Unit 22 in *National Real Estate Principles* software. The chart also provides students with a useful reference to the *Guide to Passing the PSI Real Estate Exam*, 4th Edition, by Lawrence Sager.

Chapter Conversion Table

Massachusetts Real Estate: Practice & Law, 7th Edition		Modern Real Estate Practice, 17th Edition	Real Estate Fundamentals, 7th Edition	Mastering Real Estate Principles, 4th Edition	National Real Estate Principles Version 2.0	Guide to Passing the Promissor Exam, 8th Edition
1.	Real Estate Brokerage	4, 5	7	13	4, 5	7
2.	Seller and Buyer Representation Agreements	6	7, 8	15	6	4
3.	Interests in Real Estate	7	3	7	7	3, 8
4.	Forms of Real Estate Ownership	8	5	9	8	1
5.	Legal Descriptions	9	2	6	9	1
6.	Real Estate Taxes and Other Liens	10	10	5, 25	10	2
7.	Real Estate Contracts	11	8	14	11	4
8.	Transfer of Title	12	4	10	12	2
9.	Title Records	13	6	11	13	—
10.	Massachusetts Real Estate License Laws	—	—	16	—	—
11.	Real Estate Financing: Principles and Practice	14, 15	12, 13	Unit VII	14, 15	6
12.	Leases	16	9	8	16	7
13.	Real Estate Appraisal	18	11	Unit VI	18	3
14.	Land-Use Controls and Property Development	19	14	3	19	2
15.	Fair Housing and Ethical Practices	20	15	17	20	5, 7
16.	Environmental Issues and the Real Estate Transaction	21	16	3	—	2

Acknowledgments

The publisher would like to thank Robert Sawyer, Craig Tattan, and Jody O'Brien. These individuals provided vital professional guidance and expertise from which everyone benefits.

Thanks also goes to attorney Steve Ryan, counsel for the Massachusetts Association of REALTORS®, for his tireless efforts in helping us secure forms, and permissions to use those forms, in this edition.

■ ABOUT THE AUTHOR

Anita C. Hill, CRB, CBR, CAI, QSC, ASR, is the owner of Anita Hill Training & Seminars and has spent the past 28 years establishing her credentials in the field of real estate with an emphasis on training and education. She provides training to a variety of organizations and companies throughout New England. She has been a guest speaker at several Massachusetts Association of REALTORS® conventions and education conferences. Anita is one of two instructors in Massachusetts for the Certified Buyers Representative (CBR) course. She is also an instructor for the Accredited Sellers Representative (ASR) course and for continuing education classes throughout Massachusetts.

As the former Director of Professional Development for Carlson GMAC Real Estate, she developed, coordinated, and supervised an educational curriculum for a 1,400-agent company in four training locations. She is a current member of the Board of Registration of Real Estate Brokers and Salesperson License School and Instructor Approval Review Committee, as well as a member of the Northeast Association of REALTORS®, the Massachusetts Association of REALTORS®, the National Association of REALTORS®, and Real Estate Educators Association (REEA). Most notably, she worked as the consulting editor of the 6th edition of *Massachusetts Practice and Law.*

Preparing for the Real Estate License Examination

In Massachusetts, as in most other states, the real estate profession is regulated. *Regulation* means that the state of Massachusetts, through the Board of Registration of Real Estate Brokers and Salespersons, has established certain standards for real estate professionals. As a broker or salesperson, you will be expected to be aware of those standards and to comply with them. You are already complying with Massachusetts General Law, Chapter 112, Section 87SS by taking an approved prelicense real estate course. Your next step will probably be to take the state licensing exam.

The Massachusetts Real Estate License Examination tests your knowledge of general and state-specific real estate principles and practices—knowledge you will need as a real estate broker or salesperson. Can you locate and identify a property from the legal description on the deed? Can you explain to your client the difference between real estate and personal property? Are you aware of your responsibilities as an agent and of your ethical and legal duties to both buyers and sellers? The Board of Registration needs to determine the extent of your real estate knowledge to find out whether you meet the standard expected of real estate professionals in Massachusetts.

■ ABOUT THE MASSACHUSETTS REAL ESTATE LICENSE EXAMINATION

The Promissor Format

The Massachusetts Real Estate License Examination is prepared and administered by an independent testing service, Promissor, Inc. (formerly ASI), under the supervision of the Massachusetts Board of Real Estate Brokers and Salespersons. Promissor offers licensing exams nationwide, but each exam is adapted to local real estate laws and practices and the priorities of the state's licensing agency. All questions are multiple choice, and the test is completely automated—you'll get your results on the spot. The examinations for both brokers and salespersons are given in two parts. The first section on either examination is called the *Uniform Test* and consists of 80 general real estate questions on which your scaled score of 70 will be based. (70 is the passing score, and scores can range from 1 to 100.) Most of those questions will determine your score, while at least 5 questions, scattered throughout the exam, are being tested by Promissor for future use. Therefore, carefully answer all questions because you do not know which of the 80 questions count toward your score. The future test questions do not affect your score in any way. The second section, the *State Test*, consists of approximately 30 questions on Massachusetts law and practice on which your scaled score of 70 will be based. Here, too, an additional 5 to 8 questions are test questions and will not count toward your score. Answer all questions carefully—30 questions on which your score will be based, plus 5 to

10 uncounted test questions. Candidates who pass one portion of the examination and fail the other need retake only the portion they failed. The failed portion must be successfully completed within two years from the completion date on the Education Certification Form.

Following is a description of the examination content for real estate salespersons, brokers, and affiliate brokers.

General Exam

The general exam covers the following topics:

- Real property definitions, characteristics, ownership, transfer, and restrictions (sales: 20 percent—16 questions; brokers:19 percent—15 questions)
- Assessing and explaining property valuation and the property appraisal process (sales and brokers: 8 percent—6 questions)
- Agency relationships with buyers and sellers, and contracts, (sales and brokers: 26 percent—21 questions)
- Disclosures and property conditions (sales and brokers: 8 percent—6 questions)
- Real estate activities governed by Federal Laws such as Federal Fair Housing Act, ADA, Antitrust, marketing controls (sales: 8 percent—6 questions; brokers: 10 percent—8 questions)
- Financing components and settlement (sales: 21 percent—17 questions; brokers: 18 percent—14 questions)
- Leases, rents, and property management (sales and brokers: 8 percent—6 questions)
- Operating a Real Estate Brokerage (sales: 3 percent—2 questions; brokers: 5 percent—4 questions)

Massachusetts Exam

The Massachusetts-specific section of the exam tests the following topics:

- Duties and powers of the Board of Registration of Real Estate Brokers and Salespersons (5 percent—1 to 2 questions)
- Licensing requirements (10 percent—3 questions)
- Requirements governing licensees (45 percent—13 to 14 questions)
- Additional topics, including landlord/tenant issues, Massachusetts fair housing law, property taxes, zoning and land-use regulations, condominiums, cooperatives, time-shares, Massachusetts Consumer Protection law, and environmental issues (40 percent—12 questions)

The Promissor approach to testing is designed to test your reasoning process as well as your real estate knowledge. The examination includes questions on general real estate information and the Massachusetts Real Estate License Law and Rules and Regulations, as well as math problems and several kinds of comprehension problems.

While the Massachusetts Real Estate License Examination is designed to find out how much you know, it also is designed to find out how well you can think and apply your knowledge in appropriate situations. Many of these questions involve reading comprehension: Can you read a statement or form and answer questions based on what you have read? Other questions involve reading comprehension in combination with application: Can you read a selection or problem and answer questions based on what you have read and what you know about certain real estate principles?

Throughout this book you will find multiple-choice questions that follow the chapter sections. These questions are in the Promissor test format. This format presents the question and four possible answers in a straightforward manner. There is only one correct answer to each question.

Math

Math problems relating to real estate transactions make up approximately 10 percent of the general portion of the examination. You may use a silent, hand-held, *battery-operated* calculator during the broker's and salesperson's license examinations.

The problems you will be asked to solve deal with the following subjects:

- Financing
- Tax Assessment
- Commissions
- Area Calculations
- Settlement Statement
- Profit and Loss
- Tax Ramifications

■ RELATED WEB SITES

License Testing Corporation, Promissor   *www.promissor.com*

Massachusetts Association of REALTORS®   *www.marealtor.com*

Massachusetts Board of Registration of Real Estate Brokers and Salespersons *www.mass.gov/dpl/boards/re*

Real Estate Brokerage

■ NATURE OF THE BROKERAGE BUSINESS

Brokers and Salespersons

Massachusetts law distinguishes between two types of real estate professionals: real estate brokers and real estate salespersons.

The statutory definition of a **real estate broker** is "any person who for another person and for a fee, commission, or other valuable consideration, or with the intention or in the expectation or upon the promise of receiving or collecting a fee, commission, or other valuable consideration, does any of the following: sells, exchanges, purchases, rents or leases, or negotiates, or offers, attempts or agrees to negotiate the sale, exchange, purchase, rental, or leasing of any real estate, or lists or offers, attempts or agrees to list any real estate, or advertises or holds himself or herself out as engaged in the business of selling, exchanging, purchasing, renting, or leasing real estate, or assists or directs in the procuring of prospects or the negotiation or completion of any agreement or transaction that results or is intended to result in the sale, exchange, purchase, leasing, or renting of any real estate."

The statutory definition of a **real estate salesperson** is identical to that of a broker, except that a salesperson does not engage in completing the negotiation of agreements or transactions that result or are intended to result in the sale, exchange, purchase, rental, or lease of any real estate.

In Massachusetts, no salesperson may conduct or operate his or her own real estate business. All salespersons are required to affiliate with only one broker at a time, either as an employee or independent contractor, and the broker must approve any transaction entered into by the salesperson. Salespersons are not entitled to commissions from anyone other than the broker who holds his or her license. Brokers are responsible for regulatory violations by their salespersons.

Because of the relationship between brokers and salespersons in Massachusetts, we will refer only to "brokers" throughout this Chapter. Readers should understand, however, that the term "broker" as used in this Chapter includes salespersons as well.

■ THE LAW OF AGENCY

The relationship between the principal and the agent results from a contract of employment. In such a contract, the principal gives the agent authority to act on the principal's behalf, and the agent consents to that authority. Generally this "hiring" may be oral, although good practice involves the use of a signed listing contract.

Because buyers of real estate often do not understand the law of agency, and typically believe that the person who drives them around town showing them properties is "their" agent, a disclosure requirement exists that requires each broker to have consumers sign the Massachusetts Mandatory Licensee-Consumer Relationship Disclosure form at the *first personal meeting*. (See Figure 1.1.)

This form was designed to make the consumer aware of the different types of relationships available, to provide choices to the consumer, and to require real estate licensees to disclose their relationship to the prospective purchaser or seller of real estate at the first personal meeting.

The Massachusetts Mandatory Licensee-Consumer Relationship Disclosure form that became effective July 1, 2005, defines the types of relationships that may exist between a licensee and a consumer and are explained on the back of the form. They are seller's agent, buyer's agent, facilitator (nonagent), designated seller's and buyer's agent, and disclosed dual agent. The front of the disclosure form describes the relationship the licensee has with others in their firm. This disclosure of a company's business model lets the consumer know whether everyone in the firm represents the consumer (Traditional Agency firm) or only the agent identified along with the principal broker represents the consumer (Designated Agency firm).

Seller's Agent

A seller who engages the services of a listing broker is the broker's client, and the broker is the **seller's agent**. The broker/agent owes the seller/principal the traditional *fiduciary responsibilities* of Obedience, Loyalty, Disclosure, Confidentiality, Accountability, and Reasonable care (the acronym "OLDCAR") and must put the seller's lawful interests ahead of all others. The seller's agent must negotiate the best possible price and terms for the seller.

FIGURE 1.1

Sample Massachusetts Mandatory Licensee-Consumer Relationship Disclosure Form

MASSACHUSETTS MANDATORY LICENSEE-CONSUMER RELATIONSHIP DISCLOSURE

This disclosure is provided to you, the consumer, by the real estate agent listed on this form. Make sure you read both sides of this form. The reverse side contains a more detailed description of the different types of relationships available to you. This is not a contract.

THE TIME WHEN THE LICENSEE MUST PROVIDE THIS NOTICE TO THE CONSUMER:

All real estate licensees must present this form to you at the first personal meeting with you to discuss a specific property. The licensee can represent you as the seller (Seller's Agent) or represent you as the buyer (Buyer's Agent) and also can assist you as a facilitator.

CONSUMER INFORMATION AND RESPONSIBILITY:

Whether you are the buyer or seller you can choose to have the advice, assistance and representation of your own agent who works for you. **Do not assume that a real estate agent works solely for you unless you have an agreement for that relationship.** With your consent, licensees from the same firm may represent a buyer and seller in the same transaction. These agents are referred to as dual agents.

Also a buyer and seller may be represented by agents in the same real estate firm as designated agents. The "designated seller or buyer agent" is your sole representative. However where *both* the seller and buyer provide written consent to have a designated agent represent them then the agent making such designation becomes a "dual agent" for the buyer and seller. All real estate agents must, by law, present properties honestly and accurately. They must also disclose known material defects in the real estate.

The duties of a real estate agent do not relieve the consumers of the responsibility to protect their own interests. If you need advice for legal, tax, insurance or land survey matters it is your responsibility to consult a professional in those areas. Real Estate agents do not have a duty to perform home, lead paint or insect inspections nor do they perform septic system, wetlands or environmental evaluations.

RELATIONSHIP OF REAL ESTATE LICENSEE WITH THE CONSUMER

(Check one)   ____ **Seller's agent**   ____ **Buyer's agent**   ____ **Facilitator**

IF A SELLER'S OR BUYER'S AGENT IS CHECKED ABOVE COMPLETE THE SECTION BELOW:

Relationship with others affiliated with _____
                                                    (Print name of real estate firm or business and license number)

(Check one)   ____ The real estate agent listed below, the real estate firm or business listed above and all other affiliated agents have the same relationship with the consumer named herein **(seller or buyer agency, not designated agency).**

____ Only the real estate agent listed below represents the consumer named in this form **(designated seller or buyer agency).** In this situation any firm or business listed above and other agents affiliated with the firm or business do not represent you and may represent another party in your real estate transaction.

By signing below I, the real estate licensee, acknowledge that this disclosure has been provided timely to the consumer named herein.

_____   _____   _____   _____
(Signature of real estate agent)   (Printed name of real estate agent)   (License Number/Type)   (Today's Date)

By signing below I, the consumer, acknowledge that I have received and read the information in this disclosure.

_____   _____   _____
(Signature of consumer)   (Printed name of consumer)   (Today's Date)

_____   _____   _____
(Signature of consumer)   (Printed name of consumer)   (Today's Date)

____ Check here if the consumer declines to sign this notice.

Massachusetts Association of REALTORS 256 Second Ave, Waltham MA 02451
Phone: 7818903700   Fax: 7818904919   MAR

Form No. 705
sdf.zfx

Produced with ZipForm™ by RE FormsNet, LLC 18025 Fifteen Mile Road, Clinton Township, Michigan 48035   www.zipform.com

F I G U R E 1.1 (Continued)

Sample Massachusetts Mandatory Licensee-Consumer Relationship Disclosure Form

TYPES OF AGENCY REPRESENTATION

SELLER'S AGENT

A seller can engage the services of a real estate agent to sell his property (called the listing agent) and the real estate agent is then the agent for the seller who becomes the agent's client. This means that the real estate agent represents the seller. The agent owes the seller undivided loyalty, reasonable care, disclosure, obedience to lawful instruction, confidentiality and accountability, provided, however, that the agent must disclose known material defects in the real estate. The agent must put the seller's interests first and negotiate for the best price and terms for their client, the seller. (The seller may authorize sub-agents to represent him/her in marketing its property to buyers, however the seller should be aware that wrongful action by the real estate agent or sub-agents may subject the seller to legal liability for those wrongful actions).

BUYER'S AGENT

A buyer can engage the services of a real estate agent to purchase property and the real estate agent is then the agent for the buyer who becomes the agent's client. This means that the real estate agent represents the buyer. The agent owes the buyer undivided loyalty, reasonable care, disclosure, obedience to lawful instruction, confidentiality and accountability, provided, however, that the agent must disclose known material defects in the real estate. The agent must put the buyer's interests first and negotiate for the best price and terms for their client, the buyer. (The buyer may also authorize sub-agents to represent him/her in purchasing property, however the buyer should be aware that wrongful action by the real estate agent or sub-agents may subject the buyer to legal liability for those wrongful actions).

(NON-AGENT) FACILITATOR

When a real estate agent works as a facilitator that agent assists the seller and buyer in reaching an agreement but does not represent either the seller or buyer in the transaction. The facilitator and the broker with whom the facilitator is affiliated owe the seller and buyer a duty to present each property honestly and accurately by disclosing known material defects about the property and owe a duty to account for funds. Unless otherwise agreed, the facilitator has no duty to keep information received from a seller or buyer confidential. The role of facilitator applies only to the seller and buyer in the particular property transaction involving the seller and buyer. Should the seller and buyer expressly agree a facilitator relationship can be changed to become an exclusive agency relationship with either the seller or the buyer.

DESIGNATED SELLER'S AND BUYER'S AGENT

A real estate agent can be designated by another real estate agent (the appointing or designating agent) to represent either the buyer or seller, provided the buyer or seller expressly agrees to such designation. The real estate agent once so designated is then the agent for either the buyer or seller who becomes their client. The designated agent owes the buyer or seller undivided loyalty, reasonable care, disclosure, obedience to lawful instruction, confidentiality and accountability, provided, however, that the agent must disclose known material defects in the real estate. The agent must put their client's interests first and negotiate for the best price and terms for their client. In situations where the appointing agent designates another agent to represent the seller and an agent to represent the buyer then the appointing agent becomes a dual agent. Consequently a dual agent cannot satisfy fully the duties of loyalty, full disclosure, obedience to lawful instructions which is required of an exclusive seller or buyer agent. The dual agent does not represent either the buyer or the seller solely only your designated agent represents your interests. The written consent for designated agency must contain the information provided for in the regulations of the Massachusetts Board of Registration of Real Estate Brokers and Salespeople (Board). A sample designated agency consent is available at the Board's website at www.mass.gov/dpl/re.

DUAL AGENT

A real estate agent may act as a dual agent representing both the seller and buyer in a transaction but only with the express and informed consent of both the seller and buyer. Written consent to dual agency must be obtained by the real estate agent prior to the execution of an offer to purchase a specific property. A dual agent shall be neutral with regard to any conflicting interest of the seller and buyer. Consequently a dual agent cannot satisfy fully the duties of loyalty, full disclosure, obedience to lawful instructions which is required of an exclusive seller or buyer agent. A dual agent does, however, still owe a duty of confidentiality of material information and accounting for funds. The written consent for dual agency must contain the information provided for in the regulations of the Massachusetts Board of Registration of Real Estate Brokers and Salespeople (Board). A sample dual agency consent is available at the Board's website at www.mass.gov/dpl/re.

Buyer's Agent

A buyer who engages the services of a broker becomes the broker's client, and the broker is the **buyer's agent**. The broker/agent owes the buyer/principal the traditional fiduciary responsibilities of Obedience, Loyalty, Disclosure, Confidentiality, Accountability, and Reasonable care (the acronym "OLDCAR") and must negotiate the best price and terms for the buyer, whose lawful interests must be put ahead of all others.

Disclosed Dual Agent

A broker may represent both the buyer and the seller on the same property. To act as a dual agent, the broker must first obtain the informed written consent of both parties. Fiduciary duties are owed to both parties with a modification in the duties of Obedience, Loyalty, Disclosure, and Reasonable care. While the disclosed **dual agent** is obliged to treat both parties equally and honestly, neither can expect the broker's undivided loyalty, full disclosure, or obedience to lawful instructions that is required of an exclusive seller or buyer agent. A dual agent must still account for funds received on behalf of a client and must maintain the confidentiality of material information received from either client.

Agents associated with a traditional brokerage firm offering dual agency must disclose, using the disclosure form currently mandated, that when hired by the consumer all the agents associated with the brokerage firm will represent the consumer. The agent must obtain written consent to dual agency using either the Massachusetts Consent to Dual Agency form (see Figure 1.2) or may include the information, as required in the regulation, in either the Seller or Buyer Agency Agreement. In addition, the agents must provide a written notice to their respective client(s) when dual agency is identified.

Undisclosed dual agency is illegal, and a broker who acts on behalf of more than one party to a transaction without disclosure may lose his or her license.

Subagent

A **subagent** is the agent of an agent. If the original agency agreement permits it, an agent may delegate some of his or her authority or responsibility to a third party. A subagency is created when one broker, usually the seller's agent, appoints another broker (with the seller's permission) to help perform client-based functions on the principal's behalf. The subagent is also an agent of the principal and therefore can create vicarious liability for the seller. Massachusetts requires agents to obtain written permission from their client (seller or buyer) prior to offering subagency. The written notice must state that "vicarious liability is the potential for a seller or buyer to be held liable for a misrepresentation of an act or omission of the subagent" and that in signing the notice, the seller or buyer authorizes the agent to offer subagency.

Nonagent

A *nonagent* is also referred to as a *facilitator*. A **nonagent** is a "middleman" between a buyer and seller (or landlord and tenant) who assists both parties with the transaction without representing either party's interests. A *facilitator* has the duty to present all properties honestly and accurately, disclosing known material defects and accounting for funds. The facilitator does not have a duty of confidentiality with regard to any information received from the seller or purchaser.

FIGURE 1.2

Sample Massachusetts Consent to Dual Agency

MASSACHUSETTS CONSENT TO DUAL AGENCY

A real estate broker or salesperson may act as a dual agent who represents both prospective buyer and seller with their informed written consent. A dual agent is authorized to assist the buyer and seller in a transaction, but shall be neutral with regard to any conflicting interest of the buyer and seller. Consequently, a dual agent will not have the ability to satisfy fully the duties of loyalty, full disclosure, reasonable care and obedience to lawful instructions, but shall still owe the duty of confidentiality of material information and the duty to account for funds.

Buyers and sellers should understand that material information received from either client that is confidential may not be disclosed by a dual agent, except: (1) if disclosure is expressly authorized; (2) if such disclosure is required by law; (3) if such disclosure is intended to prevent illegal conduct; or (4) if such disclosure is necessary to prosecute a claim against a person represented or to defend a claim against the broker or salesperson. This duty of confidentiality shall continue after termination of the brokerage relationship.

BUYER/SELLER ACKNOWLEDGMENT

I acknowledge and agree that _____ {insert name of licensee} is (are) authorized to represent both the buyer and seller as a dual agent. I hereby consent to dual agency.

_____
Signature of ☐ Buyer ☐ Seller   Print Name   Today's Date
       (check one)

_____
Signature of ☐ Buyer ☐ Seller   Print Name   Today's Date
       (check one)

BROKER/SALESPERSON ACKNOWLEDGMENT

I acknowledge and agree to represent the above named consumer as a dual agent and my signature below signifies that I understand the duties and responsibilities of that relationship, and explained to the consumer that I am a dual agent and therefore will assist the buyer and seller in a transaction, but shall be neutral with regard to any conflicting interest of the buyer and seller.

_____
Signature of Broker/Salesperson   License Number   Today's Date

MASSACHUSETTS ASSOCIATION OF REALTORS®
03.25.05/3483

MassForms
Statewide Standard Real Estate Forms

Massachusetts Association of REALTORS 256 Second Ave, Waltham MA 02451
Phone: 7818903700   Fax: 7818904949   Brian Doherty

Form No. 710

m.zfx

Produced with ZipForm™ by RE FormsNet, LLC 18025 Fifteen Mile Road, Clinton Township, Michigan 48035   www.zipform.com

Designated Buyer's or Seller's Agent

A *designated agent* is a licensee in a brokerage firm who is appointed by the broker or another real estate agent (the designating agent) to represent a seller or buyer. One licensee within the same firm is appointed to represent the seller, and one licensee within the same firm is appointed to represent the buyer. The licensees are then the agents of the persons for whom they were designated.

The agent designated to represent the buyer will owe the buyer/principal the traditional fiduciary responsibilities of Obedience, Loyalty, Disclosure, Confidentiality, Accountability, and Reasonable care (the acronym "OLDCAR") and must negotiate the best price and terms for the buyer, whose lawful interests must be put ahead of all others.

The agent designated to represent the seller will owe the seller/principal the traditional fiduciary responsibilities of Obedience, Loyalty, Disclosure, Confidentiality, Accountability, and Reasonable care ("OLDCAR") and must negotiate the best price and terms for the seller, whose lawful interests must be put ahead of all others.

The broker or appointing agent becomes a dual agent and does not represent either the buyer or seller solely and, therefore, must remain neutral in regards to any conflicting interests of the buyer and seller. All other licensees associated with the firm will not represent either buyer or seller unless so appointed.

Agents associated with a brokerage firm that offers designated agency must disclose to the consumer, using the disclosure form currently mandated, that the brokerage practices designated agency. The agent must obtain written consent to designated agency using either the Massachusetts Consent to Designated Agency form (see Figure 1.3) or may include the information, as required in the regulation, in either the Seller or Buyer Agency Agreement. In addition, the agent(s) must provide a written notice to their respective client(s) when designated agency is identified.

When an agency relationship is created, the principal is called the *client*. Agents *work for* clients. The *customer* is the third party for whom some level of service is provided. Agents *work with* customers.

■ CONSUMER PROTECTION LAW

In addition to the obligations placed on the broker by the fiduciary relationship, Massachusetts brokers must comply with the provisions of the *Massachusetts Consumer Protection Act* (MCPA) (Massachusetts General Law, Chapter 93A). The purpose of the MCPA is to level the playing field between consumers and businesses in all areas, not just real estate. The MCPA outlaws unfair and deceptive acts or practices in the conduct of any trade or commerce, including advertising, offering for sale, rent, or lease; or selling, renting, leasing, or distributing any service or property whether real or personal, tangible or intangible.

FIGURE 1.3

Sample Massachusetts Consent to Designated Agency

MASSACHUSETTS CONSENT TO DESIGNATED AGENCY

A designated agent is a real estate licensee who has been appointed by a broker or salesperson to represent a buyer as a "designated buyer's agent" or to represent a seller as a "designated seller's agent." When a buyer or seller consents to designated agency only that designated agent represents the buyer or seller. Any other agents affiliated with the broker may represent another party to the transaction and by consenting to designated agency the buyer or seller permits those agents to represent another party. Individuals who are designated agents owe fiduciary duties to their respective clients.

If you are a **seller** you are advised that:
    a) the designated seller's agent will represent the seller and will owe the seller the duties of loyalty, full disclosure, confidentiality, to account for funds, reasonable care and obedience to lawful instruction;
    b) all other licensees affiliated with the appointing broker will not represent the seller nor will they owe the other duties specified in paragraph (a) to that seller, and may potentially represent the buyer; and
    c) if designated agents affiliated with the same broker represent the seller and buyer in a transaction, the appointing broker shall be a dual agent and neutral as to any conflicting interests of the seller and buyer, but will continue to owe the seller and buyer the duties of confidentiality of material information and to account for funds.

Conversely, if you are a **buyer** you are advised that:
    a) the designated buyer's agent will represent the buyer and will owe the buyer the duties of loyalty, full disclosure, confidentiality, to account for funds, reasonable care and obedience to lawful instruction;
    b) all other licensees affiliated with the appointing broker will not represent the buyer nor will they have the other duties specified in paragraph (a) to that buyer, and potentially may represent the seller; and
    c) if designated agents affiliated with the same broker represent the seller and buyer in a transaction, the appointing broker shall be a dual agent and neutral as to any conflicting interests of the seller and buyer, but will continue to owe the seller and buyer the duties of confidentiality of material information and to account for funds.

BUYER/SELLER ACKNOWLEDGMENT

I acknowledge and agree that _____ *[insert name of licensee]* is authorized to represent me as a designated agent. I hereby consent to designated agency.

_____ _____ _____
Signature of ☐ Buyer ☐ Seller   Print Name   Date
    (check one)

_____ _____ _____
Signature of ☐ Buyer ☐ Seller   Print Name   Date
    (check one)

BROKER/SALESPERSON ACKNOWLEDGMENT

I acknowledge and agree to represent the above named consumer as a designated agent and my signature below signifies that I understand the duties and responsibilities of that relationship, and explained to the consumer that I am their agent, together with any other licensees expressly appointed as their designated agent; and that the appointing broker/salesperson may become a "dual agent;" and that no one else affiliated with my firm represents them.

_____ _____ _____
Signature of Broker/Saleperson   License Number   Date

MASSFORMS
Statewide Standard Real Estate Forms

MASSACHUSETTS ASSOCIATION OF REALTORS®
03.25.05/3483

Form No. 711

Massachusetts Association of REALTORS 256 Second Ave, Waltham MA 02451   Phone: 7818903700   Fax: 7818904919   dis.zfx
Brian Doherty   Produced with ZipForm™ by RE FormsNet, LLC 18025 Fifteen Mile Road, Clinton Township, Michigan 48035 www.zipform.com

The major significance of the Act to the real estate broker is that it increases the broker's responsibility for his or her statements and omissions. Under common law, a broker could be held liable only for *intentional* misstatements he or she made to the buyer. If the broker received inaccurate information from the seller and passed it on in good faith to the buyer, the broker generally could not be found guilty of misrepresentation. But under the MCPA, the broker can be held liable for *any* untrue claim or representation made to the buyer, whether directly, indirectly, or by implication, as well as for omissions and nonstatements. *Fraudulent intent need not be proven for such a claim to be considered illegal.* In practice this means that if a seller gives a broker false information and the broker then presents this information as fact, the broker can be held liable for misrepresentation.

Because the MCPA is designed to provide equal bargaining power, facts that a broker *should* know or have reason to know need to be disclosed if they would tend to caution a buyer against entering into a contract. The fact that the buyer never asked a question about something important relating to the property does not relieve the broker of the responsibility to disclose relevant information.

In addition to this broad statement of liability, the MCPA lists specific actions considered to be *misrepresentations*. These include

- making false claims about a product's construction, durability, safety, or strength;
- making false claims concerning the ease with which a product can be repaired or maintained;
- making false claims about financing terms or availability;
- advertising that something has a quality, value, or usability that it does not have;
- substituting different goods for those advertised ("bait and switch"); and
- offering guarantees without disclosing the nature and extent of the guarantees.

The MCPA does not define what are *unfair or deceptive acts or practices*, but rather the Act leaves it up to the courts to look at the circumstances of each case. In general, the courts have found that a behavior is considered deceptive if it could reasonably be found to have caused a person to act differently from the way he or she otherwise would have acted.

The MCPA makes no exception for "puffing" in advertising or otherwise. *Puffing* is an exaggerated or superlative comment or opinion not made as a representation of fact. Under common law, puffing is permitted; fraudulent misrepresentation of fact is not. But the MCPA makes no distinction between claims presented as fact and those presented as opinion.

The broker may be held liable for a misstatement in an advertisement even if he or she later informs the prospective buyer that the statement was incorrect.

IN PRACTICE

All representations that have the capacity to deceive buyers or influence them in any way have been declared illegal, including those that were previously considered to be mere sales rhetoric.

Affirmative Disclosure

Equally important under the MCPA is the broker's duty to disclose all facts relating to the sale. In the past, sellers and brokers were required under common law to disclose only defects they knew about that could not be discovered in a normal inspection of the premises. Now, however, it is illegal to fail to disclose to a buyer or prospective buyer any fact that might influence the buyer or prospective buyer not to enter into the transaction, *whether or not the buyer or prospective buyer requests the information*. However, with stigmatized property issues, absent a specific inquiry about an incident by the prospective buyer, there is no duty for the broker to either investigate or affirmatively disclose murders, suicides, allegations of ghosts, or other potential stigmas. The broker must answer to the best of his or her knowledge any question posed by the prospective buyer.

Whether the buyer actually would have refused to complete the transaction if certain facts were disclosed appears to be immaterial—the possibility alone of such a refusal seems to constitute a violation of the law on the broker's part. A broker may also be held responsible even if the buyer agrees to purchase the property under conditions other than those originally agreed on (such as a lower price).

Under the *New Home Inspection Law* of Massachusetts, real estate agents are prohibited from making direct referrals. Upon request, they may provide a complete list of home inspectors prepared by the Consumer Affairs Board. A real estate agent acting as a buyer's agent with a written contractual agreement between the agent and buyer may make direct referrals. All real estate agents are required to provide to the consumer a copy of the brochure, "Home Inspectors Facts for Consumers." (See Figure 1.4.)

Persons Affected by the Law

The MCPA applies to all listing, selling, and cooperating brokers and all salespersons affiliated with these brokers as either employees or independent contractors. Sellers, developers, and builders also come under the Act's authority. However, *the law does not apply to owners who sell their homes privately*. The Massachusetts Supreme Court has reasoned that because buyers and private sellers enjoy equal rights under the common law, extending the Act's protection to buyers involved in private sales would give them an unnecessary advantage.

The broker is also a vendor of services, and the degree to which he or she advertises or makes claims about the speed, quality, or diligence of these services brings the broker/owner (and broker/seller) relationship under the MCPA. The substantial impact on the landlord/tenant relationship under this Act is discussed in Chapter 12.

Enforcement

The attorney general of Massachusetts has the power to issue rules and regulations for interpreting and enforcing the Act. Although the attorney general may intervene whenever a violation occurs, usually this only happens when a violation involves a large number of consumers. Individuals who have sustained losses as a result of unfair or deceptive practices may bring a lawsuit themselves. A consumer must first give the alleged violator 30 days' written notice of the claim, describing the unfair practice and the resulting loss so that the accused can investigate the claim and offer to settle it out of court. *If the consumer rejects the offer and a court finds that it was indeed reasonable, the consumer may recover no more than the amount of the offer.*

FIGURE 1.4

"Facts for Consumers" Brochure

Commonwealth of Massachusetts ~ Office of Consumer Affairs ~ Division of Professional Licensure

Board of Registration of Home Inspectors

www.mass.gov/dpl/boards/hi

The Board of Registration of Home Inspectors is charged with evaluating the qualifications of applicants and granting licensure to those who qualify. It establishes rules and regulations to ensure the integrity and competence of licensees. The Board protects the public health and welfare through regulation of the profession in accordance with the state statutes and board regulations.

The Board is responsible for insuring that licensed home inspectors have proper training and experience through an education program and meet minimum inspection requirements in each inspection performed. Applicants are required to pass a board approved examination prior to licensure and fulfill continuing education requirements for license renewal.

The Board publishes a Standards of Practice and Code of Ethics for home inspectors.

Contents:
- **About Home Inspections**
- **Timing of the Home Inspection**
- **Selecting a Home Inspector**
- **During the Home Inspection**
- **Other Inspections and Tests to Consider**
- **Filing a Complaint**

Contents

General Tips

Board Pages

About Home Inspections

A standard home inspection is a visual examination of the physical structure and major interior systems of a residential building consisting of one to four dwelling units. An inspection can be likened to a physical exam by a physician; however, it should be clearly understood that a home inspection is not to be confused with an appraisal, a building code inspection, a guarantee of any kind, and/or an insurance policy on the condition of the property.

During an inspection, the inspector will review the readily accessible

F I G U R E   1.4 (Continued)

"Facts for Consumers" Brochure

exposed portions of the structure of the home, including the roof, the attic, walls, ceilings, floors, windows, doors, basement, and foundation as well as the heating/air conditioning systems, interior plumbing and electrical systems for potential problems.

Home inspections are not intended to point out every small problem or any invisible or latent defect in a home. Most minor or cosmetic flaws, for example, should be apparent to the buyer without the aid of a professional.

Timing of the Home Inspection

A home inspector is typically hired by a potential homebuyer right after the offer to purchase contract is signed, prior to executing the final purchase and sales agreement. However, before the potential buyer signs the offer to purchase contract, he/she should be sure that there is an inspection clause in the contract making the purchase obligation contingent upon the findings of a professional home inspection. This clause should specify the terms to which both the buyer and seller are obligated.

Selecting a Home Inspector

Good referral sources for home inspection services are friends, neighbors, or business acquaintances who have been satisfied with a home inspector. In addition, lawyers and mortgage brokers may also recommend a home inspector. The names of local inspectors can be found by searching the Division of Professional Licensure website at http://license.reg.state.ma.us/public/licque.asp?color=green&Board=HI, or in the Yellow Pages where many advertise under "Building Inspection Service" or "Home Inspection Service."

Real estate brokers and salesmen may not directly recommend a specific home inspection company or home inspector unless representing the buyer as a buyer's broker. Brokers, however, may provide assistance to buyers in accessing information on licensed home inspectors.

A current home owner may also want to get a home inspection to identify any problems, especially if the owner plans to sell the home in the near future.

Following are additional tips when searching for a home inspector:

F I G U R E   1.4 (Continued)

"Facts for Consumers" Brochure

- As of May 2001, home inspectors are required to be licensed in the Commonwealth of Massachusetts. A home inspector's license should be verified prior to hiring. Consumers should not be confused by home inspector "certifications" offered by, or sold by home inspection trade societies or companies, obtained via home study courses, or provided by home inspection companies that certify their own home inspectors. Since the home inspection business is unregulated in most states, certifications are available to anyone. A home inspector's license can be verified with the Board of Registration of Home Inspectors at its <u>website</u> or by calling the Board at (617) 727-4459.
- The home inspection company that is retained should welcome the potential buyer's presence at the home inspection. The home inspector should be willing to address all of the buyer's questions and provide a full verbal and written report.
- Those hiring an inspector should expect an open door policy from the home inspection company to be able to ask questions about the content of the home inspection report in the future.

During the Home Inspection

While not necessary, it is recommended that the buyer be present for the inspection. This allows the buyer to observe the inspector, ask questions directly, and obtain a better understanding of the condition of the home, how its systems work, and how to maintain it. The written report may be easier to understand if the buyer was present during the inspection.

It is important that safe access and sufficient lighting is provided so that the inspector can inspect the property.

Inspectors must provide a written evaluation report based on the standards of compliance in accordance with Massachusetts General Laws Chapter 146.

At the conclusion of the home inspection, the buyer should be well informed of the condition of the home. It should be known if there are visible, apparent problems, if repairs need to be made, or whether or not there are any risks of concealed damage, and whether further investigation is recommended and/or required.

F I G U R E   1.4 (Continued)

"Facts for Consumers" Brochure

Other Inspections and Tests to Consider

It is strongly recommended that potential buyers consider having the following inspections and/or tests performed prior to signing the final purchase agreement:

- Lead paint, the **seller**, under 105 CMR 460.750(A) shall disclose if the property has been inspected for lead paint and provide copies of any lead paint reports concerning the residential premises or any dwelling unit therein.
- Water quality (is it drinkable)
- Wood destroying insects, including termites
- Air quality, including radon gases
- Fungi, mold and allergens
- **Seller** required, by Department of Public Health, under 105 CMR 651.010, to provide the potential buyer with an affidavit disclosing the presence of Urea Formaldehyde Insulation if it exists.

While some home inspectors are qualified to offer these services, these inspections and tests are not part of the basic home inspection and should be contracted through qualified licensed professionals in those fields.

Filing a Complaint

While most licensees conduct themselves as true professionals, the Division of Professional Licensure will take action against those licensees who fail to maintain acceptable standards of competence and integrity. In some cases, complaints are made by dissatisfied consumers, however, dissatisfaction alone is not proof of incompetence or sufficient grounds for disciplinary action.

If you have a serious complaint about a home inspector, call or write the Division's Office of Investigations and ask for a complaint form. The Division's Office of Investigations is located at 239 Causeway Street, Boston, MA 02114. The phone number is 617-727-7406. A copy of the complaint form can also be downloaded from the Division's website (www.mass.gov/dpl/).

If the court does not consider the offer reasonable, the consumer may be awarded the amount of actual damages or $25, whichever is greater. The court may double or triple the amount of damages if (1) the unfair or deceptive act or practice was a willful and knowing violation, or (2) the accused refuses in bad faith to make a reasonable offer to settle. In addition, the court can offer equitable relief, including an injunction to prevent the defendant from engaging in future unfair or deceptive acts, or willfully and knowingly violating the statute. Multiple damages will not be awarded if the accused did not violate the Act willfully, although the consumer will still receive attorney's fees.

Recommendations

If the broker knows of a problem or discovers one during an inspection, he or she must disclose that information to the buyer or prospective buyer, identify its source, and state whether or not he or she has verified it. When the broker makes any sort of claim or representation, he or she should disclose both the source and whether or not he or she has made an attempt to personally verify that information. *The broker cannot be held responsible for the truthfulness of the claims if he or she has not tried to verify them.* However, if the broker has tried to verify the claims or received information that could be used for verification, he or she must say so. The broker is not required to conduct any investigation of property that is beyond his or her level of competence.

Cooperating brokers also must identify the source of their representations and disclose their attempts at verification and any facts that might cause the prospective buyer not to complete the transaction. Cooperating brokers should make independent investigations of property they are involved with whenever possible.

The MCPA overrides the common-law agency duty of confidentiality in some circumstances. A broker must disclose *facts about the property* to the buyer even if the seller revealed them to the broker in confidence. If the seller has stated that the roof leaks, for example, the broker must pass on this information to the prospective buyer. But the broker need not reveal any personal information about the seller, such as the seller's willingness to accept an offer that is less than the listing price.

For a buyer to recover damages for the nondisclosure of a material fact, the buyer must prove that: (1) the seller or broker knew of the material defect, (2) the seller or broker failed to disclose the problem, and (3) he or she would not have purchased the property if he or she had known of the defect.

To help the broker prove that he or she did not mislead the buyer, a special clause has been added to some purchase-and-sale agreements issued by real estate boards. The clause requires buyers to list the representations the broker has made that they relied on when deciding to make the purchase.

■ **FOR EXAMPLE**

Seller knows that 20 acres of his 100-acre property have been used as a dumping ground for hazardous and toxic materials since 1974. When he sells to Buyer, who plans to build a health spa and retreat center on the land, both Seller and his Broker "forget" to mention the contamination. Seller will be liable to Buyer. The Broker will be liable as well.

II

In a 1994 case, Broker showed Purchasers a house in their price range. They were new to the city and asked about the safety of the neighborhood. Broker replied that it was "okay." Three days after they moved in, the Purchasers' new home was burglarized, and they sued Broker for misrepresentation. The court found Broker to not be liable because he had no knowledge—and had no reason to know—of any facts suggesting that the neighborhood was unsafe. *Grynowicki v. Silvia* (1994), 1994 Mass. App. Div. 173.

■ AGENCY TERMINATION

The agency relationship may be terminated at will by either the principal or the agent. Neither party has to have a reason to terminate the agency, and the broker cannot claim expenses from the principal unless this was specifically provided for in the hiring contract. If, however, the agency contract provides that the relationship is to continue for a specific period of time, such as an exclusive-right-to-sell listing for 90 days, early termination exposes the seller to a potential lawsuit for expenses and damages by the broker. If the broker has done something wrong that gives the seller "good cause" to terminate the contract, or if the seller removes the property from the market, then the likelihood that the broker will recover compensation for expenses incurred or a commission if the property is sold is considerably lessened.

Compensation

A real estate broker works under a contractual agreement with his or her employer. In Massachusetts, this agreement may be created in one of three ways:

1. *Orally*
2. *In writing*
3. *By implication*, where the broker and the seller *behave* as if they have an agreement

A written agreement between the broker and the principal is not necessary to create an enforceable brokerage contract. The *statute of frauds* requirement of a written agreement applies to conveyances of property, but it does not apply to employment agreements such as listing contracts. Note, however, that an *exclusive-right-to-sell listing agreement* must be in writing to be enforceable in court. Brokers and salespersons are advised always to execute a written contract.

IN PRACTICE

Students should clearly understand that several contracts are typically involved in a real estate transaction: the *listing agreement,* which is a service contract between the seller and the broker; and/or a *buyer representation agreement,* which is a service contract between the buyer and the broker; the *Offer to Purchase,* which is the initial contract between the seller and the buyer; and the *Purchase and Sales Agreement,* which is the final contract between the seller and the buyer. Both the Offer to Purchase and the Purchase and Sales Agreement are required to be in writing, although an exclusive-right-to-represent agreement must also be written to be enforceable in court.

The essence of a listing contract between a seller and a broker is that the real estate professional will use his or her knowledge and skill to find a buyer who is ready, willing, and able to purchase the property under the terms and conditions stated in the contract.

The broker must be careful to properly "list the property" (see Chapter 2) and to find out all the seller's terms and conditions. Such conditions include: (1) the asking price for the property, (2) any special financial considerations that may be involved, and (3) what personal property will be conveyed along with the house.

After a broker has done the job he or she was hired to do, he or she should be entitled to compensation. It sometimes bothers an owner when a broker rushes back to the office immediately after being hired, calls a prospective buyer whom he or she knows is looking for the type of property involved, and obtains a signed contract of sale with no apparent effort. Of course, the same owner is likely to squawk if the broker seems to be taking too long to find a buyer. However, the broker is paid for the *result*, whether it takes hours, days, weeks, or months to produce a ready, willing, and able buyer.

In the past, the general rule was that as soon as a broker produced a ready, willing, and able buyer and a binding contract was signed, the commission was earned, whether or not the sale ever went to closing. Owners always have been able to protect themselves by including in the listing or the sales contract a provision that no commission is payable until the sale actually closes. A seller may also reserve the right, in the listing agreement, to reject any purchaser or to condition the commission on producing a buyer who meets certain specified requirements.

The Massachusetts Supreme Court in *Tristram's Landing v. Wait*, 367 Mass. 622, 327 N.E.2d 727 (1975) held that a broker is entitled to his or her commission only when the following three conditions are met:

1. The broker produces a purchaser ready, willing, and able to buy on the terms fixed by the owner.
2. The purchaser enters into a binding contract with the owner to purchase the property.
3. The purchaser completes the transaction by closing the title in accordance with the provisions of the contract.

A real estate broker under a brokerage agreement is entitled to a commission from the seller only if these three requirements are met. This is known as the "Tristram's Landing" rule.

If the contract is not consummated because of the buyer's financial inability to perform, or because of any other buyer default, the broker has no right to a commission from the seller. However, a seller and a broker could agree in the written listing or sales contract on the extent to which the forfeited earnest money deposit might be shared in the event of a buyer's default. On the other hand, a narrow exception to the Tristram's Landing rule exists: if the failure to complete the contract is the result of the seller's wrongful act or interference. In this situation the broker is entitled to receive a commission based on the contract presented. However, for the broker to receive commission, the first two conditions of the Tristram's Landing rule must be met: production of a purchaser willing and able to buy on terms fixed by the owner and formation of a binding contract for purchase. The seller's wrongful act or interference must have upset the completion of a sale—the third Tristram's Landing condition—that was called for by a binding purchase and sale agreement entered into between a broker's client and the seller. Conduct is considered "wrongful" if it is in itself a violation of an existing legal duty or obligation. The listing contract might also include terms that a commission must be paid if the broker presents a customer who is ready, willing, and able and the seller refuses to sign a contract.

Even if the broker succeeds in finding a ready, willing, and able buyer who meets all the terms and conditions of sale described by the seller in the listing contract, however, he or she still has not earned a commission unless the seller signs a contract to sell. Should the owner refuse to sign a contract of sale, and as long as there is no bad faith in the refusal, no commission is earned (of course, the seller may be liable to the broker for damages). The practical reality of this rule is: Get the seller's signature.

A broker can earn a commission, then, if the sale is not consummated because of the seller's default or the seller's decision not to complete the transaction. But remember: The seller must enter into a contract to sell and then either refuse to comply or be dealing in bad faith.

Procuring Cause

In some cases, a broker may claim a commission by showing that he or she was the **procuring cause** of a sale even though the broker did not actually complete the terms of the employment agreement. Generally, the mere introduction of a potential buyer to a property does not entitle the broker to a commission. The broker needs to demonstrate that he or she was the efficient, effective, or final cause or force of bringing about the actual sale. This requires that the agent has set into operation a continuing and uninterrupted chain of events resulting in the agreed objective of the parties: the sale. Introducing a seller to a prospective buyer or interesting a customer in a property that he or she later buys may satisfy that test. The broker's case is particularly strong if the seller impedes or precludes the broker from negotiations or involvement in the sale.

■ **FOR EXAMPLE**   Broker is hired with an open listing for an indefinite period of time and a 6 percent commission. On Monday, Broker shows Owner's house to Buyer. On Tuesday, Owner fires Broker. On Wednesday, Owner calls Buyer and negotiates the sale of the property.

Technically, Broker has not done her job: she did not present Owner with an offer from a ready, willing, and able buyer. However, Broker was the *procuring cause* of the sale: she was responsible for Owner and Buyer getting together and for the property being sold. Broker could sue for a commission and would likely win.

Normally, the courts examine the broker's continued efforts to consummate the sale as well as the good faith of both the buyer and the seller. A broker may often have a provision in the listing contract that says that he or she is entitled to a commission if the property is sold to a customer of the broker *within a specified period of time after the listing ends*. This is known as a *protection clause*. To protect all parties, owners should be provided with notices or lists of potential buyers to whom the property has been shown. The most difficult problem occurs when a buyer inquires about the property because of a sign that the broker has placed on it and then buys the property directly from the owner.

Massachusetts courts will not generally allow a broker to collect a commission if the transaction that results is different from the original transaction. *How* it is different and *why* it is different are important considerations in determining the broker's entitlement to a commission. The court will consider whether or not some new force instigated the sale after the broker ended his or her efforts. The court examines each case on its own facts.

Multiple Commissions

Where one broker is the procuring cause and another broker succeeds in getting the seller and the buyer to sign the sales contract, the owner could end up having to pay more than one commission. While possibly burdensome for sellers, this ensures that both brokers are compensated for doing their job. For instance, if the owner changes real estate agents after the expiration of a listing agreement and the new agent sells the property to a buyer who originally contacted the first agent, the owner may owe commissions to both agents. The original broker's right to a commission is clear because he or she introduced the buyer to the property and thus was the procuring cause. The second broker is entitled to a commission because he or she did exactly what was specified. There is no obligation to split a single commission. This is an excellent argument in favor of the exclusive-right-to-sell listing contract that will avoid this problem. In Massachusetts, if the owner has exclusively engaged a new agent after the expiration of a listing agreement, the owner will not be liable for commissions to both current and former agents. This is discussed further in Chapter 2.

Brokers or salespersons who are REALTORS® resolve these disputes by the rules of the REALTORS® Association, so there are no multiple commission situations.

Attachment

When a broker is entitled to a commission and the seller refuses to pay, a writ of *attachment* may be filed against the seller's property. An *attachment* is a legal writ or proceeding by which property is made subject to a lien pending the outcome of a suit. Note, however, that an attachment is not itself a lien but rather a court injunction preventing a seller's conveyance of the property while litigation is pending. By means of an attachment, the sale of the real estate is prohibited until the suit has been heard in court. If the owner attempts to close the sale, he or she will be obligated either to settle the suit by paying the commission or to somehow guarantee that the amount can be paid. The owner will not be able to transfer or sell the property until it is free of the attachment. Often, an owner cannot afford to wait for the suit to be heard and is forced to pay the commission.

When an attachment is sought, the courts may demand that notice be given the owner and that a hearing be held prior to the issuance of the writ of attachment.

This process ensures that an owner will have an opportunity to demonstrate why the attachment is improper or to make other arrangements for guaranteeing the potential financial obligation.

■ THE MASSACHUSETTS REAL ESTATE LICENSE LAW

The *Massachusetts Real Estate License Law* and the rules and regulations of the Board of Registration of Real Estate Brokers and Salespersons will be the subject matter of questions on your state license examination and the law that governs your professional life after you are licensed. (See Chapter 10.)

■ RELATED WEB SITES

Massachusetts Association of REALTORS®   *www.marealtor.com*

Massachusetts Board of Registration of Real Estate Brokers and Salespersons *www.mass.gov/dpl/boards/re/index.htm*

Massachusetts Consumer Affairs Fact Sheet on Home Inspection *www.mass.gov/dpl/consumer/fspagehi.htm*

Massachusetts General Laws   *www.mass.gov/legis/laws/mgl*

Massachusetts Office of Consumer Affairs Division of Professional Licensure *www.mass.gov/dpl*

QUESTIONS

1. An enforceable listing agreement does *NOT* have to be in writing because the
   a. broker has a fiduciary relationship with the principal.
   b. principal has a fiduciary relationship with the broker.
   c. law of agency does not apply in the case of a listing agreement.
   d. *statute of frauds* does not apply to a listing agreement.

2. Which of the following is *NOT* necessary for a broker to be entitled to a commission?
   a. A signed listing agreement
   b. A ready, willing, and able buyer
   c. Closing of title by purchaser
   d. A binding contract between seller and purchaser

3. The *Massachusetts Consumer Protection Act* requires that the
   a. broker keep all information that the seller has provided confidential.
   b. broker disclose everything that the seller tells him or her.
   c. broker disclose known material information that might affect the sale even though the buyer does not ask for it.
   d. seller disclose all facts that might affect the sale.

4. Six months after the buyer bought a house, the roof leaked during a rainstorm. When the house was listed the seller told the broker that the roof leaked but they agreed not to tell any prospective buyers. The broker claims that the buyer did not ask about the roof. Under these facts the buyer
   a. can sue the broker under MCPA.
   b. cannot sue the broker under MCPA.
   c. can sue the seller under MCPA.
   d. cannot do anything because the leaking roof could have been discovered by inspection.

5. A buyer's agent
   a. owes the buyer the traditional fiduciary duties.
   b. retains the right to hire subagents.
   c. must obtain the informed consent of all parties.
   d. may act on behalf of both buyer and seller.

6. Obedience, loyalty, disclosure, confidentiality, accountability, and reasonable care are the
   a. responsibilities required by the MCPA.
   b. elements required to prove that an agent is entitled to a commission.
   c. traditional fiduciary duties owed by a principal to an agent.
   d. traditional fiduciary duties owed by an agent to a principal.

7. A broker is legally entitled to a commission if he or she
   a. produces a buyer who is ready, willing, and able.
   b. produces a purchaser and a binding contract, and the transaction closes.
   c. has a signed listing contract.
   d. introduces the seller to the eventual purchaser.

8. Broker Albert shows Owner's house to a Buyer on March 7. On March 10, Albert's listing expires and the Owner lists the house with Broker Betty. On March 15, the Buyer calls Betty and asks to see the house again. Broker Betty enters into an exclusive right to represent the Buyer, helps the Buyer obtain mortgage preapproval, and shows several other homes for comparison. On May 1, the sale closes. With regard to the commission, Albert
   a. is entitled to nothing.
   b. and Betty are both entitled to a full commission.
   c. is entitled to one-half of Betty's commission.
   d. is entitled to all of Betty's commission.

9. An oral agency relationship may be terminated
   a. only for good cause.
   b. only under the terms of the contract.
   c. at will by either party.
   d. only if one party breaches the contract.

10. What types of agency are *MOST* commonly practiced in Massachusetts?
    a. Seller's, buyer's, undisclosed dual
    b. Subagency, disclosed dual, seller's
    c. Seller's, buyer's, disclosed dual, designated
    d. Seller's, buyer's, full fiduciary

CHAPTER 2

Seller and Buyer Representation Agreements

■ LISTING PROPERTY

The *listing agreement* is the employment contract between the real estate broker and the seller. It contains the essential substance of the transaction: It defines the relationship between the agent and principal and establishes their rights and responsibilities; it sets the price of the property and the rate of commission that will be paid to the broker. The listing agreement may establish such things as whether the seller will permit the broker to cooperate with buyers' brokers, facilitators, dual agents, whether or not a multiple listing service (MLS) may be used, and whether a lockbox may be placed on the property. In short, the listing agreement sets out the parties' responsibilities and expectations.

■ LISTING THE BUYER

The Buyer Representation Agreement is an employment contract between the real estate broker and the buyer. It defines the relationship between the agent and the buyer/principal and establishes their rights and responsibilities; it sets forth the length of the relationship, the type and scope of the agency relationship, the type and method of compensation, the management of offers from multiple-buyer clients, the consent to dual or designated agency (if applicable), and any other agreed upon terms.

Representation Agreements

The types of representation agreements commonly used in Massachusetts include the exclusive-right-to-represent listing, the exclusive-agency listing, the open listing, and the cobroker listing.

Exclusive-right-to-represent listing (Seller).   In an *exclusive-right-to-sell listing* with a seller, the broker has sole control over the sale of the property. This type of listing is the most desirable for brokers because, in addition to total control over the transaction, it provides them with the greatest protection. By law, the contract must be *in writing* and signed by the parties involved. A definite period of time must be stated, at the end of which the exclusive-right-to-sell agreement terminates. As with all written documents that a broker asks anyone to sign, the broker must furnish the parties with a copy. Figure 2.1 contains an example of an exclusive-right-to-sell agreement.

Exclusive-right-to-represent agreement (Buyer).   An *exclusive-right-to-represent* a buyer gives to the buyer's agent the sole right to represent the buyer. On behalf of the buyer client, the buyer agent accepts the responsibility of searching for a property acceptable to the buyer. The buyer agent is entitled to compensation, as defined in the written agreement, if the buyer purchases a property from anyone at any time during the period of the agreement. By law, the contract must be *in writing* and signed by the parties involved. A definite period of time must be stated, at the end of which the exclusive-right-to-represent agreement terminates. As with all written documents that a broker asks anyone to sign, the broker must furnish the parties with a copy. (See Figure 2.2.)

Exclusive-agency agreement (Seller).   An *exclusive-agency agreement* is similar to the exclusive-right-to-sell agreement in that it strictly limits the parties by whom the property may be sold. In this listing arrangement, however, the owner reserves the right to sell the property without the broker's assistance, in which case the owner keeps the commission. The broker, on the other hand, is hired as the only broker who represents the owner in the sale and is entitled to the commission if he or she produces a ready, willing, and able buyer. The contract should be in writing and for a specific term. An exclusive-agency agreement for a seller is illustrated in Figure 2.3.

Exclusive-agency agreement (Buyer).   An *exclusive-agency agreement* with a buyer client is similar to the exclusive-right-to-represent agreement. However, the buyer reserves the right to purchase a property directly from the seller and without the broker's assistance. In this case the buyer would not owe the agent a commission. The broker, on the other hand, is hired as the only broker who will represent the buyer in the purchase and is entitled to the commission if the broker locates and assists the buyer in purchasing a property not directly from a seller. The contract should be in writing and for a specific term.

Open listing.   *Seller*—Under an open listing, the owner retains the right to hire as many brokers as he or she pleases. The first broker to present a ready, willing, and able buyer earns the commission, and the other brokers are automatically discharged. An open listing hiring contract may be oral or written.

FIGURE 2.1

Sample Exclusive-Right-To-Sell Listing Agreement

EXCLUSIVE RIGHT TO SELL LISTING AGREEMENT
[With Consent To Dual Agency]

MASSACHUSETTS ASSOCIATION of REALTORS®

I/We _____ ("SELLER"), hereby grant to _____ , a real estate broker licensed under the laws of the Commonwealth of Massachusetts ("BROKER") the exclusive right to sell the property described as _____ _____ and recorded in the _____ County Registry Of Deeds at Book _____ , Page _____ ("PROPERTY") on the following terms and conditions:

1. **Seller's Duties And Representations.** The BROKER is granted the exclusive right to sell the PROPERTY, as the SELLER'S agent, during the term of the Agreement and the SELLER agrees to refer all inquiries to the BROKER, to cooperate in marketing the PROPERTY, including completing lead paint (if property built before 1978) and other forms. If the PROPERTY is sold to a buyer procured by the BROKER, by the SELLER or by anyone else, the fee described in paragraph 4 shall be due. The BROKER is authorized, but is not required: (a) to offer compensation to other licensed brokers as buyer's agents or facilitators; (b) to place a listing for the PROPERTY in any multiple listing service; (c) to place a sign on the PROPERTY; (d) to photograph and advertise the PROPERTY in such media as the BROKER may select; and (e) to place a lock box on the PROPERTY. The SELLER authorizes the BROKER to disclose to prospective buyers all information about the PROPERTY provided to the BROKER by the SELLER, all of which the SELLER represents to be accurate. **The SELLER acknowledges receipt of a Mandatory Licensee-Consumer Relationship Disclosure form.** According to the Code of Ethics and Standards of Practice of the National Association of REALTORS®, the SELLER has been advised of (1) the broker's general company policies regarding cooperation with and compensation to subagents, buyer's agents and facilitators; (2) the fact that a buyer's agent, even if compensated by the listing broker or seller will represent the interest of the buyer; and (3) any potential for the listing broker to act as a disclosed dual agent on behalf of the seller and buyer. The SELLER agrees to comply with all applicable fair housing laws.
2. **Listing Price.** The listing price for the PROPERTY shall be _____ dollars or such other price and terms as the SELLER may approve.
3. **Listing Period.** This Agreement shall begin on _____ and end on _____ and may be extended by agreement.
4. **Broker's Fee.** If within the term of this Agreement or any extension the PROPERTY is sold or the BROKER procures a buyer who is ready, willing and able to buy at a price and on the terms set forth herein or on such other price and terms as the SELLER may agree, the BROKER shall be due a fee of _____ percent of the selling price, whether or not the transaction is completed or title passes. Said fee shall be paid at the time set for closing and may be deducted from amounts held by BROKER as escrow agent. The aforesaid fee shall also be due upon sale within _____ months after expiration of this Agreement or any extension to any person who is introduced to the PROPERTY during the aforesaid term or any extension, except if the SELLER has entered into an exclusive agreement with another broker in good faith, in which case the BROKER shall be entitled to receive only the difference between the fee set forth herein and any lesser fee paid to the other broker. If any deposit is retained by the SELLER as liquidated damages for default by the buyer under any agreement for sale of the PROPERTY, the BROKER shall be due one-half (1/2) of the amount so retained, but not more than an amount equal to the full commission that would have been paid to BROKER if a sale had been completed.
5. **Broker Cooperation.** BROKER hereby advises SELLER that BROKER will offer compensation to cooperating real estate licensees as follows: buyer's agents _____ % of the selling price; facilitators (non-agents) _____ % of the selling price. If subagency will be offered, Consent To Subagency form must be signed.
6. **Broker's Duties.** The BROKER agrees to use reasonable efforts in marketing the PROPERTY and agrees to list the PROPERTY with the _____ multiple listing service. The BROKER shall have no obligation to continue to market the PROPERTY after an offer has been accepted and shall have no obligation to present any offer once an offer has been accepted and while a transaction is pending. The BROKER is not hired as a property inspector, tax advisor or attorney and if such services are desired SELLER should hire professionals.
7. **Consent To Dual Agency.** The SELLER understands that BROKER also represents buyers and that if BROKER introduces a buyer-client to the PROPERTY a "dual agency" will be created. The BROKER may act as a dual agent who represents both prospective buyer and seller with their informed written consent. A dual agent is authorized to assist the buyer and seller in a transaction, but shall be neutral with regard to any conflicting interest of the buyer and seller. Consequently, a dual agent will not have the ability to satisfy fully the duties of loyalty, full disclosure, reasonable care and obedience to lawful instructions, but shall still owe the duty of confidentiality of material information and the duty to account for funds. SELLER understands that material information received from either client that is confidential may not be disclosed by a dual agent, except: (1) if disclosure is expressly authorized; (2) if such disclosure is required by law; (3) if such disclosure is intended to prevent illegal conduct; or (4) if such disclosure is necessary to prosecute a claim against a person represented or to defend a claim against the broker or salesperson. This duty of confidentiality shall continue after termination of the brokerage relationship. **By signing this agreement, SELLER authorizes BROKER to act as a dual agent and consents to dual agency.** If dual agency occurs in a transaction, a notice of dual agency will be given.
8. **Additional Terms:** _____ _____

Dated: _____

_____   _____
BROKER Or Authorized Representative   SELLER Or Authorized Representative

_____
                                                SELLER Or Authorized Representative

MASSFORMS™ Statewide Standard Real Estate Forms   © 1999, 2002, 2004, 2005 MASSACHUSETTS ASSOCIATION OF REALTORS® 4.11.05/349765.1

Massachusetts Association of REALTORS 256 Second Ave, Waltham MA 02451   Phone: 7818903700   Fax: 7818904919   Form No. 707
Brian Doherty   Produced with ZipForm™ by RE FormsNet, LLC 18025 Fifteen Mile Road, Clinton Township, Michigan 48035 www.zipform.com   d.zfx

F I G U R E   2.2

Sample Exclusive Buyer Agency Agreement—Buyer

EXCLUSIVE BUYER AGENCY AGREEMENT

This Buyer Agency Agreement is made between _____
_____ ("BUYER") and _____
("BROKER"). In consideration of the mutual promises set forth below, BUYER and BROKER agree as follows:

1. <u>Exclusive Buyer Agency.</u> BUYER grants to BROKER the exclusive right to locate or procure real property acceptable for purchase/lease by BUYER. BUYER further agrees to refer all potentially acceptable real property to BROKER during the term of this Agreement and agrees to notify all other real estate agents who communicate with BUYER of BROKER'S exclusive agency relationship with BUYER. The final decision whether or not a property is acceptable for purchase shall be solely within the discretion of BUYER. **The BUYER acknowledges receipt of a Mandatory Licensee-Consumer Relationship Disclosure form.**

2. <u>Term Of Agency.</u> The term of this Agreement shall be from _____ , _____ to
_____ , _____ , unless extended verbally or in writing or terminated by completion of the purpose or by agreement.

3. <u>Broker's Services/Duties.</u> BROKER agrees to use reasonable efforts to locate real property acceptable to BUYER and to assist BUYER to negotiate terms and conditions of a contract acceptable to BUYER for the acquisition of the real property (the "Contract"). The Contract may consist of an accepted offer, purchase and sale agreement, option, deed, exchange agreement, lease or similar instrument. BROKER agrees to assist in locating properties, arrange showings, analyze financing alternatives, give advice concerning real estate practices and procedures, assist in negotiations, arrange inspections requested by BUYER and coordinate activities throughout the process. BUYER agrees that such services do not constitute a guarantee or warranty concerning any real property. BUYER agrees that BROKER has not been retained as an attorney, inspector, home inspector, pest/termite inspector, septic inspector, surveyor or to determine the condition of the real property and has not been retained to provide legal advice, to provide an opinion concerning lawfulness of current or anticipated uses, to perform a title search or to act as a mortgage broker. BUYER agrees that BROKER shall have no duty to disclose any matter or condition outside the boundaries of the real property being considered for purchase, including, but not limited to, present conditions and anticipated changes in the neighborhood where the property is located. BROKER recommends that an attorney and other professionals be hired for such services as BUYER deems appropriate and that BUYER personally investigate particular matters which may be of importance, including, but not limited to, neighborhood composition, the level of crime and presence of sex offenders. BROKER agrees to preserve confidential information of BUYER, making disclosure of confidential information solely to the extent necessary to establish BUYER'S financial qualifications. BROKER represents that BROKER is duly licensed as a real estate broker by the Commonwealth of Massachusetts.

4. <u>Buyer's Duties.</u> BUYER agrees to work exclusively with BROKER during the term of this agreement. BUYER agrees to conduct all negotiations with the knowledge and assistance of BROKER. BUYER agrees to cooperate with BROKER by providing relevant personal and financial information and to cooperate in scheduling and attending showings. BUYER agrees to advise BROKER of any interest in purchase or lease of real property about which BUYER was previously advised by any other person. BUYER shall provide any lender's letter of pre-approval or pre-qualification to BROKER within seven (7) days of receipt. BUYER agrees not to attend any open house without advance notice and approval of BROKER and agrees to advise each listing broker at each open house of BUYER'S agency relationship with BROKER. BUYER represents that BUYER is

©1999, 2002, 2005 MASSACHUSETTS ASSOCIATION OF REALTORS®
03.25.05/348357.1

MassForms™
Statewide Standard Real Estate Forms

Massachusetts Association of REALTORS 256 Second Ave, Waltham MA 02451
Phone: 7818903700   Fax: 7818904919   Brian Doherty

Form No. 701

d.zfx

Produced with ZipForm™ by RE FormsNet, LLC 18025 Fifteen Mile Road, Clinton Township, Michigan 48035 www.zipform.com

F I G U R E   2.2 (Continued)

Sample Exclusive Buyer Agency Agreement—Buyer

not subject to any earlier agency agreement with any other broker or any protection period. BUYER understands that this agreement does not relieve BUYER of the duty to exercise due diligence for BUYER'S own protection, including the duty to investigate any information of importance to the BUYER.

5. <u>Broker's Compensation.</u> BUYER agrees to pay BROKER:
   (a) <u>Retainer.</u> BUYER shall pay BROKER a retainer in the amount of $ _____ upon signing this Agreement as compensation for professional counseling, consultation, and research. Such retainer is non-refundable and shall (__) shall not (__) be credited against any Success Fee.

   (b) <u>Success Fee.</u> The parties agree that compensation equal to _____ *(insert percent of purchase price or other amount)* shall be due BROKER upon successful completion of this Agreement or in the event that, within _____ days following the term of this Agreement, BUYER or any person acting for or with BUYER purchases, leases or otherwise acquires an interest in the real property after becoming aware of the availability of the real property or receiving information about the real property during said term. The parties agree that BROKER shall first seek compensation, if any, offered by the listing agent or otherwise from the transaction (listing broker/seller). If obtained, such amount shall be credited to the amount of the Success Fee. If such fee cannot be obtained in whole or in part from the transaction, BUYER agrees to pay BROKER the Success Fee, due at the time set for closing.

6. <u>Disclosure Of Identity/Other Brokers/Other Potential Buyers.</u> BROKER is authorized to disclose BUYER'S identity. BROKER is authorized to cooperate with and pay compensation to other brokers in connection with the performance of BROKER'S services. BUYER understands that BROKER may represent other buyers interested in purchasing the same or a similar property. BUYER consents to such representation.

7. <u>Entire Agreement/Governing Law.</u> This Agreement is the entire agreement between the parties. It is binding upon the parties' heirs, successors, and personal representatives. Assignment shall not limit the rights of BROKER. This Agreement shall be governed by the laws of the Commonwealth of Massachusetts. Unless otherwise stated, this Agreement may not be modified, except in writing signed by both parties.

8. <u>Other Provisions.</u> _____
_____
_____
_____

This document creates binding legal obligations. For legal advice, consult an attorney.

Dated: _____   _____
                                                  BUYER or Authorized Representative

_____   _____
BROKER or Authorized Representative   BUYER or Authorized Representative

Produced with ZipForm™ by RE FormsNet, LLC 18025 Fifteen Mile Road, Clinton Township, Michigan 48035   www.zipform.com   d.zfx

FIGURE 2.3

Sample Exclusive-Agency Listing Agreement—Seller

MASSACHUSETTS ASSOCIATION of REALTORS ®

EXCLUSIVE AGENCY LISTING AGREEMENT #692

I/We _____ ("OWNER"), hereby grant to

_____ , a real estate broker licensed under the laws

of the Commonwealth of Massachusetts ("BROKER"), the EXCLUSIVE AGENCY to sell the property described as

_____

_____ and recorded in the _____ County Registry Of Deeds

at Book _____ , Page _____ ("PROPERTY") on the following terms and conditions:

1. <u>Owner's Duties And Representations</u>. The BROKER is granted the right to sell the PROPERTY, as the OWNER'S exclusive agent, during the term of the Agreement and to cooperate in marketing the PROPERTY, including completing UFFI, lead paint (for residences built before 1978) and other forms. If the PROPERTY is sold to a buyer procured by the BROKER the fee described in paragraph 4 shall be due. The OWNER reserves the right to sell the PROPERTY himself during the Listing Period without owing a fee. If the OWNER places the PROPERTY under agreement with a Buyer, the OWNER shall notify the BROKER promptly. The BROKER is authorized, but is not required: (a) to offer compensation to other licensed brokers as subagents of OWNER, buyer's agents or otherwise; (b) to place a listing for the PROPERTY in any multiple listing service; (c) to place a sign on the PROPERTY; (d) to photograph and advertise the PROPERTY in such media as the BROKER may select; and (e) to place a lock box on the PROPERTY. The OWNER authorizes the BROKER to disclose to prospective buyers all information about the PROPERTY provided to the BROKER by the OWNER, all of which the OWNER represents to be accurate. **The OWNER acknowledges receipt of an agency disclosure form** and, according to the Code of Ethics and Standards of Practice of the National Association of REALTORS®, has been advised of (1) the broker's general company policies regarding cooperation with and compensation to subagents, buyer's agents and other licensees; (2) the fact that a buyer's agent, even if compensated by the listing broker or seller will represent the interest of the buyer; and (3) any potential for the listing broker to act as a disclosed dual agent on behalf of the seller and buyer. The OWNER agrees to comply with all applicable fair housing laws.

2. <u>Listing Price</u>. The listing price for the PROPERTY shall be _____ dollars or such other price and terms as the OWNER may approve.

3. <u>Listing Period</u>. This Agreement shall begin on _____ and end on _____ and may be extended by agreement.

4. <u>Broker's Fee</u>. If within the term of this Agreement or any extension the PROPERTY is sold to a buyer introduced by the BROKER or the BROKER procures a buyer who is ready, willing and able to buy at a price and on the terms set forth herein or on such other price and terms as the OWNER may agree, the BROKER shall be due a fee of _____ percent of the purchase price, whether or not the transaction is completed or title passes. Said fee shall be paid at the time set for closing and may be deducted from amounts held as escrow agent. The aforesaid fee shall be due upon sale within _____ months after expiration of this Agreement or any extension to any person who is introduced to the PROPERTY during the aforesaid term or any extension, except if the OWNER has entered into an exclusive agreement with another broker in good faith, in which case the BROKER shall be entitled to receive only the difference between the fee set forth herein and any lesser fee paid to the other broker. If any deposit is retained by the OWNER as liquidated damages for default by the buyer under any agreement for sale of the PROPERTY, the BROKER shall be due one-half (1/2) of the amount so retained, but not more than an amount equal to the full commission that would have been paid to BROKER if a sale had been completed.

5. <u>Broker's Duties</u>. The Broker agrees to use reasonable efforts in marketing the PROPERTY and agrees to list the PROPERTY with the _____ multiple listing service. The BROKER shall have no obligation to continue to market the PROPERTY after an offer has been accepted and while a transaction is pending. The BROKER is not hired as a property inspector, septic inspector, surveyor, tax advisor or attorney and if such services are desired OWNER should hire professionals.

6. <u>Additional Terms</u>. _____

_____

_____

Dated: _____

_____
OWNER or Authorized Representative

_____
BROKER or Authorized Representative

_____
OWNER or Authorized Representative

MASSForms™
Statewide Standard Real Estate Forms
Massachusetts Association of REALTORS 256 Second Ave, Waltham MA 02451
Phone: 7818903700   Fax: 7818904919   Brian Doherty

©1999, 2000 MASSACHUSETTS ASSOCIATION OF REALTORS®

7.05.00/160352

d.zfx

Produced with ZipForm™ by RE FormsNet, LLC 18025 Fifteen Mile Road, Clinton Township, Michigan 48035   www.zipform.com

Buyer—Under an open buyer-agency agreement, the buyer retains the right to hire as many brokers as he or she pleases at any given time. The buyer is only required to compensate the broker who ultimately sells the buyer a property. An open listing hiring contract may be oral or written.

Cobroker cooperation.   It is not unusual for one broker to have a property listed that meets the needs of a buyer found by another broker. Cooperation between brokers is created when a brokerage submits a listing to the multiple-listing service and offers cooperation to other brokerage firms who want to show the property to potential buyers and compensation to the brokerage firm that brings a buyer who purchases the property. If the customer buys the property, the listing broker will divide the commission between the two brokers in whatever proportion is agreed to. The listing broker retains control of the listing, and the cooperating broker acts in the capacity of a salesperson bringing a customer to the listing broker. It is the listing broker, however, who must complete the transaction. The cobroker agreement should be expressed in writing even if the two brokers have had previous dealings. Note, however, that if the cooperating broker does not have an agency relationship with the buyer, the cooperating broker may be called a *subagent*. As a subagent of the listing broker, she or he has the same fiduciary duties toward the seller as the listing broker. The cooperating broker may also be a *nonagent,* in which case she or he facilitates the sales process and owes no fiduciary duties to either principal. In order to protect the best interest of the client, sellers agents should always inform the seller of the status of the cooperating broker when a property is being shown.

Net listing.   Under the Massachusetts Real Estate License Law, a net listing is forbidden. A *net listing* results when an owner specifies a particular dollar amount that he or she must net from the sale of the property; any sum exceeding that amount will constitute the broker's commission. In those states in which such arrangements are legal, they often result in disagreements between owners and brokers on methods of payment and in claims that brokers have set prices low and made exorbitant profits. Under a net listing, it is difficult to balance the broker's fiduciary responsibility to the principal with the broker's own ability to make a profit. Because the practice of net listing is illegal in Massachusetts, brokers must inform owners that their fee will be either a percentage of the selling price or a flat fee for services. Then the broker presents the seller with information about comparable sales in the area, and the seller then determines the proper sales price based on the broker's advice and expertise.

■ **FOR EXAMPLE**   Ben Bottomline called Doris Doright, a Boston real estate broker, and told her that he wanted to sell his house.

"I don't want to be bothered with percentages and bargaining and offers and counteroffers," he explained, "I just need to walk out of this deal with $200,000 in my pocket. You sell this place for any more than that, and you keep the rest."

Doright knew that homes such as Bottomline's in his neighborhood were selling for over $250,000. On the other hand, she knew that a net listing is illegal in Massachusetts. What should she do?

■ PRICING THE PROPERTY

Brokers are often asked for their opinion of a property's market value before it is listed for sale. Sellers rightly assume that a broker should be generally knowledgeable about local property values. In order to protect the seller's interests and to ensure that a fair and reasonable price is set, a broker should prepare a *competitive market analysis (CMA)* that compares the seller's property with similar properties that have sold recently. The broker may advise the seller of how the price the seller has set compares with other known values and may encourage the seller to consider such factors as how quickly he or she wants to sell. However, a licensed broker should avoid recommending or setting a price on the listed property. *It is the seller's responsibility to set the selling price.*

A CMA is *not* an appraisal and must not be presented as one. In Massachusetts, no one other than a state-certified residential real estate appraiser or state-licensed real estate appraiser may appraise real estate. (See Chapter 13.) Real estate brokers or salespersons, however, are permitted to give price opinions in the normal course of their business *as long as the opinion is not referred to as an appraisal.* Nonappraisers may appraise property in non-federally related transactions, such as those not involving federal mortgage insurance or guarantees. While a listing agreement or a strictly cash sale is not a federally related transaction, most mortgage applications are likely to be. Therefore, they would require the involvement of a certified or licensed appraiser. (See Chapter 13.)

Whether or not they are licensed appraisers, brokers should disclose to sellers whatever information they have about a property's value. If necessary, they should express concern about a seller's price, although they may not give an opinion as to what the proper selling price should be.

While counseling sellers about a property's price, brokers should emphasize that any information they present is neither an opinion of value nor an appraisal, but merely important information that they feel should be shared with the seller. If further questions arise, or if the seller is insistent, the broker should recommend that a licensed appraiser be consulted. Figure 2.4 contains an example of the Seller's Statement of Property Condition.

FIGURE 2.4

Sample Seller's Statement of Property Condition

MASSACHUSETTS ASSOCIATION OF REALTORS®
SELLER'S STATEMENT OF PROPERTY CONDITION

THE SELLER AUTHORIZES THE BROKERS OR SALESPERSONS TO PROVIDE THE FOLLOWING INFORMATION TO PROSPECTIVE BUYERS. THIS INFORMATION IS BASED UPON THE SELLER'S KNOWLEDGE, BUT IS NOT INTENDED AS A GUARANTEE OF THE CONDITION OF THE PROPERTY OR THE CONTINUED SATISFACTORY OPERATION OF ANY SYSTEM.
THE BUYER SHOULD INDEPENDENTLY VERIFY ALL INFORMATION BEFORE PURCHASE.

Property Address _____

ANSWERS

YES	NO	UNKN	**I. TITLE/ZONING/BUILDING INFORMATION**
☐	☐	☐	1. Seller/Owner _____ How long owned? _____
			2. How long occupied? _____ Approximate year built? _____
			3. Have you been advised of any title problems or limitations (for example, deed restriction, lot line dispute, order of conditions)? If yes, please explain _____
☐	☐	☐	a) Do you know of any easement, common driveway, or right of way? If yes, please explain _____
			4. Zoning classification of property (if known) _____
☐	☐	☐	5. Has your city/town issued a notice of any violation which is still outstanding? If yes, explain _____
☐	☐	☐	a) Have you been advised that the current use is nonconforming in any way? Explain _____
☐	☐	☐	6. Do you know of any variances or special permits? Explain _____
☐	☐	☐	7. During Seller's ownership, has work been done for which a permit was required? If yes, explain _____
☐	☐	☐	a) Were permits obtained?
☐	☐	☐	b) Was the work approved by inspector?
☐	☐	☐	c) Is there an outstanding notice of any building code violation? Yes ____ No ____ Explain _____
☐	☐	☐	8. Have you been informed that any part of the property is in a designated flood zone or wetlands? Explain _____
			(See Flood Zone disclosure Page 4)
☐	☐	☐	9. Water drainage problems? Explain _____

YES	NO	UNKN	**II. SYSTEM AND UTILITIES INFORMATION**
			DO YOU KNOW OF ANY CURRENT PROBLEM WITH ANY SYSTEM LISTED BELOW?
☐	☐	☐	10. Has there ever been an UNDERGROUND FUEL TANK?
			If yes, is it still in use? _____
			If not used, was it removed? _____
			(See Hazardous Materials Disclosure Page 4)
☐	☐	☐	11. HEATING SYSTEM: Problems? Explain _____
			a) Identify any unheated room or area _____
			b) Approximate date of last service _____
			c) Reason _____
			12. DOMESTIC HOT WATER: Type _____ Age _____ Problems? Explain _____ Burners Owned or rented?
☐	☐	☐	13. SEWAGE SYSTEM: Problems? Explain _____
			Type: Municipal Sewer ____ Private ____ If private, describe type of system: (cesspool, septic tank, etc.) _____
			Name of service company _____
			Date it was last pumped _____ Frequency _____
☐	☐	☐	During your ownership has sewage backed up into house or onto yard? Yes ____ No ____ Explain _____
☐	☐	☐	Is system shared with other homes?
			Date a Title 5 inspection last performed _____ Copy attached. Yes ____ No ____

SELLER'S INITIALS _____ _____   BUYER'S INITIALS _____ _____

1 of 4

F I G U R E 2.4 (Continued)

Sample Seller's Statement of Property Condition

<u>ANSWERS</u>

☐ ☐ ☐   14. PLUMBING SYSTEM: Problems/Leaks/Freezing? Explain _____

Bathroom ventilation problems? Explain _____

15. DRINKING WATER SOURCE: Public _____ Private _____ If private:

☐ ☐ ☐   a) Location _____
    b) Date last tested _____ Report Attached _____ Not attached _____
    c) Water quality problems? Explain _____
    d) Water quantity problems? Explain _____
    e) Flow rate (gal. min.) _____
    f) Age of pump _____

☐ ☐ ☐   g) Is there a filtration system? _____ Age/Type of filtration system _____

16. ELECTRICAL SYSTEM: Problems? Explain _____

☐ ☐ ☐   17. APPLIANCES: List appliances that are included _____
Any known problems? _____
If yes, explain _____

☐ ☐ ☐   18. SECURITY SYSTEM: None _____ Type _____ Age _____ Company _____
Problems? Explain _____

☐ ☐ ☐   19. AIR CONDITIONING: Central _____ Window _____ Other _____ None _____
Problems? Explain _____

YES **NO** **UNKN**   **III. BUILDING/STRUCTURAL IMPROVEMENTS INFORMATION**

☐ ☐ ☐   20. FOUNDATION/SLAB:
Problems? Explain _____

☐ ☐ ☐   21. BASEMENT: Water _____ Seepage _____ Dampness _____
Explain amount, frequency, and location _____
    a) Sump pump? If yes, age _____ location _____ Problems? _____

☐ ☐ ☐   22. ROOF:
Problems? Explain _____
Location of leaks/repairs _____

☐ ☐ ☐   23. CHIMNEY/FIREPLACE: Date last cleaned _____ Problems? _____
Wood/Coal/Pellet Stove in compliance with installation regulations/code/bylaws?_____
If not, explain _____

☐ ☐ ☐   24. History of smoke/fire damage to structure, if any? Explain _____

☐ ☐ ☐   25. FLOORS: Type of floors under carpet/linoleum? _____
Problems with floors (buckling, sagging, etc.)? Explain _____

☐ ☐ ☐   26. WALLS:
    a) INTERIOR Walls: Problems? Explain _____
    b) EXTERIOR Walls: Problems? Explain _____

☐ ☐ ☐   27. WINDOWS/SLIDING DOORS/DOORS:
Problems or leaks? Explain _____

☐ ☐ ☐   28. INSULATION: Does house have insulation? If yes, type _____ Date installed _____ Location _____

☐ ☐ ☐   29. ASBESTOS: Do you know whether asbestos is present in exterior shingles, pipecovering or boiler insulation?
Has a fiber count been performed?
If yes, attach copy _____
    (See Asbestos disclosure Page 4)

☐ ☐ ☐   30. LEAD PAINT: Is lead paint present?
If yes, locations (attach copy of inspection reports) _____
If yes, describe abatement plan/interim controls, if any _____
Has paint been encapsulated? If yes, when and by whom? _____
    (See Lead Paint disclosure Page 4)

☐ ☐ ☐   31. RADON: Has test for radon been performed? If yes, attach copy _____
    (See Radon disclosure Page 4)

☐ ☐ ☐   32. INSECTS: History of Termites/Wood Destroying Insects or Rodent Problems? If yes, explain treatment and dates _____
    (See Chlordane disclosure Page 4)

SELLER'S INITIALS _____ _____   BUYER'S INITIALS _____ _____

2 of 4

MassForms
Statewide Standard Real Estate Forms   ©1999 MASSACHUSETTS ASSOCIATION OF REALTORS®

F I G U R E   2.4 (Continued)

Sample Seller's Statement of Property Condition

ANSWERS

☐	☐	☐	33. SWIMMING POOL/JACUZZI: Problems? Explain _____
☐	☐	☐	Name of service company _____
			34. GARAGE/SHED/OR OTHER STRUCTURE: Problems, explain _____

YES   NO   UNKN   **IV. MISCELLANEOUS INFORMATION**

☐   ☐   ☐   35. Do you know of any other problem which may affect the value or use of the property which may not be obvious to a prospective buyer?
Explain _____

YES   NO   UNKN   **V. CONDOMINIUM INFORMATION**

☐   ☐   ☐   36. If converted to condominium, are documents recorded (Master deed/Unit deed etc.)?
☐   ☐   ☐   37. PARKING: Is parking space included? If yes, is it deeded, exclusive easement or common?
☐   ☐   ☐   38. CONDO FEES: Current monthly fees for Unit are $ _____
☐   ☐   ☐   Heat included? Yes ____ No ____
☐   ☐   ☐   Electricity included? Yes ____ No ____
☐   ☐   ☐   39. RESERVE FUND: Has an advance payment been made to a condo reserve fund?
If yes, how much $ _____

☐   ☐   ☐   40. CONDO ASSOC. INFO: Is owners' association currently involved in any litigation? _____
If yes, explain _____

☐   ☐   ☐   41. Have you been advised of any matter which is likely to result in a special assessment or substantially increase condominium fees?
Explain _____

YES   NO   UNKN   **VI. RENTAL PROPERTY INFORMATION**

42. NUMBER OF UNITS: _____
☐   ☐   ☐   Has a unit been added/subdivided since original construction?
If yes, was a permit for new/added unit obtained? _____
43. RENTS: Number of units occupied _____ Rents $ _____ /month
Expiration date of each lease _____
☐   ☐   ☐   Any tenants without leases?
☐   ☐   ☐   Is owner holding last month's rent _____ security deposit? _____
If yes, has interest been paid? _____
If security deposit held attach a copy of statements of condition.. Attached _____ Not attached _____
☐   ☐   ☐   44. Is there any outstanding notice of any sanitary code violation? Yes ____ No ____ Explain _____

VII. ACKNOWLEDGMENT

Seller(s) hereby acknowledge that the information set forth above is true and accurate to the best of my (our) knowledge. I (we) further agree to defend and indemnify the broker(s) and any subagents for disclosure of any on the information contained herein. Seller(s) further acknowledge receipt of copy of Seller's Statement of Property Condition.

Date _____   Seller _____   Seller _____

Buyer/Prospective Buyer acknowledges receipt of Seller's Statement of Property Condition before purchase. Buyer acknowledges that Broker has not verified the information herein and Buyer has been advised to verify information independently.

Date _____   Buyer _____   Buyer _____

SELLER'S INITIALS _____ _____   BUYER'S INITIALS _____ _____

3 of 4

F I G U R E   2.4 (Continued)

Sample Seller's Statement of Property Condition

VIII. EXPLANATORY MATERIAL

The following clauses are provided for descriptive purposes only. For detailed information, consult the Massachusetts Department of Public Health, the Massachusetts Department of Environmental Protection, or other appropriate agency, or your attorney.

A. Flood Hazard Insurance Disclosure Clause   (Question #8)
The lender may require Flood Hazard Insurance as a condition of the mortgage loan if the lender determines that the property is in a flood hazard zone.

B. Hazardous Materials Disclosure Clause   (Question #10)
In certain circumstances Massachusetts law can hold an owner of real estate liable to pay for the cost of removing hazardous or toxic materials from real estate and for damages resulting from the release of such materials, according to the Massachusetts Oil and Hazardous Material Release and Response Act, General Laws, Chapter 21E. The buyer acknowledges that he may have the property professionally inspected for the presence of, or the substantial likelihood of release of oil or hazardous material and such proof of inspection may be required as a prerequisite for financing the property.

C. Asbestos Disclosure Clause   (Question #29)
The United States Consumer Product Safety Commission has maintained that asbestos materials are hazardous if they release separate fibers which can be inhaled. Asbestos is a common insulation material on heating pipes, boilers, and furnaces. It may also be present in certain types of floor and ceiling materials, shingles, plaster products, cements and other building materials. The buyer may have the property professionally inspected for the presence of asbestos and if repair or removal of asbestos is desired, proper safety guidelines must be observed.

D. Lead Paint Disclosure Clause   (Question #30)
Whenever a child under six years of age resides in any residential premises in which any paint, plaster or other accessible material contains dangerous levels of lead, the owner is required by law, to remove all said paint, plaster or cover with appropriate materials so as to make it inaccessible to a child under six years of age. Consumption of lead is poisonous and may cause serious personal injury. Whenever such residential premises containing dangerous levels of lead undergoes a change of ownership, as a result, a child under six years of age will become a resident, the new owner is required by law to remove said paint, plaster cover or encapsulate it with appropriate materials so as to make it inaccessible to such child. Buyer should receive information pamphlet from Department of Public Health.

E. Radon Disclosure Clause   (Question #31)
Radon is an odorless, colorless, tasteless gas produced naturally in the ground by the normal decay of uranium and radium. Radon can lead to the development of radioactive particles which can be inhaled. Studies indicate the result of extended exposure to high levels of radon may increase the risk of developing lung cancer.

F. Chlordane Disclosure Clause   (Question #32)
Pesticide products containing chlordane were banned in Massachusetts on June 11, 1985, following a determination by the Department of Food and Agriculture that the use of chlordane may cause unreasonable adverse effects on the environment including risk of cancer. Although existing data does not conclusively prove that significant health effects have occurred as a direct result of chlordane use, the long-term potential health risks are such that is prudent public health policy, according to the Department, to eliminate the further introduction of chlordane into the environment.

G. Mold Information
Molds are naturally occurring organisms that exist both indoors and outdoors. More than 1000 different kinds of mold have been found in homes in the United States. Molds are fungi that reproduce by making spores. Spores are small and lightweight and able to travel through the air. Molds need moisture and food to grow and their growth is stimulated by warm, damp and humid conditions. Molds can use materials such as wood, paper, drywall and carpet as food sources. Reducing dampness indoors is often key to reducing the growth of mold. Depending on the level of mold, allergies, respiratory problems and other health consequences can be triggered in sensitive individuals. However, exposure to mold does not always result in health problems. As of July of 2002, U.S. governmental agencies reported that a determination had not been made what quantity of mold was acceptable in an indoor environment. For more information on mold, contact an engineer or other qualified mold inspector. Information may also be found at the web site for the U. S. Environmental Protection Agency, www.epa.gov.

H. Fair Housing Notice
It is unlawful to discriminate on the basis of race, color, religious creed, national origin, age, gender, sex, ancestry, marital status, veteran status, sexual orientation, disability, presence of a child, receipt of public assistance or other protected classification in the sale or rental of covered housing.

SELLER'S INITIALS _____ _____   BUYER'S INITIALS _____ _____

4 of 4

MassForms
Statewide Standard Real Estate Forms   ©1999 MASSACHUSETTS ASSOCIATION OF REALTORS®

Produced with ZipForm™ by RE FormsNet, LLC 18025 Fifteen Mile Road, Clinton Township, Michigan 48035 www.zipform.com   gf.zfx

QUESTIONS

1. A listing agreement
   a. is an employment contract between a broker and a seller.
   b. is an agreement to purchase property signed by the buyer.
   c. must not specify a price for the property.
   d. may not state a specific commission.

2. Which type of listing agreement is illegal in Massachusetts?
   a. Open listing
   b. Net listing
   c. Exclusive-right-to-sell listing
   d. Exclusive-agency listing

3. Which of the following agreements need *NOT* be in writing?
   a. Exclusive-agency listing
   b. Open listing
   c. Exclusive-right-to-sell listing
   d. Multiple listing

4. Under which of the following relationships may an owner *NOT* sell his or her home without compensating a broker?
   a. Open listing
   b. Exclusive-right-to-sell listing
   c. Exclusive-agency listing
   d. Multiple listing

5. Sally Seller told Bill Broker that she wanted to receive $50,000 when she sold her house. Bill accepted the listing and sold the house for $160,000. Since Sally has no mortgage or other debt on the home Bill gave Sally the $50,000 she wanted and kept the rest. Which of the following is correct?
   a. Bill should have given Sally a better appraisal of the value of her house.
   b. Bill's commission exceeds statutory and NAR guidelines.
   c. Bill accepted an illegal net listing.
   d. As Sally's agent, Bill had a duty to sell the house for as much as possible.

6. In a cobroker agreement the
   a. selling broker shows a listing broker's property to a potential buyer.
   b. selling broker may complete the transaction if he or she produces the buyer.
   c. listing broker is the "cooperating broker."
   d. listing broker divides the commission with the finding broker.

7. CMA is the acronym for which of the following?
   a. Comparative market appraisal
   b. Comparative marketing agreement
   c. Competitive market analysis
   d. Competitive market accounting

8. The sales price of a house
   a. is set by the selling broker in the listing agreement.
   b. should be based on a licensed broker's recommendation.
   c. is based on a licensed broker's appraisal.
   d. should be set by the seller.

9. Paula is buying a house near Springfield, using FHA financing. The appraisal may only be performed by
   a. a licensed real estate broker.
   b. a licensed or certified real estate appraiser.
   c. any resident of Massachusetts.
   d. a comparative market analyst.

10. A broker should *NOT* do which of the following in regard to sales price.
    a. Give the seller advice
    b. Provide information about comparable values
    c. Express an opinion of what the proper selling price should be
    d. Express concern about the seller's selected price

CHAPTER

Interests in Real Estate

■ ESTATES IN LAND

When a valid deed is delivered, the law presumes that a fee simple estate has been conveyed with the delivery of the deed, unless the deed specifically states otherwise.

Legal Life Estates

Dower and curtesy.   The purpose underlying dower and curtesy is the protection of one spouse against disinheritance by the other. At common law, *dower* was the right of a widow to an interest for life in one-third of all real estate owned by her husband during their marriage. *Curtesy* was the right of a widower to an interest for life in all (i.e., not one-third) of the real estate owned by his wife during their marriage. The Massachusetts legislature has abolished the distinction between dower and curtesy (i.e., now all rights are called dower) and has abolished the rights of dower except as to those lands owned at the time of death. Therefore, it is no longer necessary to obtain a release of dower or curtesy rights in a deed.

Dower rights are rarely exercised. Persons who are dissatisfied with their treatment under their deceased spouses' wills generally choose to exercise their waiver right under the Massachusetts Law of Descent and take the minimum statutory share of the estate. (See Chapter 8.) Further, because most married couples hold their property as tenants by the entirety or joint tenants, succession is not usually an issue. Only if an individual dies insolvent may dower arise: the surviving spouse's right comes before the claims of creditors.

Homestead. The homestead right entitles a homeowner and his or her surviving spouse and minor children to a life estate in the land and buildings occupied as their principal residence as a protection against attachment, levy on execution, or sale to satisfy debts to the extent of $500,000 per residence, per family. Disabled and elderly persons filing jointly are entitled to a maximum amount of $500,000 per individual, regardless of whether such declaration is filed individually or jointly with another. Over the years, these allowances have increased. If a homeowner has already filed a homestead under a former allowance, the homeowner gets the increased protection without needing to file a new declaration.

The purpose of homestead is to protect an individual's equity in his or her home. A declaration of homestead exempts certain property (e.g., land, buildings, and manufactured homes) from the laws of conveyance, descent, devise, attachment, levy on execution, and sale for payment of debts or legacies up to the homestead value except in the following six cases:

1. Sale for taxes
2. For a debt contracted prior to the acquisition of said estate of homestead
3. For a debt contracted for the purchase of said home
4. Upon an execution issued from the probate court to enforce its judgment that a spouse pay a certain amount weekly or otherwise for the support of a spouse or minor children
5. Where buildings on land not owned by the owner of a homestead estate are attached, levied upon, or sold for the ground rent of the lot whereon they stand
6. Upon an execution issued from a court of competent jurisdiction to enforce its judgment based upon fraud, mistake, duress, undue influence, or lack of capacity

To acquire a homestead right, the deed of conveyance must include a statement or "declaration" that the principal residence will be held as a homestead. Homestead may also be invoked by recording a signed declaration in the Registry of Deeds for the county in which the land is located.

■ ENCUMBRANCES

Easements

Following are the three ways easements are commonly created in Massachusetts:

1. By deed
2. By prescription
3. By necessity (implied easements)

Easement by deed. An easement can be created by deed when a grantor (1) conveys a limited easement right to his or her property or (2) conveys all his or her rights in a specific property but retains or reserves an easement. The grantor can use either a quitclaim or a warranty deed to create an easement. (See Chapter 8.) A quitclaim deed may be used to convey an easement when the grantor is conveying no other interest. In Massachusetts, the quitclaim deed has special warranty deed status because of the title search process.

An easement may be granted for a specific, limited period of time to a specific individual, or to the grantee or his or her heirs and assignees forever.

Easement by prescription. An easement by prescription is the equivalent of adverse possession. In Massachusetts, the following five factors must be established in order to establish an easement by prescription:

1. Use or possession must endure for 20 years.
2. Use must be continuous and uninterrupted.
3. Use occurred without the owner's permission.
4. The owner knew (or should have known) of the use and took no action to prevent it.
5. A benefited parcel of land, usually abutting or adjacent, must exist.

The final factor is intended to prevent the public from obtaining an easement. The 20-year period may include previous users of the easement, which is referred to as *tacking*.

■ **FOR EXAMPLE**

I

For the past 20 years, Jim has driven across his neighbor Fred's property several times a day in order to reach his garage from a more comfortable direction or angle. Jim has an easement by prescription.

II

For 25 years, Lulu has driven across Fred's property two or three times a year to reach her property when she's in a hurry. She does not have an easement by prescription because her use was not continuous.

III

Twenty years ago, Edna arranged a line of colored stones marking the path she would like to use to cross Fred's property, but she never used the path. She does not have an easement.

IV

For 15 years, Anna parked her car next to Fred's garage. Five years ago, she sold her house to Nick, who continued to park his car next to Fred's garage. Nick now has a permanent easement by prescription.

But what if instead of parking his car next to the garage, Nick simply recorded his easement in the county in which Fred's property is located? Nick would not have an easement because recording documents or deeds does not, by itself, give notice to the owner.

Easement by necessity. An easement by necessity is created when a seller conveys a parcel of land and the buyer has no way to reach the property except by crossing the seller's land or that of a neighboring owner. In determining whether or not an easement by necessity exists, courts will consider the intent of the parties at the time of the conveyance.

In particular, courts will consider the

■ specific geographic condition of the property (the "lay of the land");
■ buyer's and the seller's actual knowledge of the limited access; and
■ references (or the absence of references) to an easement or right of access made in the conveyance document (deed).

The easement by necessity is not automatic as is the 20-year prescriptive easement. If a court determines that the parties did not intend an easement, none will be imposed. Nor will an easement be imposed if the grantee, by spending a reasonable amount of time and money, would be able to create another means of access to and from the property. Massachusetts courts consider each case on its own merits: There is no hard-line rule.

■ **FOR EXAMPLE**   Lou conveys a portion of his land to Bud. Bud's property is completely surrounded by Lou's land, with Road 1 separated from Bud's property by a rapidly flowing river and Road 2 on the other side of Lou's field. If the conveyance included an easement to the road, Bud would obviously have one. But if the conveyance expressly said "without any easement across Lou's property," Bud would not have an easement.

IN PRACTICE

In general, easements remain in effect against property and are not abandoned by nonuse. By statute and case law, however, the failure to rerecord an easement at least once every 50 years can cause the easement to be unenforceable against a new owner of the property who has no knowledge of its existence. Usually, attorneys will restate or refer to easements in deeds as a title is transferred, giving notice of the continuing encumbrance.

License

A *license* is the smallest right a person can have in real estate. It arises out of a contract, not from a grant of ownership. A parking place, a hotel room, and a movie seat are examples of licenses.

If a person rents a parking space for a few hours, he or she has contracted for certain rights in the land: he or she has the right to park his or her car there, for instance, and the right to enter the property to recover the car. However, where the license is *gratuitous*—without payment or the underlying contractual elements—the license may be canceled without notice and with no legal recourse for the licensee (i.e., the person who used the license).

■ **FOR EXAMPLE**   Herman's friend Ahab buys a boat in February. Ahab asks Herman for permission to leave the boat in Herman's backyard until the harbor opens in May. By permitting Ahab to store the boat on his property, Herman has given Ahab a license. But if Herman buys his own boat in March, he can tell Ahab to remove his boat, and Ahab will have no legal remedy.

■ RIPARIAN RIGHTS

Owners of property that includes or lies alongside bodies of water face particular ownership issues, called *riparian rights*. In Massachusetts, there are three types of common riparian rights situations: streams, surface waters, and tidal waters.

The word *riparian* refers to the rights of an owner along a river or watercourse, but when the rights are adjacent to a lake or the ocean they may be called *littoral* rights. The terms "riparian rights" and "riparian owner" are often used in conjunction with all water-related issues. For study purposes, just remember that *Riparian* refers to *Rivers* (and other flowing bodies of water), and *Littoral* refers to *Lakes* (and other standing waters).

Streams

If the stream is navigable, that is, if a boat can be floated down it, then the public owns both the water and the land under the water. The Commonwealth is responsible for the care and supervision of the stream. The owner of the land next to the stream, or through which the stream runs, owns the land *up to the bank* of the stream.

An owner of land abutting a navigable waterway owns the right to use the water as it passes, but he or she cannot obstruct it or prevent it from flowing in its natural course or from being used for navigation.

If the stream is not navigable, ownership may be held in one of two ways. First, if the stream separates two properties, the adjacent landowners own the water and the land under the water to the center of the stream. Second, if the stream runs through a single property, then the riparian owner owns the water all the way across and all the land on both sides and underneath.

Ponds and Lakes

Surface waters—such as ponds, swamps, and lakes—are controlled by the state and are regulated according to antipollution statutes. Adjacent property owners own the land up to the shore and do not have an unlimited right to fill in a wetland or lakeshore. Use of the water must be approved under the state environmental laws.

Tidal Water

An owner whose property abuts tidal waters (that is, oceanfront property) owns the land to the mean low water line or 100 rods below mean high water, whichever is less. The land between low water and high water is reserved for the use of the public by state law and is regulated by the state.

QUESTIONS

1. When a valid deed is delivered, unless stated otherwise, it is assumed that which of the following estates is delivered?
   a. Life
   b. Leasehold
   c. Fee simple
   d. Freehold

2. In Massachusetts, dower rights become effective
   a. at the time of the marriage.
   b. at the moment of a spouse's death.
   c. when a creditor lays claim to the property.
   d. when the couple is divorced.

3. Which of the following statements is NOT true regarding the homestead right?
   a. The amount of the mortgage is exempt from the debt.
   b. The home must be the principal residence of the family.
   c. The homeowner, surviving spouse, and minor children have a life estate.
   d. The homestead right does not have to be recorded.

4. If an easement is to be acquired by prescription, it must be proved that which of the following is TRUE?
   a. The owner's permission was given.
   b. The easement was used for 15 years.
   c. Only one person used the easement.
   d. There was a benefited parcel of land.

5. When Lorenzo sold the back half of his property to Mike, he granted to Mike an easement allowing Mike the ability to cross Lorenzo's land in order to access his property. Lorenzo should
   a. have the easement written into the deed when title is conveyed.
   b. just tell Mike that he can drive across the strip.
   c. give Mike a notarized letter granting him permission to use the strip.
   d. let Mike use the strip for 20 years.

6. Which of the following statements about a license is NOT true?
   a. A license can be canceled without notice.
   b. A license is a grant of ownership.
   c. A license arises out of a contract.
   d. A licensee has purchased certain rights.

7. The smallest right that a person can have in real estate is a(n)
   a. license.
   b. life estate.
   c. lease.
   d. easement.

8. Littoral rights would be of interest to someone living in which of the following situations?
   a. On the bank of a river
   b. On the side of a hill
   c. On the edge of a forest
   d. On an ocean beach

9. If a river is navigable, the adjacent landowner owns the
   a. land and water to the middle of the river.
   b. water in the river.
   c. land under the river.
   d. land to the bank of the river.

10. The purpose of homestead is to
    a. protect spouses against disinheritance.
    b. ensure the payment of taxes, claims, and liens.
    c. protect a person's equity in his or her home.
    d. permit a surviving spouse to retain the home.

11. Owners whose property is adjacent to a large pond own the
    a. property to the shore, with their use of the water limited by environmental laws.
    b. property to the center of the pond, but they may use the water only for recreation.
    c. property up to 100 rods from the shoreline.
    d. entire pond if they agree to comply with the appropriate environmental regulations.

CHAPTER 4

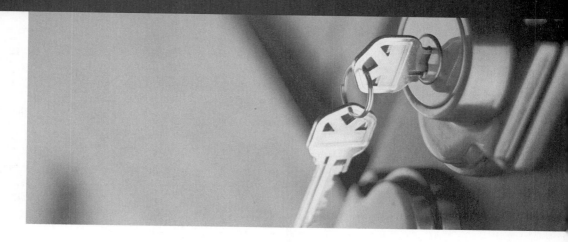

Forms of Real Estate Ownership

■ FORMS OF OWNERSHIP

Massachusetts recognizes estate in common, joint tenancy, tenancy by the entirety, and partnership ownership. The deed usually states the form of ownership.

Estate in Common

In Massachusetts, it is presumed that when a deed conveys land to two or more people or to a husband and a wife—except if it is a mortgage, a devise, or a conveyance in trust—it is conveying ownership as an estate in common, unless there is evidence that another form of ownership was intended.

Joint Tenancy

In Massachusetts, a conveyance or devise of land to a person and his or her spouse that expressly states that the grantees or devisees shall take jointly, or as joint tenants, or in joint tenancy, or to them and the survivor of them shall create an estate in joint tenancy. In a conveyance or devise to three or more persons, words creating a joint tenancy shall be construed as applying to all of the grantees, or devisees, regardless of marital status, unless a contrary intent appears from the instrument.

Note: A grant of land to two people who are not married that specifies that they shall hold the land as tenants by the entirety will result in a joint tenancy.

Tenancy by the Entirety

A tenancy by the entirety is created when

1. the conveying deed *expressly* transfers the property "to X and Y as tenants by the entirety"; and
2. the conveyance is to a *married couple*.

It is important to note that there must be an *express* statement that a tenancy by the entirety is being created. The mere fact that a property's owners are married does not automatically mean it is held by the entirety.

IN   PRACTICE

In Massachusetts, property is presumed to be held as an estate in common unless the deed explicitly states otherwise.

An advantage of tenancies by the entirety created after February 1980 is that a creditor of either spouse cannot take action against property that is used as their home because the ownership is indivisible. The disadvantage of this form of ownership, and the reason why some couples choose joint tenancy, is that neither individual may sell his or her share without destroying the tenancy by the entirety. A joint tenant may sell his or her share, and the purchaser becomes a tenant in common with the other joint tenant. In a tenancy by the entirety, however, the parties must be married to each other: conveying an interest to a nonmarital party destroys the tenancy, creating a tenancy in common. Similarly, if a married couple divorces, a tenancy by the entirety converts to a tenancy in common. Just remember that this form of ownership is limited to two married persons who cannot convey or partition their interest without destroying the tenancy.

Because both husband and wife own the entire property, the surviving spouse will be the sole owner. If there is confusion in a deed about which estate is created by a husband and wife, but it is clear that a survivorship right is desired, courts will construe ownership as being a joint tenancy, not a tenancy by the entirety.

Partnership Ownership

Partnership ownership results if partnership funds are used in the purchase of property by persons who are partners. Massachusetts has adopted the Uniform Partnership Act, under the terms of which a partner may purchase property with partnership funds in his or her own individual name. The property does not have to be in the partnership's name.

■ COOPERATIVES, CONDOMINIUMS, AND TIME-SHARES

Cooperative Housing Corporations

To foster the development of safe, decent, and affordable housing, the state encourages the establishment of multiple-family housing cooperative associations. Following statutory requirements, a special kind of corporation is established in which individual unit residents own stock in the corporation and receive a *proprietary lease* entitling him or her to occupy a specific unit in the building and to use the common areas.

Because an individual in a cooperative association occupies the unit under a proprietary lease but does not own the unit, his or her interest is treated as personal property.

Condominiums

Condominium ownership is a real-property interest combining mixed forms of ownership, for example, joint tenancy with an estate in common. *Condominium* means to "exercise dominion with others."

Condominium conversion. Massachusetts has specific laws governing the conversion of existing rental property to condominium ownership. At both the state and local levels, these laws protect tenants who will be displaced by the sale of the property. The protections allow time for those who are dislocated to move, or they give the right of first refusal to purchase to present tenants. Some communities, faced with inadequate housing for low-income people, the elderly, or the handicapped, have placed emergency moratoriums on condominium conversions. In fact, in Massachusetts, any building containing four or more housing units that has been occupied by tenants during the prior year is covered by condominium conversion law. Under the law, the owner of such a building must give all tenants a notice of intent to convert to condominium or cooperative. The notice must contain the following three items:

1. Owner has filed or intends to file a Master Deed converting the property to a condominium.
2. The tenant shall be given a period of time to vacate based on status as elderly, low to moderate income, handicapped, or other.
3. The tenant shall be given a chance to purchase the unit he or she occupied at terms equal to or better than those offered to the general public.

Any notices given must honor any existing leases between a landlord and tenant. The procedure for offering the unit for sale to the tenants calls for the owner to provide a purchase-and-sale agreement to the tenant signed by the owner. The tenant has a minimum of 90 days to sign the agreement and accept the offer.

If the tenant elects not to purchase the unit, the tenant has one year from the owner's notice to vacate. In the case of elderly, handicapped, and low-income to moderate-income tenants, the period to vacate is two years. The owner is required to assist any tenant in the protected categories (i.e., elderly, handicapped, low income to moderate income) in finding comparable housing. If comparable housing cannot be found, the time to vacate is increased from two years to four years. Rent during this period can only be increased by an amount controlled by the Consumer Price Index (CPI) as published by the U.S. Department of Labor.

Any tenant who elects not to purchase the unit shall be reimbursed by the owner for moving expenses. Reimbursement for these actual expenses shall not exceed $750, or in the case of the elderly, handicapped, or low-income to moderate-income tenants, $1,000. Tenants are to be reimbursed within ten days of moving.

Condominium closing requirements. In addition to normal property closing requirements, a condominium requires two items:

1. *6D Certificate*—This is a statement, obtained from the Condominium Association Management Office, stating whether there are any unpaid condominium fees due from the current unit owner. A 6D Certificate showing that all fees have been paid to date is necessary to provide a unit title that is free of any condominium fee lien. It is usually the responsibility of the broker or salesperson to obtain the 6D Certificate.
2. *Master Insurance Policy*—Most lending institutions require that a statement covering the overall condominium building or buildings be prepared showing amounts of coverage, the new unit owner, and the new unit owner's bank as the loss payee in the event of damage. A copy of the Master Insurance Policy is obtained from the insurance company handling the policy, and it is usually the responsibility of the broker or salesperson to obtain the policy.

Condominium financing. Condominium buyers are often surprised to find their bank will allow them to buy a house that costs more than a condominium. In calculating how much a buyer can afford, most lenders will include the condominium fee as a monthly expense. Therefore, when calculating how much of a buyer's monthly income is available to carry a mortgage, include the condominium fee.

Condominium Super Lien. In 1993, Massachusetts passed a new law improving a condominium association's right to collect unpaid condominium fees in the case of foreclosure. This change is referred to as the Condominium Super Lien. It allows the condominium association to collect up to six month's overdue condominium fees after taxes and municipal debts have been paid but before any mortgage obligations are paid. This is true even if the condominium association lien is recorded after the mortgage at the Registry of Deeds.

Time-Share Ownership

Massachusetts has adopted the Model Real Estate Time-Share Act that establishes uniform laws and procedures governing time-share estates.

In a time-share arrangement, a parcel is held by several owners in common. Each owner has the right to use the property for a certain period of time, which may be either fixed or variable. In Massachusetts, an *ownership interest in a unit that includes the right of possession during a potentially infinite number of separate periods is an estate in fee simple, and it includes all the rights of common law fee ownership. An interest in a unit that includes the right of possession during five or more separate time periods over a limited number of years that is greater than five, including extension and renewal options, is a common law estate for years.*

Each time-share owner has financial responsibilities for the upkeep and preservation of the property. Although each interest represents a separate estate in real property, the time-share property is considered a single parcel for purposes of assessment and taxation. Owners pool their funds, and all fees and taxes are paid out from this pool. The Model Real Estate Time-Share Act provides specific regulations for the sale, ownership, and management of time-share properties.

There are numerous requirements governing how time-shares are created and offered. For example, a single property may be divided into more than 12 time-shares only by a recorded instrument that specifically describes the property, time periods of use, management provisions, and the rights and liabilities of each time-share. The public offering statement advertising the availability of time-share units must contain detailed information about the property, the managing entity, the developer, and the time-share owner's rights and liabilities. If the promotional materials and time-share instrument promise improvements, the improvements must be made. If the time-share property is promoted through the use of prizes or other inducements, the approximate fair market value of the prize must be disclosed, along with how many are available and the criteria for winning.

Time-shares may be offered or sold in Massachusetts only by a *project broker* designated by the time-share developer. The project broker must be a licensed real estate broker, and the time-share property is considered a separate real estate office for purposes of the license laws.

Quarter-share units are condominium units owned by four owners under a use agreement. Either method of sharing—time-share or quarter-share—is available by deed, lease, or contract, and the condominium laws apply.

■ RELATED WEB SITE

Massachusetts General Laws   *www.mass.gov/legis/laws/mgl*

QUESTIONS

1. Unless stated to the contrary in a deed, ownership of land by a married couple is assumed to be by
   a. severalty.
   b. joint tenancy.
   c. tenancy in common.
   d. tenancy by the entirety.

2. Sam and Maria are married and hold their property as tenants by the entirety. When Sam dies, Maria will
   a. own one-half of the property.
   b. own a personal property interest.
   c. own a legal homestead interest.
   d. be sole owner of the property.

3. Which of the following forms of ownership represents a personal property interest?
   a. Tenancy by the entirety
   b. Partnership
   c. Tenancy in common
   d. Cooperative housing

4. In Massachusetts, a tenancy by the entirety
   a. may be held only by husband and wife.
   b. continues after a spouse's death.
   c. may be partitioned.
   d. gives the husband control of the property.

5. Burt and Carole are a married couple living in Massachusetts. The deed to their property explicitly states that it is held as tenants by the entirety. In Massachusetts, they
   a. automatically hold the property as joint tenants.
   b. own the property as tenants in common.
   c. may not hold the property as tenants by the entirety.
   d. hold the property as tenants by the entirety.

6. Which of the following is NOT recognized in Massachusetts?
   a. Tenancy in common
   b. Quarter-share
   c. Common property
   d. Tenancy by the entirety

7. Tenants of a building that is being converted to a condominium will
   a. be given the chance to purchase the unit they occupy.
   b. have to move.
   c. automatically become owners.
   d. be allowed to stay indefinitely.

8. Joan holds ownership in a cooperative building. She owns
   a. in fee simple.
   b. in severalty.
   c. stock in a corporation.
   d. a partnership share.

9. Taxes on a time-share unit are
   a. paid individually, by each owner.
   b. paid out of a common pool of funds.
   c. assessed against the board.
   d. paid only upon transfer.

10. Jack bought a condominium. When title is conveyed to Jack, he will
    a. own his unit in fee simple.
    b. own stock in the association.
    c. pay his taxes to the board.
    d. not have to pay an assessment.

11. In a building containing four or more units that has been occupied by tenants during the prior year and is currently being converted to condominiums, how long does a tenant have to sign a purchase-and-sale agreement and accept the offer from the landlord?
    a. 30 days
    b. 10 days
    c. 45 days
    d. 90 days

CHAPTER 5

Legal Descriptions

■ METHODS OF DESCRIBING REAL ESTATE

Massachusetts does not use the rectangular survey system for the description of property. It has been impractical to attempt to change all existing metes-and-bounds descriptions, and the land is far too irregular in contour to allow the rectangular survey system to function effectively.

In Massachusetts, the land is described using what is known as a *full legal description*. The full legal description consists of the following three elements:

1. Street or designated *address* of the property involved
2. *Metes-and-bounds description*—a description of the location and length of the various boundaries, including the identification of ownership of adjacent tracts of land
3. *Reference description*—a description directing the reader to some other recorded document that gives a more complete definition of the location, shape, and size of the property, such as a previous deed reference (by book, page, and date); the plan, normally the map and parcel number, or plat number from the Registry of Deeds; or a certificate number from the Land Court Records

The use of the full legal description depends on a fixed set of boundary markers. Generally, each survey or description will begin at a *monument*, sometimes called a *benchmark*, which is a fixed, permanent marker. Then the description proceeds around the property, going from monument to monument. In Massachusetts, monuments are commonly iron pipes, granite blocks, trees, boulders, walls, telephone poles, or buildings.

Many monuments that seemed fixed and permanent at one time have been moved, changed, or have become lost over a period of years. This has made a current survey almost mandatory in many land transactions, and the broker should find out who in the area is qualified to conduct such a survey. While a current survey is not essential, without one the buyer never really knows what he or she is buying. A survey *must* be ordered and a plat obtained when the property will be subdivided. The top of a plat is usually considered to be north, and it is customary for the direction north to be indicated by an arrow. (See Figure 5.1.)

Although it is possible to use fewer than all three of these elements to describe land in a contract, real estate brokers and salespersons should make every effort to ensure that the full legal description is used in all real estate documents. It should also be noted that in a deed, a street address, standing alone, is not a sufficient description of a parcel of land and would not be acceptable as the sole description in a deed. The street address alone could suffice, however, in a lease.

FIGURE 5.1

Plat of Honeysuckle Hills Subdivision

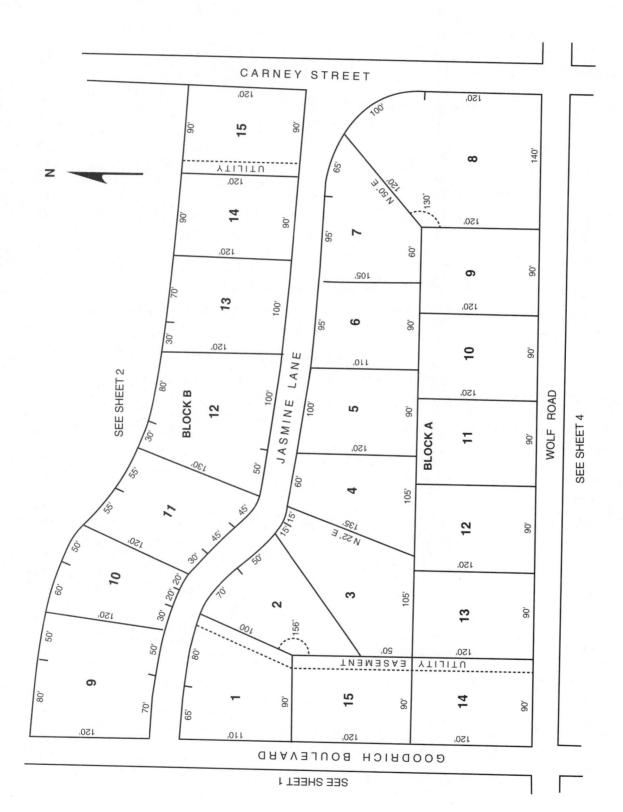

QUESTIONS

1. Which of the following is *NOT* an adequate description of land in a deed?
   a. Street address
   b. Metes-and-bounds description
   c. Reference description
   d. Street address and metes-and-bounds description

2. A metes-and-bounds description will
   a. return to the point of beginning.
   b. refer to some other recorded plan.
   c. have four sides.
   d. include a street address.

3. The data for a metes-and-bounds description is created by a
   a. landowner.
   b. bank attorney.
   c. licensed surveyor.
   d. broker.

Answer the following questions according to the plat of Honeysuckle Hills in Figure 5.1 on page 49.

4. Which lot in Block B has the *MOST* frontage on Jasmine Lane?
   a. Lot 9
   b. Lot 13
   c. Lot 12
   d. Lot 11

5. How many lots have easements?
   a. 3
   b. 1
   c. 4
   d. 0

6. Which roads run north and south?
   a. Goodrich and Jasmine
   b. Wolf and Jasmine
   c. Carney and Goodrich
   d. Goodrich and Wolf

7. Which lot in the subdivision has the *LEAST* frontage on Jasmine Lane?
   a. Block B, Lot 11
   b. Block A, Lot 4
   c. Block B, Lot 12
   d. Block A, Lot 3

8. "Beginning at the intersection of the East line of Goodrich Boulevard and the South line of Jasmine Lane and running South along the East line of Goodrich Boulevard a distance of 230 feet: thence East parallel to the North line of Wolf Road a distance of 195 feet: thence Northeasterly on a course N 22° E a distance of 135 feet: and thence Northwesterly along the South line of Jasmine Lane to the point of beginning."

   Which lots are described here?

   a. Lots 13, 14, and 15, Block A
   b. Lots 9, 10, and 11, Block B
   c. Lots 1, 2, 3, and 15, Block A
   d. Lots 7, 8, and 9, Block A

9. Which lot has the *MOST* street exposure?
   a. Lot 15, Block A
   b. Lot 14, Block B
   c. Lot 8, Block A
   d. Lot 9, Block B

10. Assume that the bold number "15" in the middle of Lot 15 represents the location of a monument. The monument marks the southeast corner of a subdivided parcel. If the parcel is bounded by Goodrich and Lot 1, approximately how many square feet is the subdivided parcel?
    a. 1,210 square feet
    b. 2,700 square feet
    c. 4,500 square feet
    d. 5,400 square feet

CHAPTER

Real Estate Taxes and Other Liens

■ LIENS

Massachusetts Real Estate Taxes

Each town and city in the state is responsible for raising revenue through a property tax. The tax year begins January 1, although for budgeting and appropriation purposes a community may use the fiscal year from July 1 to the following June 30.

The purpose of real estate taxes is to fund a community's budget. Once the spending plan has been decided, the community must determine how to most fairly distribute the cost of programs and services among property owners. All property within a community is assessed at the same time; all property is assessed at 100 percent of its full cash value or fair market value. Then the amount of the community's budget that will be raised from real estate taxes is divided by the total of all the assessed values. The result is the amount of the budget each dollar's worth of property will bear, generally quoted as X dollars per $1,000 of assessed value.

■ **FOR EXAMPLE** The town of Bedford Falls has an annual budget of $500,000. There are 75 property owners in the town, and each property has an assessed fair market value of $150,000. To determine the real estate tax, perform the following calculation:

$$500,000 \div (\$150,000 \times 75 = \$11,250,000) = 0.04$$

$0.04 is the amount each owner must pay for every dollar's worth of property he or she owns. So, each owner must pay $40 per $1,000 assessed value, or $6,000 in real estate taxes.

Annual real estate tax bills are prepared by the local municipalities. Most cities and towns mail out tax bills in quarterly installments. Bills for improvements made by the municipality are due annually on November 1.

"Proposition 2½" is the title given to an initiative petition adopted by the voters of the Commonwealth of Massachusetts in 1980. The primary feature of "Proposition 2½" relates to the total amount of property taxes a city or town can raise each year. The increase in property taxes cannot exceed more than 2½ percent of the full cash value of all taxable property in the city/town nor can it increase more than 2½ percent from year to year. Because the cap may adversely affect tax-dependent bodies such as schools and emergency services, individual communities may vote to override it.

Unpaid Real Estate Taxes

Real estate taxes that remain unpaid two years after they are due may be collected by a tax sale of the property. Because the owner has one year from the date of the tax sale to redeem the property, called a *right of redemption*, the purchaser of a tax deed cannot be assured of acquiring title. If no redemption is made within two years from the date of the tax sale, the new owner can bring an action in the land court to register the title and confirm ownership. Land court registration and the Torrens system are described in Chapter 9.

Other Liens

Municipal liens. Municipal liens on a property may be ascertained by checking the records at the Registry of Deeds for the county in which the land is located or by securing a municipal lien certificate from the local tax collector. The lien certificate indicates unpaid real estate taxes, water charges, betterments, assessments, and other unpaid or current financial obligations levied by the town or city against the land.

Mechanic's lien. The Massachusetts Mechanic's Lien Statute, revised in 1996 and effective in 1997, extends mechanic's lien protection to a broader range of persons providing labor and materials. It now gives statutory rights to

- persons/parties involved in the alteration, erection, repair, or removal of a building, structure, or *other improvement to real property;*
- persons/parties furnishing material or *rental equipment, appliances, or equipment;* and
- *persons/parties providing construction management and general contractor services.*

Under the revised statute, a mechanic's lien can attach to a leasehold interest of a contracting party, whereas the prior version of the statute required the contracting party to be the "owner of land" to which the lien was to attach. In addition, it is no longer necessary that the lien relate to work on a building or structure, giving lien rights to site work contractors such as landscapers, parking lot surfacers, and utility contractors.

If a contractor has a *written* contract with the owner of a property, a Notice of Contract must be recorded at the appropriate Registry no later than the earliest of the following dates:

- 60 days after the recording of a Notice of Substantial Completion executed by the project owner and the general contractor
- 90 days after the recording of a Notice of Termination (if the contract is terminated before completion), executed by the project owner
- 90 days after the last of the labor and materials has been furnished by the general contractor (or anyone claiming through the general contractor)

A contractor, to enforce his or her lien rights, must also file a Statement of Account at the appropriate registry no later than the earliest of the following dates:

- 90 days after the owner and the general contractor file or record the Notice of Substantial Completion
- 120 days after the owner records the Notice of Termination
- 120 days after the general contractor last performed or furnished labor or materials or both labor and materials or furnished rental equipment, appliances, or tools

The statute also creates new procedures that subcontractors must follow to perfect their mechanics' liens. In addition to the procedures applicable to contractors, a subcontractor must also (1) include a brief accounting of its claim in the recorded Notice of Contract and (2) serve a copy of the Notice of Contract on the project owner by certified mail. If the subcontractor does not have a direct contractual relationship with the general contractor, he or she must also provide the general contractor with a Notice of Identification within 30 days of commencement of the subcontractor's work on the project to put the general contractor on notice to provide the subcontractor with a copy of the Notice of Substantial Completion.

A lien shall be dissolved unless the contractor or subcontractor begins a civil action within 90 days of recording of the Statement of Account and record an attested-to copy of the complaint within 30 days after he or she sued.

Contractors or subcontractors who provide services without a written contract can claim a mechanic's lien for up to 30 days' work during the 90 days preceding recording.

Although complicated, when properly used, mechanics' liens can help a contractor or subcontractor get paid for his or her products, services, or equipment.

IN PRACTICE

From the owner's point of view, the mechanic's lien provides an obstacle that should be circumvented by using release forms that relieve the owner from claims by subcontractors in the event the contractor fails to pay them. A high risk of claims—and clouds on a property's title—exists without the use of releases.

Title 5 betterments. Most title transfers in Massachusetts now require a "Title 5 inspection" of private on-site sewage disposal systems. If the existing system is found to be deficient, the homeowner must repair or upgrade the system to meet environmental standards. (See Chapter 16.) In Massachusetts, if the private system cannot be inspected due to frozen ground, the inspection can be performed up to six months after closing. Lenders will usually allow the closing but may hold back (some of) the seller's funds (equal to the cost of replacing the system) in escrow pending the inspection results.

The Massachusetts Legislature has created a $10 million long-term loan program to assist homeowners who lack sufficient funds to have the Title 5 repair or upgrade work performed. The loan appears as a betterment assessment on the tax bill, which is similar to the way sidewalks or street improvements appear. The presence of such an assessment has led some banks to refuse mortgages for homes subject to Title 5 assessments.

Condominium certificates and Condominium Super Liens.   If the property is a condominium, in addition to the usual closing documents, a condominium must have a 6D Certificate stating the unit owner's condominium fee balance of payment. The certificate is required to establish that the title of the unit is free of association fee liens. Since April of 1993, the Condominium Super Lien law allows the condominium association to collect up to six months of fees after taxes and municipal debts have been paid but before any other mortgage obligations.

Other Tax Credits and Deductions

Tenant deduction.   Anyone who rents property located in the Commonwealth as a principal residence is entitled to an income tax deduction from Part B adjusted gross income equal to 50 percent of rent paid to the landlord. The maximum deduction a tenant may take is $2,500.

Renewable energy source credit.   Any owner of residential property in the Commonwealth who is not a dependent of another taxpayer and who occupies the property as his or her principal residence is allowed a credit equal to 35 percent of the net expenditure for renewable energy source property or $1,000, whichever is less.

Lead paint removal credit.   After January 1, 1994, a homeowner who pays for the "de-leading" of the premises for the purpose of bringing the premises into full compliance with Massachusetts law may claim a de-leading credit equal to the lesser cost of de-leading or $1,500 per dwelling unit. For interim control pending full compliance, the credit is equal to the lesser of one-half the cost of de-leading or $500 per dwelling unit. (See Chapter 16.)

■ RELATED WEB SITES

Code of Massachusetts Regulations   *www.lawlib.state.ma.us/cmrindex.html*
Massachusetts Department of Revenue   *www.dor.state.ma.us*

QUESTIONS

1. Property taxes are assessed and collected by the
   a. individual municipalities.
   b. county where the property is located.
   c. state tax officer.
   d. land court.

2. Property in Massachusetts must be reassessed at
   a. 80 percent of the market value.
   b. 60 percent of the market value.
   c. 100 percent of the market value.
   d. 90 percent of the market value.

3. If there is no redemption of the property, how long must a tax sale purchaser wait before starting action to obtain title to the land?
   a. Two years after the unpaid taxes are due
   b. One year from the date of the tax sale
   c. Three years from the date of the tax sale
   d. Two years from the date of the tax sale

4. To acquire title to the land, a tax sale purchaser
   a. registers the deed to the property at the Registry of Deeds.
   b. files a tax certificate with the Registry of Deeds.
   c. brings action in the land court to register title and confirm ownership.
   d. pays the back taxes and files a tax release at the Registry of Deeds.

5. To ensure that a property is free from municipal liens, the attorney for the purchaser will obtain a municipal lien certificate from the
   a. local tax collector.
   b. Registry of Deeds.
   c. state tax office.
   d. local courthouse.

6. How long does an owner have to redeem property sold for back taxes?
   a. 1 year
   b. 2 years
   c. 40 days
   d. 18 months

7. Shoddy Construction Co. was hired to remodel the Browns' kitchen. It agreed to work without a written contract. To obtain a mechanic's lien it must
   a. file a lien at the town hall.
   b. file a lis pendens.
   c. hire someone to collect the monies for it.
   d. file within 90 days of completing the job.

8. How many days after the recording of a Statement of Account does a contractor or subcontractor have to file a mechanic's lien?
   a. 30 days
   b. 60 days
   c. 90 days
   d. 120 days

9. All of the following can file a mechanic's lien EXCEPT
   a. a contractor.
   b. a subcontractor
   c. the owner.
   d. a subcontractor of a subcontractor.

10. A subcontractor worked for 22 days on a project at a daily cost of $500. The contractor failed to pay the subcontractor, who properly filed a lien 33 days after work was completed. What is the value of the work protected by the lien?
    a. $9,000
    b. $11,000
    c. $16,500
    d. $500

11. A foreclosure has taken place on a condominium property. Four months of condominium association fees have not been paid to the association. In the settlement, these fees will be paid
    a. before any other debts are paid.
    b. after taxes are paid, but before the mortgage is paid.
    c. after the taxes and the mortgage are paid.
    d. after the taxes, mortgage, and all other liens are paid.

CHAPTER

7

Real Estate Contracts

■ CONTRACT LAW

In Massachusetts, to be enforceable, a written contract for the sale of real estate is required. The statute of frauds requires a written memorandum to include

- the identity of the parties;
- a description of the property;
- a recital of the consideration;
- the date of the agreement; and
- the signatures of the parties.

The signatures of both parties always should be obtained because a party cannot be sued for any breach of a contract unless the contract has been signed. Any contract reduced to writing must be a complete document and include all the terms of the agreement. The statute of frauds' requirements represent only the bare minimum. From a practical standpoint, brokers are not properly fulfilling their obligation to the principal or being attentive to their own interest if a complete and legally enforceable contract is not prepared and executed. Oral contracts for the sale of real estate are legal but not enforceable in a court of law.

Legally competent parties. In Massachusetts, a person becomes of age and can be held responsible for his or her contracts upon reaching 18 years of age. A contract executed by someone under the age of 18 is a voidable contract.

Broker's Authority to Prepare Documents

In Massachusetts, a broker may only fill in the blanks on preprinted forms—such as contract-to-purchase agreements and purchase-and-sale agreements—that are available from stationery stores, the Massachusetts Association of REALTORS®, and regional real estate boards/associations. (See Figure 7.1 and Figure 7.2.)

Real estate brokers and salespersons who are not licensed attorneys must not attempt to draft legal documents. A salesperson or broker may not recommend that an attorney *not* be used.

Sales Contracts

Offer to purchase. In *McCarthy v. Tobin* (1999), the Massachusetts Supreme Judicial Court found that under certain situations an offer to purchase may be considered a contract that creates binding obligations even if the offer to purchase states that it is subject to the execution of a purchase-and-sales agreement satisfactory to the buyer and seller.

In this instance, the Supreme Judicial Court ruled that even though many of the terms of the purchase-and-sale agreement may still require negotiation, the terms upon which the parties had already agreed in the offer to purchase were the relevant terms of the agreement and that any other terms that would be added to the purchase-and-sale agreement would be "non-essential and ministerial." The court also took into consideration the *NOTICE* printed on the offer-to-purchase agreement that warned both parties that the document created legally binding obligations and that if the consumers did not understand they should consult an attorney.

As a result of *McCarthy v. Tobin*, licensees should recognize that an offer to purchase may be deemed binding notwithstanding contingencies. In fact the Supreme Judicial Court identified suggested language for the offer to purchase if the parties clearly want this document to be non-binding.

Earnest money deposits. Massachusetts license law requires brokers to deposit earnest money and other customer's monies "in a separate bank account maintained by the broker." The account should be outside the reach of a broker's creditors. Some buyers and sellers request that the earnest money be put in an interest-bearing account. It is important that this be stated in the purchase-and-sale agreement and that it be clearly indicated who will receive the interest. A deposit is usually customary but not required for a valid contract.

A real estate broker or agent's responsibilities regarding the handling of others' funds are discussed in Chapter 10.

IN PRACTICE

Most purchase-and-sale agreements include a clause stating that if a dispute should occur between the buyer and seller concerning to whom the escrowed funds should be paid, the broker (escrow agent) may retain the funds pending mutually agreed upon written instructions by the buyer and the seller.

FIGURE 7.1

Sample Contract-to-Purchase Agreement

CONTRACT TO PURCHASE REAL ESTATE *#501*
(With Contingencies)
(Binding Contract. If Legal Advice Is Desired, Consult An Attorney.)

From: BUYER(S):   To: OWNER OF RECORD ("SELLER"):

Name(s): _____   Name(s): _____

_____   _____

Address: _____   Address: _____

_____   _____

The BUYER offers to purchase the real property described as _____

_____

together with all buildings and improvements thereon (the "Premises") to which I have been introduced by _____

_____ upon the following terms and conditions:

1. **Purchase Price:** The BUYER agrees to pay the sum of $ _____ to the SELLER for the purchase of the Premises, due as follows:
   i. $ _____ as a deposit to bind this Offer;
   ii. $ _____ as an additional deposit upon executing the Purchase And Sale Agreement;
   iii. Balance by bank's, cashier's, treasurer's or certified check or wire transfer at time for closing.

2. **Duration Of Offer.** This Offer is valid until _____ ☐ a.m. ☐ p.m. on _____ by which time a copy of this Offer shall be signed by the SELLER, accepting this Offer and returned to the BUYER, otherwise this Offer shall be deemed rejected and the money tendered herewith shall be returned to the BUYER. Upon written notice to the BUYER or BUYER'S agent of the SELLER'S acceptance, the accepted Offer shall form a binding agreement. Time is of the essence as to each provision.

3. **Purchase And Sale Agreement.** The SELLER and the BUYER shall, on or before _____ ☐ a.m. ☐ p.m. on _____ execute the Standard Purchase and Sale Agreement of the MASSACHUSETTS ASSOCIATION OF REALTORS® or substantial equivalent which, when executed, shall become the entire agreement between the parties and this Offer shall have no further force and effect.

4. **Closing.** The SELLER agrees to deliver a good and sufficient deed conveying good and clear record and marketable title at _____ ☐ a.m. ☐ p.m. on _____ at the _____ County Registry of Deeds or such other time or place as may be mutually agreed upon by the parties.

5. **Escrow.** The deposit shall be held by _____ , as escrow agent, subject to the terms hereof. Endorsement or negotiation of this deposit by the real estate broker shall not be deemed acceptance of the terms of the Offer. In the event of any disagreement between the parties concerning to whom escrowed funds should be paid, the escrow agent may retain said deposit pending written instructions mutually given by the BUYER and SELLER. The escrow agent shall abide by any Court decision concerning to whom the funds shall be paid and shall not be made a party to a pending lawsuit solely as a result of holding escrowed funds. Should the escrow agent be made a party in violation of this paragraph, the escrow agent shall be dismissed and the party asserting a claim against the escrow agent shall pay the agent's reasonable attorneys' fees and costs.

6. **Contingencies.** It is agreed that the BUYER'S obligations under this Offer and any Purchase and Sale Agreement signed pursuant to this Offer are expressly conditioned upon the following terms and conditions:
   a. **Mortgage.** *(Delete if Waived)* The BUYER'S obligation to purchase is conditioned upon obtaining a written commitment for financing in the amount of $ _____ at prevailing rates, terms and conditions by _____ . The BUYER shall have an obligation to act reasonably diligently to satisfy any condition within the BUYER'S control. If, despite reasonable efforts, the BUYER has been unable to obtain such written commitment the BUYER may terminate this agreement by giving written notice that is received by 5:00 p.m. on the calendar day after the date set forth above. In the event that notice has not been received, this condition is deemed waived. In the event that due notice has been received, the obligations of the parties shall cease and this agreement shall be void; and all monies deposited by the BUYER shall be returned. In no event shall the BUYER be deemed to have used reasonable efforts to obtain financing unless the BUYER has submitted one application by _____ and acted reasonably promptly in providing additional information requested by the mortgage lender.

#501 6.06.02/214648

MassForms
Statewide Standard Real Estate Forms
©1999, 2000, 2001, 2002 MASSACHUSETTS ASSOCIATION OF REALTORS®
Massachusetts Association of REALTORS 256 Second Ave, Waltham MA 02451
Phone: 7818903700   Fax: 7818904919   MAR

ssf.zfx

Produced with ZipForm™ by RE FormsNet, LLC 18025 Fifteen Mile Road, Clinton Township, Michigan 48035   www.zipform.com

FIGURE 7.1 (Continued)

Sample Contract-to-Purchase Agreement

    b. <u>Inspections</u>. *(Delete if Waived)* The BUYER'S obligations under this agreement are subject to the right to obtain inspection(s) of the Premises or any aspect thereof, including, but not limited to, home, pest, radon, lead paint, septic/sewer, water quality, and water drainage by consultant(s) regularly in the business of conducting said inspections, of BUYER'S own choosing, and at BUYER'S sole cost within _____ days after SELLER'S acceptance of this agreement. If the results are not satisfactory to BUYER, in BUYER'S sole discretion, BUYER shall have the right to give written notice received by the SELLER OR SELLER'S agent by 5:00 p.m. on the calendar day after the date set forth above, terminating this agreement. Upon receipt of such notice this agreement shall be void and all monies deposited by the BUYER shall be returned. Failure to provide timely notice of termination shall constitute a waiver. In the event that the BUYER does not exercise the right to have such inspection(s) or to so terminate, the SELLER and the listing broker are each released from claims relating to the condition of the Premises that the BUYER or the BUYER'S consultants could reasonably have discovered.

    7. <u>Representations/Acknowledgments</u>. The BUYER acknowledges receipt of an agency disclosure, lead paint disclosure (for residences built before 1978), and Home Inspectors Facts For Consumers brochure (prepared by the Office of Consumer Affairs). The BUYER acknowledges that there are no warranties or representations on which BUYER relies in making this Offer, previously made in writing and the following: (if none, write "NONE")

_____

_____

    8. <u>Buyer's Default</u>. If the BUYER defaults in BUYER'S obligations, all monies tendered as a deposit shall be paid to the SELLER as liquidated damages and this shall be SELLER'S sole remedy.

    9. <u>Additional Terms</u>.

_____

_____

_____

_____

_____   _____
BUYER   BUYER

****

SELLER'S REPLY

SELLER(S): (check one and sign below)
_____ (a) ACCEPT(S) the Offer as set forth above at _____ ☐ a.m. ☐ p.m. on this _____ day of _____.
_____ (b) REJECT(S) the Offer.
_____ (c) Reject(s) the Offer and MAKE(S) A COUNTEROFFER on the following terms: _____

_____

_____

This Counteroffer shall expire at _____ ☐ a.m. ☐ p.m. on _____ if not withdrawn earlier.

_____   _____
SELLER, *or spouse*   SELLER

****

(IF COUNTEROFFER FROM SELLER) BUYER'S REPLY

The BUYER: (check one and sign below):
_____ (a) ACCEPT(S) the Counteroffer as set forth above at _____ ☐ a.m. ☐ p.m. on this _____ day of
_____ (b) REJECT(S) the Counteroffer.

_____   _____
BUYER   BUYER

****

RECEIPT FOR DEPOSIT

I hereby acknowledge receipt of a deposit in the amount of $ _____ from the BUYER this _____ day of

_____

_____
Escrow Agent or Authorized representative

FIGURE 7.2

Sample Purchase-and-Sale Agreement

STANDARD PURCHASE AND SALE AGREEMENT *[#503]*
(With Contingencies)

The parties make this Agreement this _____ day of _____ , _____ . This Agreement supersedes and replaces all obligations made in any prior Contract To Purchase or agreement for sale entered into by the parties.

1. **Parties.**

_____

_____ *[insert name],*
the "SELLER," agrees to sell and _____
_____ *[insert name],*
the "BUYER," agrees to buy, the premises described in paragraph 2 on the terms set forth below. BUYER may require the conveyance to be made to another person or entity ("Nominee") upon notification in writing to SELLER at least five business days prior to the date for performance set forth in paragraph 5. Designation of a Nominee shall not discharge the BUYER from any obligation under this Agreement and BUYER hereby agrees to guarantee performance by the Nominee.

2. **Description Of Premises.** The premises (the "Premises") consist of:
(a) the land with any and all buildings thereon known as _____

_____ , as more specifically described in a deed recorded in the _____ Registry of Deeds at Book _____ , Page_____ , [Certificate No. _____], a copy of which ☐ is ☐ is not *[choose one]* attached; and
(b) all structures, and improvements on the land and the fixtures, including, but not limited to: any and all storm windows and doors, screens, screen doors, awnings, shutters, window shades and blinds, curtain rods, furnaces, heaters, heating equipment, oil and gas burners and fixtures, hot water heaters, plumbing and bathroom fixtures, towel racks, built-in dishwashers, garbage disposals and trash compactors, stoves, ranges, chandeliers, electric and other lighting fixtures, burglar and fire alarm systems, mantelpieces, wall-to-wall carpets, stair carpets, exterior television antennas and satellite dishes, fences, gates, landscaping including trees, shrubs, flowers; and the following built-in components, if any: air conditioners, vacuums systems, cabinets, shelves, bookcases and stereo speakers, and _____
_____ ,
but excluding _____ .
[insert references to refrigerators, dishwashers, microwave ovens, washing machines, dryers or other items, where appropriate]

3. **Purchase Price.** The purchase price for the Premises is _____ dollars of which
$_____ were paid as a deposit with Contract To Purchase; and
$_____ are paid with this Agreement;
$_____ are to be paid _____ ; and
$_____ are to be paid at the time for performance by bank's, cashier's, treasurer's or certified check or by wire transfer.
$_____ Total

4. **Escrow.** All funds deposited or paid by the BUYER shall be held in a non-interest bearing escrow account, by _____ , as escrow agent, subject to the terms of this Agreement and shall be paid or otherwise duly accounted for at the time for performance. If a

_____ _____ _____   _____ _____ _____
BUYER'S Initials   BUYER'S Initials   BUYER'S Initials   SELLER'S Initials SELLER'S Initials SELLER'S Initials

#503 6.06.02/214650

MASSFORMS™
Statewide Standard Real Estate Forms
Massachusetts Association of REALTORS 256 Second Ave, Waltham MA 02451
Phone: 7818903700   Fax: 7818904919   Brian Doherty

©1999, 2000, 2002 MASSACHUSETTS ASSOCIATION OF REALTORS®

Produced with ZipForm™ by RE FormsNet, LLC 18025 Fifteen Mile Road, Clinton Township, Michigan 48035 www.zipform.com

p.zfx

F I G U R E   7.2 (Continued)

Sample Purchase-and-Sale Agreement

dispute arises between the BUYER and SELLER concerning to whom escrowed funds should be paid, the escrow agent may retain all escrowed funds pending written instructions mutually given by the BUYER and the SELLER. The escrow agent shall abide by any Court decision concerning to whom the funds shall be paid and shall not be made a party to a lawsuit solely as a result of holding escrowed funds. Should the escrow agent be made a party in violation of this paragraph, the escrow agent shall be dismissed and the party asserting a claim against the escrow agent shall pay the agent's reasonable attorneys' fees and costs. *[If interest is to accrue on escrowed funds, indicate to whom it shall be paid.]*

5. __Time For Performance__. The SELLER shall deliver the deed and the BUYER shall pay the balance of the purchase price at _____ o'clock _____ . m. on the _____ day of _____ . at the _____ Registry of Deeds, or at such other time and place as is mutually agreed in writing. TIME IS OF THE ESSENCE AS TO EACH PROVISION OF THIS AGREEMENT. Unless the deed and other documents required by this Agreement are recorded at the time for performance, all documents and funds are to be held in escrow, pending prompt rundown of the title and recording (or registration in the case of registered land). SELLER'S attorney or other escrow agent shall disburse funds the next business day following the date for performance, provided that the recording attorney has not reported a problem outside the recording attorney's control.

6. __Title/Plans__. The SELLER shall convey the Premises by a good and sufficient quitclaim deed running to the Buyer or to the BUYER'S nominee, conveying good and clear record and marketable title to the Premises, free from liens and encumbrances, except:
(a) Real estate taxes assessed on the Premises which are not yet due and payable;
(b) Betterment assessments, if any, which are not a recorded lien on the date of this Agreement;
(c) Federal, state and local laws, ordinances, bylaws, rules and regulations regulating use of land, including building codes, zoning bylaws, health and environmental laws;
(d) Rights and obligations in party walls;
(e) Any easement, restriction or agreement of record presently in force which does not interfere with the reasonable use of the Premises as now used;
(f) Utility easements in the adjoining ways;
(g) Matters that would be disclosed by an accurate survey of the Premises; and
(h) _____
[insert in (h) references to any other easement, restriction, lease or encumbrance which may continue after title is transferred]
If the deed refers to a plan needed to be recorded with it, at the time for performance the SELLER shall deliver the plan with the deed in proper form for recording or registration.

7. __Title Insurance__. BUYER'S obligations are contingent upon the availability (at normal premium rates) of an owner's title insurance policy insuring BUYER'S title to the premises without exceptions other than the standard exclusions from coverage printed in the current American Land Title Association ("ALTA") policy cover, the standard printed exceptions contained in the ALTA form currently in use for survey matters and real estate taxes (which shall only except real estate taxes not yet due and payable) and those exceptions permitted by paragraph 6 of this Agreement.

8. __Closing Certifications and Documents__. The SELLER shall execute and deliver simultaneously with the delivery of the deed such certifications and documents as may customarily and reasonably be required by the BUYER'S attorney.

2

BUYER'S Initials _____ BUYER'S Initials _____ BUYER'S Initials _____   SELLER'S Initials _____ SELLER'S Initials _____ SELLER'S Initials _____

F I G U R E   7.2 (Continued)

Sample Purchase-and-Sale Agreement

BUYER'S lender, BUYER'S lender's attorney or any title insurance company insuring the BUYER'S title to the Premises, including, without limitation, certifications and documents relating to: (a) parties in possession of the premises; (b) the creation of mechanics or materialmen's liens; (c) the absence or presence of urea formaldehyde foam insulation ("UFFI"), and SELLER'S satisfaction of requirements concerning UFFI imposed upon residential sellers by statute and applicable regulations; (d) the HUD-1 Settlement Statement and other financial affidavits and agreements as may reasonably be required by the lender or lender's attorney; (e) the citizenship and residency of SELLER as requried by law; and (f) information required to permit the closing agent to report the transaction to the Internal Revenue Service. At the time of delivery of the deed, the SELLER may use monies from the purchase to clear the title, provided that all documents related thereto are recorded with the deed or within a reasonable time thereafter acceptable to the BUYER and, provided further, that discharges of mortgages from banks, credit unions, insurance companies and other institutional lenders may be recorded within a reasonable time after recording of the deed in accordance with usual conveyancing practices. The SELLER'S spouse hereby agrees to release all statutory, common law or other rights or interest in the Premises and to execute the deed, if necessary.

9. **Possession And Condition Of Premises.** At the time for performance the SELLER shall give the BUYER possession of the entire Premises, free of all occupants and tenants and of all personal property, except property included in the sale or tenants permitted to remain. At the time for performance the Premises also shall comply with the requirements of paragraph 6, and be broom clean and in the same condition as the Premises now are, reasonable wear and tear excepted, with the SELLER to have performed all maintenance customarily undertaken by the SELLER between the date of this Agreement and the time for performance, and there shall be no outstanding notices of violation of any building, zoning, health or environmental law, bylaw, code or regulation, except as agreed. The BUYER shall have the right to enter the Premises within forty-eight (48) hours prior to the time for performance or such other time as may be agreed and upon reasonable notice to SELLER for the purpose of determining compliance with this paragraph. At the time of recording of the deed, or as otherwise agreed, the SELLER shall deliver to BUYER all keys to the Premises, garage door openers and any security codes. Until delivery of the deed, the SELLER shall maintain fire and extended coverage insurance on the Premises in the same amount as currently insured.

10. **Extension Of Time For Performance.** If the SELLER cannot convey title as required by this Agreement or cannot deliver possession of the Premises as agreed, or if at the time of the delivery of the deed the Premises do not conform with the requirements set forth in this Agreement or the BUYER is unable to obtain title insurance in accordance with paragraph 7, upon written notice given no later than the time for performance from either party to the other, the time for performance shall be automatically extended for thirty (30) days, except that if BUYER'S mortgage commitment expires or the terms will materially and adversely change in fewer than thirty (30) days, the time for performance set forth in paragraph 5 shall be extended to one business day before expiration of the mortgage commitment. SELLER shall use reasonable efforts to make title conform or to deliver possession as agreed, or to make the Premises conform to the requirements of this Agreement. Excluding discharge of mortgages and liens, about which the SELLER has actual knowledge at the time of signing this Agreement, the SELLER shall not be required to incur costs or expenses totaling in excess of one-half (1/2) of one percent of the purchase price to make the title or the Premises conform or to deliver possession as agreed. If at the expiration of the time for performance, or if there has been an extension, at the expiration of the time for performance as extended, the SELLER, despite reasonable efforts, cannot make the title or Premises conform, as agreed, or cannot deliver possession, as agreed, or if during the period of this Agreement or any extension thereof, the SELLER has been unable to use proceeds from an insurance claim, if any, to make the Premises conform, then, at the BUYER'S election, any payments

3

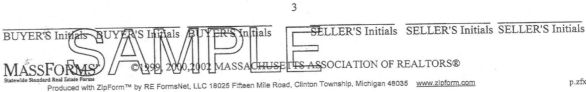

BUYER'S Initials   BUYER'S Initials   BUYER'S Initials   SELLER'S Initials   SELLER'S Initials   SELLER'S Initials

F I G U R E   7.2 (Continued)

Sample Purchase-and-Sale Agreement

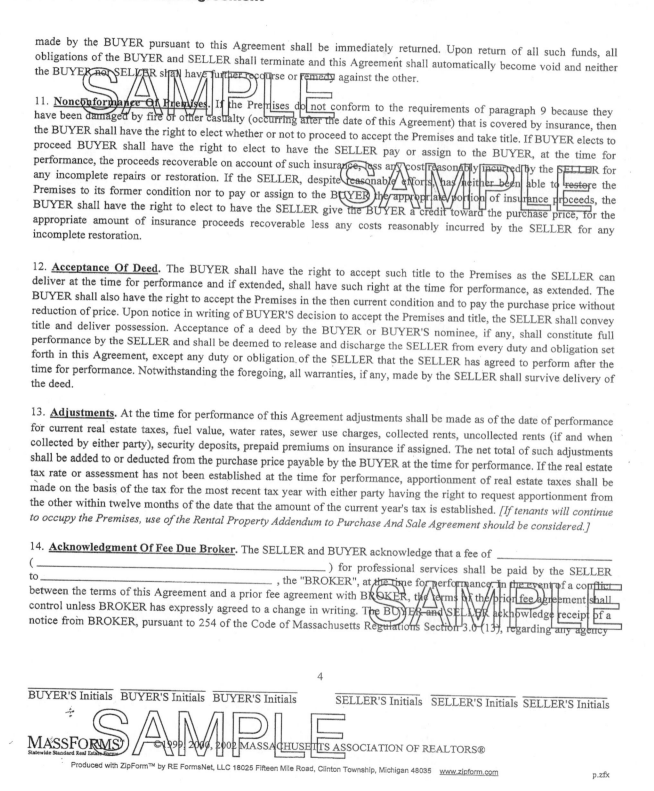

made by the BUYER pursuant to this Agreement shall be immediately returned. Upon return of all such funds, all obligations of the BUYER and SELLER shall terminate and this Agreement shall automatically become void and neither the BUYER nor SELLER shall have further recourse or remedy against the other.

11. **Nonconformance Of Premises.** If the Premises do not conform to the requirements of paragraph 9 because they have been damaged by fire or other casualty (occurring after the date of this Agreement) that is covered by insurance, then the BUYER shall have the right to elect whether or not to proceed to accept the Premises and take title. If BUYER elects to proceed BUYER shall have the right to elect to have the SELLER pay or assign to the BUYER, at the time for performance, the proceeds recoverable on account of such insurance, less any cost reasonably incurred by the SELLER for any incomplete repairs or restoration. If the SELLER, despite reasonable efforts, has neither been able to restore the Premises to its former condition nor to pay or assign to the BUYER the appropriate portion of insurance proceeds, the BUYER shall have the right to elect to have the SELLER give the BUYER a credit toward the purchase price, for the appropriate amount of insurance proceeds recoverable less any costs reasonably incurred by the SELLER for any incomplete restoration.

12. **Acceptance Of Deed.** The BUYER shall have the right to accept such title to the Premises as the SELLER can deliver at the time for performance and if extended, shall have such right at the time for performance, as extended. The BUYER shall also have the right to accept the Premises in the then current condition and to pay the purchase price without reduction of price. Upon notice in writing of BUYER'S decision to accept the Premises and title, the SELLER shall convey title and deliver possession. Acceptance of a deed by the BUYER or BUYER'S nominee, if any, shall constitute full performance by the SELLER and shall be deemed to release and discharge the SELLER from every duty and obligation set forth in this Agreement, except any duty or obligation of the SELLER that the SELLER has agreed to perform after the time for performance. Notwithstanding the foregoing, all warranties, if any, made by the SELLER shall survive delivery of the deed.

13. **Adjustments.** At the time for performance of this Agreement adjustments shall be made as of the date of performance for current real estate taxes, fuel value, water rates, sewer use charges, collected rents, uncollected rents (if and when collected by either party), security deposits, prepaid premiums on insurance if assigned. The net total of such adjustments shall be added to or deducted from the purchase price payable by the BUYER at the time for performance. If the real estate tax rate or assessment has not been established at the time for performance, apportionment of real estate taxes shall be made on the basis of the tax for the most recent tax year with either party having the right to request apportionment from the other within twelve months of the date that the amount of the current year's tax is established. *[If tenants will continue to occupy the Premises, use of the Rental Property Addendum to Purchase And Sale Agreement should be considered.]*

14. **Acknowledgment Of Fee Due Broker.** The SELLER and BUYER acknowledge that a fee of _____ (_____) for professional services shall be paid by the SELLER to _____ , the "BROKER", at the time for performance. In the event of a conflict between the terms of this Agreement and a prior fee agreement with BROKER, the terms of the prior fee agreement shall control unless BROKER has expressly agreed to a change in writing. The BUYER and SELLER acknowledge receipt of a notice from BROKER, pursuant to 254 of the Code of Massachusetts Regulations Section 3.0 (13), regarding any agency

4

BUYER'S Initials   BUYER'S Initials   BUYER'S Initials   SELLER'S Initials   SELLER'S Initials   SELLER'S Initials

FIGURE 7.2 (Continued)

Sample Purchase-and-Sale Agreement

relationship of the BROKER with the BUYER and/or the SELLER. The BUYER and SELLER understand that _____ *[insert name]*, a real estate agent, is seeking a fee from _____ *[name of listing agent, seller or buyer, if applicable]* for services rendered as a ☐ seller's subagent   ☐ buyer's agent *[choose one]*. The BUYER further represents and warrants that there is no other broker with whom BUYER has dealt in connection with the purchase of the Premises.

15. <u>Buyer's Default.</u> If the BUYER or BUYER'S Nominee breaches this Agreement, all escrowed funds paid or deposited by the BUYER shall be paid to the SELLER as liquidated damages. Receipt of such payment shall constitute the SELLER'S sole remedy, at law, in equity or otherwise, for BUYER'S default. The BUYER and SELLER agree that in the event of default by the BUYER the amount of damages suffered by the SELLER will not be easy to ascertain with certainty and, therefore, BUYER and SELLER agree that the amount of the BUYER'S deposit represents a reasonable estimate of the damages likely to be suffered.

16. <u>Buyer's Financing.</u> *(Delete if Waived)* The BUYER'S obligation to purchase is conditioned upon obtaining a written commitment for mortgage financing in the amount of $ _____ at prevailing rates, terms and conditions by _____ . The BUYER shall have an obligation to act reasonably diligently to satisfy any conditions within BUYER'S control. If, despite such diligent efforts, the BUYER has been unable to obtain such written commitment the BUYER may terminate this Agreement by giving written notice that is received by SELLER or SELLER'S agent by 5:00 p.m. on the calendar day after the date set forth above. In the event that notice has not been actually or constructively received, this condition is deemed waived. In the event that due notice has been received, all monies deposited or paid by the BUYER shall be returned and all obligations of the BUYER and SELLER pursuant to this Agreement shall cease and this Agreement shall become void. In no event shall the BUYER be deemed to have used reasonable efforts to obtain financing unless the BUYER has submitted at least one (1) application to a licensed mortgage lender by _____ and acted reasonably promptly in providing any additional information requested by the mortgage lender.

17. <u>Inspections/Survey.</u> *(Delete if Waived)* The BUYER'S obligations under this Agreement are subject to the right to obtain inspection(s) of the Premises or any aspect thereof, including, but not limited to, home, pest, radon, lead paint, septic/sewer, water quality, and water drainage by consultant(s) regularly in the business of conducting said inspections, of BUYER'S own choosing, and at BUYER'S sole cost within _____ days after SELLER'S acceptance of this agreement. If the results are not satisfactory to BUYER, in BUYER'S sole discretion, BUYER shall have the right to give written notice received by the SELLER or SELLER'S agent by 5:00 p.m. on the calendar day after the date set forth above, terminating this agreement. Upon receipt of such notice this agreement shall be void and all monies deposited by the BUYER shall be returned. Failure to provide timely notice of termination shall constitute a waiver. In the event that the BUYER does not exercise the right to have such inspection(s) or to so terminate, the SELLER and the listing broker are each released from claims relating to the condition of the Premises that the BUYER or the BUYER'S consultants could reasonably have discovered. The BUYER acknowledges receipt of the Home Inspectors Facts For Consumers brochure prepared by the Office of Consumer Affairs.

18. <u>Lead Paint Laws.</u> For premises built before 1978 BUYER acknowledges receipt of the "Department of Public Health Property Transfer Notification" regarding the Lead Law, acknowledges verbal notification of the possible presence of lead hazards and the provisions of the Federal and Massachusetts Lead Laws and regulations, including the right to inspect for dangerous levels of lead. Occupancy of premises containing dangerous levels of lead by a child under six years of age is prohibited, subjected to exceptions permitted by law. BUYER further acknowledges that neither the SELLER nor any real estate agent has made any representation, express or implied, regarding the absence of lead paint or compliance with

5

_____   _____   _____   _____   _____   _____
BUYER'S Initials   BUYER'S Initials   BUYER'S Initials   SELLER'S Initials   SELLER'S Initials   SELLER'S Initials

F I G U R E   7.2 (Continued)

Sample Purchase-and-Sale Agreement

any lead law, except as set forth in writing. BUYER assumes full responsibility for compliance with all laws relating to lead paint removal, if required by law, and related matters (in particular, without limitation, Mass. G.L., c. 111, § 197), and BUYER assumes full responsibility for all tests, lead paint removal and other costs of compliance.

19. **Smoke Detectors/Wood Stove Permit.** The SELLER shall equip the residential structure on the Premises with approved smoke detectors and furnish BUYER with Certificate of Approved Installation from the local Fire Department at the time for performance to the extent required by law as well as any wood stove permit, if any, required by law, regulation or ordinance.

20. **Warranties And Representations.** The SELLER represents and warrants that the Premises ☐ is/ ☐ is not *[choose one]* served by a septic system or cesspool. [If yes, a copy of the Title 5 Addendum is attached.] The SELLER further represents that there ☐ is/ ☐ is no ☐ has no knowledge of *[choose one]* underground storage tank. The SELLER further represents and warrants that SELLER has full authority to enter into this Agreement. The BUYER acknowledges that BUYER has not relied upon any warranties or representations other than those incorporated in this Agreement, except for the following additional warranties and representations, if any, made by either the SELLER or the SELLER'S real estate agent:

_____
_____
_____
_____
_____
_____
_____
_____
_____

[If none, state "none"; if any listed, indicate by whom the warranty or representation was made.]

21. **Notices.** All notices required or permitted to be made under this Agreement shall be in writing and delivered in hand, sent by certified mail, return receipt requested or sent by United States Postal Service overnight Express Mail or other overnight delivery service, addressed to the BUYER or SELLER or their authorized representative at the address set forth in this paragraph. Such notice shall be deemed to have been given upon delivery or, if sent by certified mail on the date of delivery set forth in the receipt or in the absence of a receipt three business days after deposited or, if sent by overnight mail or delivery, the next business day after deposit with the overnight mail or delivery service, whether or not a signature is required. Acceptance of any notice, whether by delivery or mail, shall be sufficient if accepted or signed by a person having express or implied authority to receive same. Notice shall also be deemed adequate if given in any other form permitted by law. *[If there are multiple buyers, identify the mailing address of each buyer in paragraph 23.]*

BUYER _____   SELLER _____

_____   _____

Address: _____   Address: _____

_____   _____

22. **Counterparts / Facsimilies / Construction Of Agreement.** This Agreement may be executed in counterparts. Signatures transmitted by facsimile shall have the effect of original signatures. This Agreement shall be construed as a Massachusetts contract; is to take effect as a sealed instrument; sets forth the entire agreement between the parties; is

BUYER'S Initials   BUYER'S Initials   BUYER'S Initials   SELLER'S Initials   SELLER'S Initials   SELLER'S Initials

FIGURE 7.2 (Continued)

Sample Purchase-and-Sale Agreement

binding upon and is intended to benefit the BUYER and SELLER and each of their respective heirs, devisees, executors, administrators, successors and assigns; and may be canceled, modified or amended only by a written agreement executed by both the SELLER and the BUYER. If two or more persons are named as BUYER their obligations are joint and several. If the SELLER or BUYER is a trust, corporation, limited liability company or entity whose representative executes this Agreement in a representative or fiduciary capacity, only the principal or the trust or estate represented shall be bound, and neither the trustee, officer, shareholder or beneficiary shall be personally liable for any obligation, express or implied. The captions and any notes are used only as a matter of convenience and are not to be considered a part of this Agreement and are not to be used in determining the intent of the parties. Any matter or practice which has not been addressed in this agreement and which is the subject of a Title Standard or Practice of the Real Estate Bar Association for Massachusetts, formerly known as the Massachusetts Conveyancers Association, at the time of performance shall be governed by the Standard of Practice of the Massachusetts Real Estate Bar for Massachusetts.

23. **Additional Provisions.** _____

_____

_____

_____

_____

_____

_____

_____

_____

_____

_____

_____

UPON SIGNING, THIS DOCUMENT WILL BECOME A LEGALLY BINDING AGREEMENT.
IF NOT UNDERSTOOD, SEEK ADVICE FROM AN ATTORNEY.

_____ _____   _____ _____
BUYER   Date   SELLER   Date

_____ _____   _____ _____
BUYER   Date   SELLER, *or spouse*   Date

_____ _____   _____ _____
BUYER   Date   SELLER, *or spouse*   Date

Escrow Agent. By signing below, the escrow agent agrees to perform in accordance with paragraph 4, but does not otherwise become a party to this Agreement.

_____ _____
ESCROW AGENT or representative   Date

_____   _____   _____   _____   _____   _____
BUYER'S Initials BUYER'S Initials BUYER'S Initials   SELLER'S Initials SELLER'S Initials SELLER'S Initials

Equitable title. When a buyer and seller sign a contract for the sale of real estate located in Massachusetts, the buyer immediately becomes the *equitable owner*. This does not give the buyer actual legal ownership of the property, but it gives what a court would recognize as an equitable interest. That is, the buyer has the right to become the owner or the right to have the title transferred.

Liquidated damages. Most contracts in Massachusetts contain a liquidated damages clause that permits the seller to retain all or part of the earnest money deposit as liquidated damages in the event of the buyer's default.

Usually, the clause in the contract reads:

> *Should the buyer default, the seller and the broker may divide the earnest money deposit equally as liquidated damages.*

The amount of liquidated damages must reasonably approximate what the damage might be. If the amount is excessive, the court will view it as a penalty and will not allow the seller to keep the entire amount.

If there is no clause in the contract indicating damages, then there are no liquidated damages.

Liquidated damages are a mixed bag for all parties. The benefit to buyers of having a liquidated damages clause in the contract is that their liability is defined and limited. On the other hand, buyers are guaranteed a loss in the event they breach the contract for any reason. While including a liquidated damages clause sometimes means that the seller gives up the right to sue for any actual damages, he or she is assured of compensation for the time the property was unnecessarily held off the market. In some contracts, however, the seller is entitled to take the liquidated damages *and* to pursue other remedies against the buyer, including specific performance. Brokers give up the right to sue the seller for a total commission, but brokers are entitled to some compensation for the lost income.

Reciprocal liquidated damages clauses based on seller default are rare. Normally, in the event of a seller default, the buyer would seek specific performance, sue for actual damages, or simply demand return of the deposit.

IN PRACTICE

Of course, if the transaction fails to close due to interference by the seller, the broker may sue for the commission.

Installment Contracts

Under an *installment contract*, the seller retains legal title to the property until the entire purchase price is paid, usually over a term of many years. Often the seller finances the purchase, and the buyer sends the seller monthly checks until the entire amount, including interest, is paid.

If the seller becomes insolvent during the term of the contract, the seller's creditors may attach and dispose of any property held in the seller's name, including the property the buyer is purchasing, This leaves the buyer of the property in no better position than a creditor. In many cases, however, a properly recorded equitable ownership can give the buyer a claim to the property, and creditors are limited to attaching the seller's right to receive the payments. In any event, this can be a dangerous method of purchasing property if the buyer does not obtain proper legal counsel. Installment contracts are seldom used in Massachusetts.

■ RELATED WEB SITE

Massachusetts Association of REALTORS®   *www.marealtor.com*

QUESTIONS

1. For a contract for the sale of real estate to be enforceable in a court of law, the contract must be
   a. in writing.
   b. signed by the buyer.
   c. signed by the seller.
   d. on a preprinted standard form.

2. The age of legal competence in Massachusetts is
   a. 18.
   b. 19.
   c. 20.
   d. 21.

3. The memorandum required by the statute of frauds includes all the following *EXCEPT*
   a. description of the premises.
   b. identity of the parties and their signatures.
   c. consideration.
   d. closing date.

4. Roberto makes an offer on Hidalgo's house. As soon as both parties have signed the contract, Roberto is
   a. immune from the statute of frauds.
   b. required to deposit Hidalgo's earnest money in an escrow account.
   c. the legal owner of the property.
   d. the equitable owner of the property.

5. When an earnest money deposit is received, a broker
   a. must give it to the seller.
   b. may deposit it in his checking account.
   c. must deposit it in an escrow account.
   d. must hold the check until the closing.

6. When the contract is signed, the buyer becomes the equitable owner. The buyer now has
   a. legal ownership of the property.
   b. a partnership with the seller.
   c. a deed to the property.
   d. a right to become the owner.

7. A liquidated damages clause permits the
   a. buyer to recover the earnest money deposit.
   b. seller to retain all or part of the earnest money deposit.
   c. broker to retain all of the earnest money deposit.
   d. seller to impose a fine on the buyer in case of a breach.

8. Broker Bob received a buyer's earnest money check for $5,000 and immediately cashed it. At closing, Bob handed the seller a personal check drawn on Bob's own bank account for $5,300, representing the original earnest money plus 6 percent interest. Which of the following statements is *TRUE?*
   a. Bob should have deposited the money in a special noninterest-bearing bank account.
   b. Bob properly cashed the check but should have kept the interest.
   c. Bob should have deposited the money in his personal bank account and would have been entitled to keep the interest as a service fee.
   d. Bob should have deposited the money in a special bank account and should have discussed the interest with the parties.

9. Mark and Olene made an offer on a house. The offer was accepted by the seller. The preprinted sales contract used by the broker contained a standard liquidated damages clause. Two weeks later, Mark and Olene decided that they did not want the house. Which of the following statements is *TRUE*?

a. They are bound by the sales contract they made and must proceed with the transaction.

b. The seller and broker may keep the earnest money deposit and put the house back on the market.

c. The seller may sue both Mark and Olene for breach of contract.

d. Because the broker used a preprinted form contract, the liquidated damages clause is legally void.

10. Which of the following is seldom used in Massachusetts?

a. Purchase-and-sale agreements

b. Standard preprinted form contracts

c. Installment land contracts

d. Statutory memorandum of sale

CHAPTER

Transfer of Title

■ VOLUNTARY ALIENATION

Requirements for a Valid Deed

Following are the nine basic requirements for a valid transfer of real property in Massachusetts:

1. The transfer must be evidenced by a *written document*.
2. The grantor must use the *same full name* as the one by which he or she received title by the previous conveyance. If the name has changed, both the old and new names should be indicated in the document.
3. The grantor must use language that is equivalent to the verb *grant* because that is the purpose of the document.
4. The purchase price or amount of full consideration must be *clearly and completely stated* or the document will not be recordable. Phrases such as "for one dollar and other good and valuable consideration" are not sufficient.
5. The *name of the grantee* and some means of identifying who he or she is and where he or she comes from must be included. If there is more than one grantee, it should be made clear how they are to hold the property.
6. An *accurate description* of the property must be given. (See Chapter 5.)
7. *Homestead rights* must be released.
8. *Delivery* must be made to the grantee.
9. *Recording* is mandatory in the case of registered land and optional in the case of nonregistered land. (See Chapter 9.) In the case of registered land, the registration certificate must be delivered along with the deed for title to pass to the buyer. Note that acknowledgment before a notary public must be made for recordation, but acknowledgment is not one of the requirements for a valid transfer of real property.

Types of Deeds

Massachusetts law provides for two forms of deeds for use by individual owners for transfers of property during their lifetimes (*inter vivos* transfers): the *warranty deed* and the *quitclaim deed*.

The warranty deed. When the statutory short form warranty deed is used, the grantor warrants that

- he or she held the premises in *fee simple;*
- the granted premises were *free from all encumbrances not specifically stated;*
- he or she had *good right to sell and convey;* and
- he or she *warrants and defends the title against the lawful claims and demands of all persons.*

The quitclaim deed. In a quitclaim deed the grantor warrants that *at the time of delivering the deed*

1. the premises were *free of all encumbrances made by the grantor;* and
2. the grantor will warrant and defend the title for the grantee against the lawful claims of all persons *claiming by, through, or under him or her but against no one else.*

IN PRACTICE

Note that in Massachusetts, the quitclaim deed has the status of a special warranty deed due to the title search process that is conducted prior to closing.

The acceptance of a deed generally ends a buyer's right to claim that the title is faulty. For this reason, a title search is recommended.

Contract terms that extend to issues beyond the deed—warranties or promises about the condition of the property that were part of a purchase-and-sale agreement, for instance—may survive beyond acceptance of a deed. Such terms may form the basis for a later lawsuit.

Transfer Tax Stamps

In Massachusetts, the tax levied on the conveyance of real estate is different by county. For example, $2.28 may be levied for each $500 (or fraction of $500) of real estate equity transferred from buyer to seller. The tax is paid by the seller, who must purchase *revenue stamps* (also called *excise* or *conveyance tax stamps*) at the Registry of Deeds and affix them to the deed before recording. Stamps are not required on other real estate documents, such as mortgages or leases.

■ INVOLUNTARY ALIENATION

In Massachusetts, the period for which a person must use a parcel of real estate to establish ownership by *adverse possession* is 20 years. The requirements are the same as for the easement by prescription described in Chapter 3.

The requirements are

- continuous or uninterrupted use or possession (Note that the time of possession of the prior owner's or owners' use of the property may be tacked on to the current owner's time of possession in order to establish the 20-year period.);

MATH CONCEPTS   **CALCULATING MASSACHUSETTS TRANSFER TAXES**

I

Bob purchases Sandy's home for $175,000 in cash.
There are 350 "taxable units" in 175,000.

$175,000 ÷ 500 = 350

Sandy's transfer tax is 350 × $2.28 = $798.

II

Steve buys Bill's home for $195,000, by taking over Bill's existing $100,000 mortgage and paying $95,000 in cash. Bill pays the tax only on the *equity* transferred. His equity of $95,000 is the price of $195,000 less the $100,000 mortgage, which he does not pay off at the sale but transfers with the property.
There are 190 "taxable units" in $95,000.

$95,000 ÷ 500 = 190

Bill's transfer tax is 190 × $2.28 = $433.20.

III

Sarah buys Carol's home for $175,100.
There are 351 "taxable units" in 175,100.

$175,100 ÷ 500 = 350.2

Carol's transfer tax is 351 × $2.28 = $800.28
Compare this result with example I above.

- without the permission of the owner;
- for 20 years; and
- with the actual or constructive knowledge of the owner.

Title acquired by this means is subject to legal technicalities and should not be relied on without legal advice. Adverse possession may *not* be maintained against any state-owned land or registered land. (See Chapter 9.)

■ TRANSFER OF A DECEASED PERSON'S PROPERTY

Transfer of Title by Will

In Massachusetts, any person 18 years of age or older may make a will. When a person dies having executed a valid will, they die *testate* and are referred to as the *testator*. In addition to the requirements set out in the text, a valid will must be attested by two witnesses. The witnesses do not have a right to read the will, but they must be aware that the testator is signing a document he or she knows to be his or her will. The witnesses should see the testator sign the will and should see each other sign as witnesses. Any devise or legacy given to a witness is void.

A surviving spouse has a *right of election* and may have the will's provisions for the spouse set aside. The spouse can claim his or her dower rights or may take property under the law of intestate distribution. (Dower and the spousal homestead right are discussed in Chapter 3.)

Transfer of Title by Descent

When a person dies without leaving a valid will, they die *intestate*, and his or her property passes by *intestate succession* under the terms of Massachusetts law. After payment of all debts, claims, and taxes, the estate is divided according to statute, depending on the status of the decedent. The chart in Figure 8.1 shows the most common statutory distributions.

■ RELATED WEB SITE

Massachusetts General Laws   *www.mass.gov/legis/laws/mgl*

FIGURE 8.1

Statutory Distributions

Decedent Status	Family Status	How Property Passes
Married with surviving spouse[1]	No children No other relatives	100% to surviving spouse
	Children[2]	50% to surviving spouse; 50% shared by children or descendants of deceased child
Married with no surviving spouse	Children	Children share equally, with descendants of a deceased child taking their parent's share
Unmarried with no children	Relatives	100% to father or mother, brothers or sisters, or other relatives
	No relatives	100% to Massachusetts by escheat

[1] Massachusetts law allows the decedent's spouse the right to elect a life estate of dower, as discussed in Chapter 3, in place of the share provided for in the law of descent.
[2] Adopted and biological children are treated equally.

1. The law of descent and distribution applies when a person dies
   a. testate.
   b. leaving no heirs.
   c. leaving minor children.
   d. intestate.

2. Jim was a witness to his Uncle John's will. When the will was read after John's death, Jim discovered that he was a devisee of his uncle's will. Which of the following statements is *TRUE*?
   a. Because Jim is a witness, the devise is void.
   b. As a witness, Jim should have read the will.
   c. Because Jim is a witness, the will is void.
   d. Jim has a right of election.

3. How is the voluntary transfer of real estate during a person's lifetime accomplished?
   a. By the right of election
   b. By a will
   c. By a deed
   d. By an antenuptial agreement

4. When title is conveyed using a quitclaim deed, the grantor warrants that at the time of delivery
   a. the premises are free of all encumbrances made by the grantor.
   b. the premises are free of all encumbrances made by past owners.
   c. he or she will defend the title against the claims of all people.
   d. none of the above is true.

5. For the transfer of title to be valid, which of the following requirements does *NOT* necessarily apply?
   a. There must be a written document.
   b. Language equivalent to the word *grant* must be used.
   c. The purchase price must be mentioned.
   d. The deed must be recorded at the Registry of Deeds.

6. Which of the following is *NOT* required to acquire land by adverse possession?
   a. Use with the owner's permission
   b. Use for a period of 20 years
   c. Use openly so as to be seen
   d. Use without the owner's permission

7. The Smarts sold their house to the Youngs for $203,500. The Youngs paid the entire amount out of their cash assets. If the rate for revenue stamps is $2.28 per $500 or any portion thereof, how much will the revenue stamps cost?
   a. $565.48
   b. $900.00
   c. $927.96
   d. $945.56

8. The Browns sold their house to the Greens for $150,800. The Browns had $40,000 left on their assumable mortgage, which the Greens assumed. If the rate for revenue stamps is $2.28 per $500 or any portion thereof, how much will the revenue stamps cost?
   a. $506.16
   b. $50.16
   c. $344.28
   d. $525.25

9. Which of the following is *NOT* included in a statutory short form warranty deed?
   a. The grantor held the property in fee simple.
   b. The premises are free of encumbrances.
   c. Title is warranted only against claims of persons by, through, or under the grantor.
   d. The grantor has good right to sell and convey the property.

10. For a deed to be valid, it must be delivered to the
    a. grantor.
    b. Registry of Deeds.
    c. grantee.
    d. notary public.

11. Lon accepts a statutory short-form quitclaim deed from Mary. Later a claim against the property is made by Nell, who has a valid outstanding lien against Ollie, who owned the property before Mary. Which of the following *BEST* states what can happen under these circumstances?

a. Lon can force Mary to pay the claim.
b. Mary cannot be held under her quitclaim covenants.
c. Lon can force Ollie to pay the claim.
d. No claim can be made because Lon has a valid deed.

12. Harold thought wills were unlucky, so he never had one made. Last week, Harold was struck by a meteor and died. He is survived by his wife, Wanda, and two adult children, Sam and Debbie. How is Harold's estate divided?

a. All of Harold's estate passes to Wanda.
b. One-third passes to Wanda, and one-third each goes to Sam and Debbie.
c. One-half goes to Wanda, one-quarter passes each to Sam and Debbie.
d. $200,000 passes to Wanda, and one-half of the remaining estate passes to Sam and Debbie.

13. Doug and Darryl both die, leaving estates of well over $1 million each. Neither wrote a will. Doug's parents live in Argentina and haven't spoken to him since 1980. Darryl, who has no family members, left a note in a sealed envelope stating his wish that his property be given to a local animal shelter. How will their estates be divided?

a. Both will escheat to Massachusetts.
b. Doug's estate will go to his parents, and Darryl's will go to the shelter.
c. Doug's estate will escheat to Massachusetts, and Darryl's will go to the shelter.
d. Doug's estate will go to his parents, and Darryl's will escheat to Massachusetts.

Title Records

■ PUBLIC RECORDS

Recording

The real estate recording system is a semivoluntary system in Massachusetts. A grantee is not required to record a document under the Massachusetts recording statute, although he or she may choose to do so. The law clearly places the risk that results from not recording on the person who chooses not to record. A conveyance must be recorded to be effectively executed.

There are, however, several ways in which a purchaser can get notice. Although not as effective as recordation, possession of the property, for example, may serve as notice.

Deeds, conveyances, leases, and mortgages are recorded with the Registry of Deeds of the county in which the real estate is situated. Recording establishes the order of priority of an interest or lien and also provides *constructive notice*.

Registered Land

The two kinds of real property in Massachusetts are

1. *registered land*, and
2. land that is not registered.

Registered is not the same as *recorded*. Any grantee may record his or her deed, giving notice to the world that he or she is the new owner. However, property that has been registered must have a new certificate of title issued every time it is transferred or subdivided.

System of Registration   The system of land registration used in Massachusetts is similar to the Torrens system. The *Torrens system* is a legal registration system used to verify ownership of real property and encumbrances. Registration in the Torrens system provides evidence of title without the need for an additional search of public records.

In Massachusetts, registration is commenced with an action to *quiet title*, in which the court is asked to determine who actually owns a parcel of land and what claims or liens against the property are valid. An exhaustive investigation of the history of the property's ownership is conducted. Advertising and any other possible means of reaching anyone who may have a claim on the property are used. Usually, the property will be surveyed, and its boundaries firmly established.

The court then holds a hearing at which all persons have a right to present their claims. At the conclusion of this action, the court will order the property to be registered and will issue a numbered certificate to the rightful owner. The certificate, called a *land court certificate*, will show the legal description, the owners, and their interests, as well as the valid claims and liens that the court has determined to be outstanding against the property. From that day onward, the land is registered, and a special set of rules and laws governs the title to it.

Any time registered land is conveyed, the deed must be accompanied by the land court certificate, and the deed must be presented to the land court who issues a new certificate of title in the name of the new owner. *The transfer is not valid until a new certificate of title is issued and registered.* Similarly, attempts to encumber registered land are invalid until the encumbrance is registered on the certificate in the land court office.

Normal recording of documents will not affect registered land until registered on the land court certificate. Once land has a *registered title* (also called a *land court title*), registration is mandatory and forever. The papers and documents filed in a registration action are held, recorded, and indexed by a recorder, who is appointed by the governor and under the direction of the chief justice of the land court.

IN PRACTICE   Note that the land court's records office is part of the court and is not the same as the Registry of Deeds.

■ EVIDENCE OF TITLE

In Massachusetts, it is the *buyer* who customarily has the title searched and the property surveyed. The seller does not have to share in these expenses unless he or she agrees to or unless there is a defect in the title.

Most buyers hire an attorney to make a title search, particularly because banks will not loan money on property that has not had the title searched. The attorney may make one of the following three types (see Figure 9.1) of title search:

1. A *title search and opinion*, in which the attorney searches the public records, lists the entries, and states his or her opinion of the title

2. A *full abstract*, in which the attorney copies the important parts of each document that affects the title and then states his or her opinion
3. A *certificate of title*, which is simply a brief statement of the attorney's opinion

Often, however, buyers may forgo a title search if the bank with which they will place their mortgage conducts its own. If the title is found to be faulty after the bank lends money to the buyer, the bank can sue the attorney who conducted the search to recover the mortgage amount. Similarly, if the buyer paid the bank for the lawyer's title search, and the property involved is an owner-occupied home with fewer than four families, then the attorney will be liable to the buyer for the full purchase price. In either case, the attorney will not be liable if he or she was not negligent in conducting the search.

An increasing number of lending institutions in Massachusetts require title insurance as part of the mortgage commitment. *Title insurance* is an agreement under which the policyholder is protected from losses arising from defects in the title. Unlike other insurance policies that protect against future losses, title insurance protects against events that occurred before the policy was issued. In Massachusetts, there are generally two forms of title insurance available to homeowners: the first form protects only the lender's interest, while the second more expensive form protects the interests of both the lender and the homeowner.

FIGURE 9.1

Three Types of Title Search

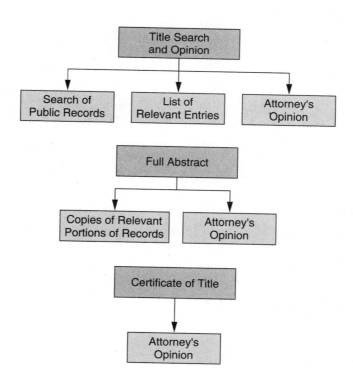

QUESTIONS

1. Mr. Hawkins buys real estate that is registered land. For the transfer to be valid he *MUST*
   a. record the deed at the Registry of Deeds.
   b. have a new certificate of title issued in his name.
   c. institute a suit to quiet title.
   d. record the land court certificate in his name.

2. In Massachusetts, who customarily pays for the title search?
   a. The bank
   b. The buyer
   c. The seller
   d. The broker

3. Which of the following is *NOT* a title search method commonly used by an attorney in Massachusetts?
   a. Land court certificate
   b. Title search and opinion
   c. Certificate of title
   d. Full abstract

4. Title insurance provides a means of financial protection if
   a. the bank had a title search conducted.
   b. the buyer did not pay the lawyer.
   c. a defect is found in the title.
   d. the seller paid for the title search.

5. Deeds, conveyances, leases, and mortgages are usually recorded
   a. with the land court recorder.
   b. in order to establish a deed's validity and to prove that delivery occurred.
   c. with the Registry of Deeds of the county in which the land is located.
   d. with the Registry of Deeds of the county in which the seller resides.

CHAPTER

10

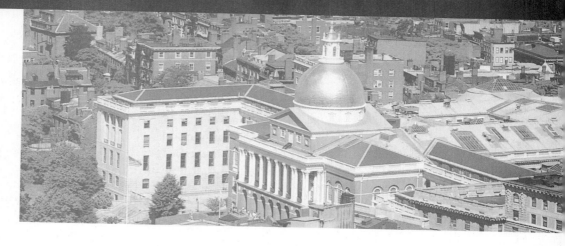

Massachusetts Real Estate License Laws

■ WHO MUST BE LICENSED

In Massachusetts, anyone who acts as a real estate broker or a real estate salesperson must be licensed. (See Chapter 1.) In an action to recover consideration owed for real estate brokerage services (that is, a commission), the person seeking to recover must prove that he or she was duly licensed at the time the services were performed. Any person who acts as a broker or salesperson without a license is subject to a fine of up to $500. Massachusetts Real Estate License Law and regulations are governed generally by the Massachusetts General Laws Chapter 13, Sections 54–57, Chapter 112, Sections 87PP-87DDD1/2, and 254 of the Code of Massachusetts Registration Sections 2.00–7.00.

Exceptions

The Massachusetts Real Estate License Law does not apply to

- persons selling, buying, exchanging, renting, leasing, or managing their own property;
- managing agents or regular employees of managing agents who perform any real estate activities as part of their regular duties;
- persons acting for themselves in negotiating a loan secured or to be secured by a mortgage or other encumbrance on real property;
- licensed auctioneers;
- persons who deal in stocks, bonds, other securities, or certificates of beneficial interests in trusts;
- public officers or employees who are performing their official duties;

- persons who are acting as attorneys-in-fact under authority of a power of attorney from an owner that authorizes them to complete a real estate transaction;
- attorneys rendering services to clients (unless they are performing the duties of a broker for a commission, in which case they must pay a fee to be licensed but do not have to take a course or licensing examination);
- receivers, trustees in bankruptcy, administrators, conservators, executors, guardians, or other persons appointed by or acting under a court order;
- trustees or their regular employees acting under written instruments of trust, deeds or declarations of trust, or wills; and
- banks, credit unions, and insurance companies acting as fiduciaries, negotiating a mortgage on real estate, or acting for themselves.

■ BOARD OF REGISTRATION OF REAL ESTATE BROKERS AND SALESPERSONS

The Massachusetts Board of Registration of Real Estate Brokers and Salespersons (referred to in this Chapter as *the board*) administers the license laws. The board consists of five members appointed by the governor to five-year terms. Three members must be full-time licensed real estate brokers who have been active in the real estate business for at least seven years. The other two members are designated representatives of the public. Members serve without compensation but are reimbursed for expenses incurred in carrying out their duties.

The board must hold at least four regular meetings each year. Written records must be kept of all meetings, and the meetings must be open to the public for inspection. The board must submit an annual report to the governor that details its proceedings and expenses.

■ LICENSING PROCEDURE

Anyone who performs real estate brokerage services, as either a broker or salesperson, must be licensed. No salesperson may conduct or operate his or her own real estate business or act in any way except as the representative of a real estate broker.

Requirements for Issuance of License

As you already know, anyone who wants to be a real estate broker or salesperson must take and pass a written examination.

Every applicant for a salesperson's license must submit proof that he or she has completed 24 classroom hours of instruction in real estate subjects approved by the board. However, for those applicants who have successfully completed a course in real property while enrolled in an accredited law school in the Commonwealth of Massachusetts may also take an examination. An applicant for a broker's license must prove that he or she has been actively associated as a salesperson with a real estate broker for at least one year at a minimum of 25 hours per week and has completed a total of 30 additional classroom hours of instruction approved by the board. The applicant must show that he or she has fulfilled the experience requirement of actively associating as a salesperson with a real estate broker within two years of taking the broker's examination. A broker must have a current Massachusetts salesperson license. Neither a broker's nor a salesperson's license may be issued to anyone younger than 18.

A nonresident may be licensed as a broker or as a salesperson in Massachusetts if he or she is licensed in another state. A nonresident may be exempt from the written examination for licensure if the laws allowing for a similar exemption are extended to licensees of the Commonwealth. In circumstances where the exemption is not permitted, the classroom study and the general portion of the exam may be waived. However, the nonresident would be required to take the state portion of the exam. A nonresident is not required to maintain an office in Massachusetts but must maintain an office in the state where he or she is licensed.

Each applicant must furnish evidence of good moral character. If a corporation, society, association, or partnership applies for a broker's license, it must furnish evidence of the good moral character of all the officers and directors, or holders of similar positions, or of all the partners.

All applications must be accompanied by the recommendations of three reputable citizens who reside in Massachusetts and are not related to the applicant. The recommendations must state that the applicant has a good reputation for honesty and fair dealing.

Massachusetts General Laws (MGL) Chapter 112 §87TT requires an applicant for a license to furnish evidence of citizenship or intent of citizenship. However, an opinion by the Attorney General's office (1975-76) declared such requirement as constitutionally defective and therefore should not be enforced. Although the state Web site still lists the requirement, the board, based upon the Attorney General's opinion, does not enforce the requirement of citizenship and has removed the requirement from the "License Law and Regulation Booklet" posted on the Web site.

Both salespersons and brokers must, to the best of their knowledge and belief, have filed all state tax returns and paid all state taxes as required by law.

Brokers must obtain a $5,000 surety bond on an original form (a copy is not acceptable), completed by the insurance agent, signed by the principal (candidate/examinee), and witnessed. The professional identification number provided by Promissor at the time of an examination reservation must be included on the original bond and entered by the insurance agent.

An applicant may be required to appear for a personal interview with the board.

The board may also require an applicant to submit a report from an independent source regarding the applicant's previous occupation or other material information.

Issuance of a Broker's License to Corporations and Other Entities

A broker's license may be held by a corporation, society, association, or partnership. At least one officer or partner must be designated as the entity's representative for the purpose of obtaining a license. Each designated officer or partner must apply to the board for a broker's license in his or her own name.

A salesperson's license, however, may not be issued to a corporation, society, association, or partnership.

Examination

The broker's or salesperson's licensing examination is prepared by Promissor (formerly ASI), the board's designated independent testing service. The examination is designed to enable the board to determine the competence of the applicant to transact the business of a real estate broker or salesperson in Massachusetts.

There is no limit on the number of applicants who may take the examination on any examination date. The broker's examination must be offered at least six times a year, and the salesperson's examination must be offered at least eight times a year. The applicant must pass the exam within two years of the date of completing the required salesperson or broker education.

To enter the examination, the examinee must have two forms of identification, one of which must be a picture identification, such as a driver's license.

The following rules apply to the examination process:

- Examinees are not permitted to bring notes, books, memoranda, dictionaries, or reference materials to the Promissor Assessment Center. Examinees who are found with these or any other aids, such as watch alarms, listening devices, or recording or photographic devices, during the exam will not be allowed to continue the exam.
- All computations must be shown on blank pages provided for that purpose. Calculators may be used only if they are hand-held, battery-operated, non-printing, and without an alphabetic key pad.
- Cellular phones, beepers, and any other electronic devices are not permitted during the exam, and there is no place for storage of personal belongings at the Promissor Assessment Center.
- Copying questions or making notes about questions is prohibited.
- No one may remove copies of the examination from the examination room either before or after the examination.
- Examinees may leave the examination room to go to the restroom, but they will not be given more time to complete the exam.
- An applicant who fails to attain a passing score may file an application for reexamination after 24 hours.

Violation of any rule may result in the disqualification of the applicant.

Issuance of License

A real estate license is valid for a period of two years. It may be renewed biennially, provided that the application for renewal is not made later than one year from the expiration date of the license. The license originally issued to an individual is valid until the licensee's next birth date occurring more than 24 months after the original date of issuance.

The fees for issuance and renewal of a broker's or salesperson's license are waived for blind persons and paraplegic veterans.

As noted above, an applicant for a broker's license must provide the board with a $5,000 bond, payable to the Commonwealth, for the benefit of any person injured by the broker's actions. The bond is renewable every five years.

In the event that a licensed broker who is the sole proprietor of a real estate business should die, the board may issue a temporary license to the deceased's personal representative.

The temporary license authorizes a licensee to continue the operation of the business for up to one year from the broker's date of death.

Continuing Education

Massachusetts law now requires 12 hours of continuing education within each 2-year renewal period in topics approved by the board in order for the license to be active. Starting January 1, 2001, for those brokers or salespersons seeking to renew their licenses, they must attend real estate classes no less than 6 hours but no more than 12 hours as determined by the board. The curriculum in such courses must contain at least 6 hours of instruction concerning compliance with laws and regulations of any of the following: fair housing, equal employment opportunity, accessibility for the disabled, agency law, environmental issues in real estate, zoning and building codes, real estate appraisal and financing, property tax assessments and valuation, and real estate board regulations.

Every broker and salesperson must provide written certification that the required courses were successfully completed. Anyone who fails to furnish, in a form satisfactory to the board, written certification that the courses were completed will be granted inactive status by the board upon renewal of a license. Anyone who provides a false or fraudulent certificate of completion of coursework will be subject to having a license suspended.

While an out-of-state licensee, who is not required to take an examination to be licensed in the commonwealth, does not need to comply with Massachusetts continuing-education requirements, such a licensee must comply with the continuing-education requirements of the licensee's home state.

Inactive Licensee

With a valid but inactive license, an agent cannot practice real estate but can earn a referral fee from active licensed brokers and can assist with or direct the procuring of prospects. A license may remain inactive for an indefinite period.

If a licensee who is inactive practices real estate, the licensee's license may be revoked. Also, a licensee who is inactive may apply to the board to reactivate the license upon demonstrating the completion of continuing-education requirements for the renewal period immediately preceding the application for reactivation.

Usual Place of Business

A licensed resident broker must maintain a usual place of business within Massachusetts and must conspicuously display his or her license (or a certified copy). The broker must promptly (within 30 days) give written notification to the board of any change of business location. Failure to notify the board is grounds for revoking the broker's license.

Suspension, Revocation, or Refusal of Renewal of License

In the event that the board receives a verified, written complaint about a broker or salesperson, his or her license may be suspended, revoked, or not renewed if the board finds that the broker or salesperson

- obtained his or her license by false or fraudulent representation;
- knowingly made any substantial misrepresentation;
- acted in the dual capacity of broker and undisclosed principal in the same transaction;
- acted for more than one party to a transaction without the knowledge and consent of all the parties;
- failed, within a reasonable time, to account for or remit any money belonging to others that has come into his or her possession as a broker or salesperson;
- paid commissions or fees to an unlicensed person who acted as a real estate broker or salesperson, and who was required to have been licensed;
- accepted, gave, or charged any undisclosed commission, rebate, or profit on expenditures for a principal;
- induced any party to break a real estate contract or lease for the personal gain of the licensee;
- commingled the money or other property of a principal with his or her own;
- failed to give both the buyer and the seller a copy of the purchase and sale agreement;
- committed any act expressly prohibited by Massachusetts Real Estate License Law;
- committed *blockbusting*, that is, affirmatively solicited residential property for sale, lease, or listing on the grounds of alleged change of value due to the presence or the prospective entry into the neighborhood of a person or persons of another race, economic level, religion, or ethnic origin, or distributed material or made statements designed to induce a residential property owner to sell or lease in response to such a change in the neighborhood. A violator is also subject to a fine of from $1,000 to $2,500 and/or up to six months in prison (see Chapter 15);
- engaged in the sale of real property that was located in a land development in another state and that was promoted or advertised in Massachusetts, the owner or developer of which failed to comply with all filing requirements, unless the owner or developer of such land submitted to the board full particulars related to the land and proposed terms of sale and deposited with the board funds to pay the expense of an investigation; or
- accepted a net listing from a prospective seller to sell real estate for a stated price that authorized the broker to keep as commission any amount of money received from the sale of said real estate in excess of the stated price.

The board may also suspend, revoke, or refuse to renew the license of a person who has been convicted of a criminal offense in Massachusetts or any other state, if the offense demonstrates his or her lack of good moral character to act as a real estate broker or salesperson.

If a licensed salesperson or broker is found to have committed unlawful discriminatory practices in violation of the Massachusetts General Laws, Chapter

151B, his or her license will be suspended for 60 days. If the violation has occurred within two years of a prior violation, the license will be suspended for 90 days. (See Chapter 15.)

IN PRACTICE

Any suspension, revocation, or refusal to renew may be reconsidered by the board. The suspension or revocation of a broker's or salesperson's license does not free him or her from liability for any other penalties or punishments provided by law.

Enforcement

The board is empowered to conduct investigations and hearings and to take other appropriate and necessary action to enforce the license law. All complaints submitted to the board must be in writing and signed by the complainant. A hearing must be held upon ten days' notice to the person charged, and no renewal of a license shall be refused and no license shall be suspended or revoked except after the hearing.

The board may summon witnesses and demand the production of books and papers. Testimony may be taken by deposition as in a civil action, and any member of the board may administer oaths, examine witnesses, and receive evidence.

In the event that a witness fails or refuses to appear and testify, the superior court has jurisdiction to issue an order compelling the witness to appear.

Decisions of the board must be by majority, expressed in writing, and signed by all the members. Copies must be sent to each interested party.

The board's decision may be appealed to the superior court within 20 days following notification of the decision.

Broker-Salesperson Relationship

A licensed salesperson must be engaged by a licensed broker. That is, *a licensed salesperson may not conduct his or her own real estate business.* A broker may not be licensed as a salesperson while retaining his or her broker's license; similarly, a salesperson may not be licensed as both a salesperson and a broker at the same time.

Brokers must furnish the board with the names, addresses, and license numbers of all brokers and salespersons engaged by them. The board must also be notified of all terminations of the broker-salesperson relationship.

A broker who is employed by another broker is called a "broker salesperson," and during the time of his or her association may not exercise his or her rights as a broker (e.g., hold escrow monies, advertise in his or her own name, sue a client for a commission, or engage any real estate salesperson). Although many states use the term "broker associate," Massachusetts does not.

Advertising

A broker may not advertise in any way that is false or misleading.

"Blind" advertising is prohibited. Any advertisement placed by a broker must affirmatively and unmistakably state that the advertiser is a real estate broker and not a private party.

Advertisements may not be limited to post office box numbers, telephone numbers, facsimile numbers, electronic address, or a street address: The broker's business name and address must appear in the advertisement.

Salespersons are prohibited from independently advertising. As with all other activities, the advertising of property must be under the direct supervision of a broker, and in the broker's name.

Brokers may not advertise to purchase, sell, rent, mortgage, or exchange any real property in a manner that indicates, either directly or indirectly, any unlawful discrimination against any individual or group. (See Chapter 15.)

Handling Other People's Money

One of the most common grounds for discipline of licensees in Massachusetts is the failure to properly handle and account for money.

Unless otherwise agreed to in writing by the parties, all money received by the broker that belongs to another party must be deposited in a fiduciary bank account, called an *escrow account*, maintained by the broker as a depository for funds. The account may be interest-bearing, but the interest must be included in the proper accounting at the end of each transaction, and the parties must agree to the earning and distribution of interest.

All deposits or payments received by a real estate salesperson, or by a broker engaged by another broker, must be turned over to the engaging broker.

Every broker must keep records of funds deposited in his or her escrow account. Every broker must also keep a copy of each check deposited into and withdrawn from the escrow account for a period of three years from the date of issuance. All such funds and records are subject to inspection by the board or its agents.

Disclosure of Interest in Property

A real estate broker or salesperson may not, either directly or indirectly, buy property in which he or she has acquired an interest or which he or she has listed without first fully disclosing his or her interest. The owner must acknowledge that disclosure has been made.

Before a real estate broker or salesperson buys property for a client in which he or she, or any relative, has an interest, the interest must be disclosed to all parties. Similarly, a real estate broker or salesperson must disclose to a purchaser any interest he or she or any relative may have in any property prior to its sale.

A broker may not take an option to purchase property for which he or she has been approached to act as a broker without first disclosing that he or she is now acting as a prospective buyer rather than as a broker or agent for the owner.

Use of Attorney

No broker or salesperson may advise against the use of an attorney's services in any real estate transaction.

Duty to Report All Offers

All offers obtained by brokers or salespersons on a property must be immediately presented to the owner. It is the owner's right to decide whether an offer is legitimate or unreasonable.

Consumer-Licensee Relationship Disclosure

All real estate brokers or salespersons must provide each prospective purchaser and seller with a form disclosing the broker's or salesperson's relationship with the prospective purchaser or seller and disclosing the licensee's relationship with others in his or her firm. (See Chapter 1.) The notice must be provided at the time of the *first personal meeting* between the broker or salesperson and the seller or purchaser where a *specific property* is discussed, where the broker or salesperson represents either the seller or the purchaser *exclusively*.

Dual agency and/or designated agency are permitted if both parties give their informed written consent and receive written notice upon the occurrence or dual or designated agency.

Permission to offer subagency is now required in writing along with an explanation of "vicarious liability."

A licensee may also work with both a seller and a buyer as a facilitator and not represent either party.

IN PRACTICE Written notice of a Consumer-Licensee relationship does not have to be given individually to each prospective purchaser who attends an open house. The Consumer-Licensee relationship disclosure provided at an open house may be made by other means, such as a poster, flyer, or property description form, provided the disclosure is more conspicuous than any other written terms.

Home Inspection Disclosure

Real estate brokers are required to distribute a brochure or fact sheet produced by the Office of Consumer Affairs about home inspections to homebuyers, and brokers are prohibited (except in the case of buyer agents) from directly recommending a home inspector. Brokers may provide a list of licensed inspectors in Massachusetts upon request. This disclosure is to be made before the buyer signs an offer to purchase agreement. (See Chapter 1, Figure 1.4.)

■ APARTMENT LISTING SERVICES

Massachusetts law no longer contains regulations for apartment listing services. It does, however, have a section on apartment rentals. Brokers and salespersons must provide a written notice to prospective tenants as to whether a fee shall be charged for procuring a rental, its amount, the manner and time of its payment, and whether it shall be paid even if a tenancy is not created. The notice is to be given at the first personal meeting between the broker or salesperson and the prospective tenant. The prospective tenant and broker or salesperson must both sign the agreement. It is to be dated and contain the broker's or salesperson's license number. If the prospective tenant declines to sign, this must be noted on the form and the tenant's name and refusal must be stipulated. This notice, all listings, checks, and written documents are to be saved for three years.

Any advertising regarding the availability of an apartment must disclose the following in print no smaller than that for the apartment itself: "The apartment advertised may no longer be available for rent."

■ PROMOTIONAL SALES OF OUT-OF-STATE PROPERTY

The promotional sale of out-of-state property is strictly regulated by the real estate license law. No real property located outside Massachusetts may be offered for sale or sold in the Commonwealth unless it is offered for sale and sold through a real estate broker licensed in Massachusetts. *Real property* includes land, buildings, fixtures, condominiums, cooperatives, and time-sharing intervals.

Out-of-state property must be registered with the board, and this registration and its accompanying fee are to be renewed annually. A broker who represents an out-of-state owner or developer shall notify the board of this agency relationship within seven days of its inception.

An out-of-state development property may not be offered for sale until the owner or developer has applied to the board for investigation of the property. The developer must provide the board with an extensive array of documentation, statements, and data regarding the property, including information on how deposits will be handled, a description of the development's topography and soil, sample advertisements, a financial statement, a price list covering specific plots to be sold, and the terms and conditions of sale offered to prospective buyers. The developers are responsible for bearing the cost of an on-site inspection by the board.

Complaint Procedure

The Division of Professional Licensure (hereinafter referred to as *the division*) of the Massachusetts Board of Registration of Real Estate Brokers and Salespersons maintains a complaint procedure for those instances when a consumer wants to issue a complaint against a licensee. An application for a complaint can be found on the board's Web site noted below.

In many cases, the division helps a consumer understand his or her rights and directs the consumer to the best resource for resolving the matter. In cases where it can be proved that it is not in the public's best interests for a licensee to continue to practice the profession, the division may elect to open a complaint and conduct an investigation.

Grounds for consumer complaints can include, among others, negligence resulting in physical harm to a consumer; misuse of client funds or records; failure to adhere to acceptable standards of practice; fraud; practice while impaired by alcohol or drugs; sexual misconduct; fraudulent procurement of a license; and practice while a license has lapsed. The division does not handle disputes over fees. Only when the division determines that it has probable cause to investigate a matter will an application for a complaint result in an investigation. Some complaints are best resolved by informal means, by court systems, or by other agencies.

■ RELATED WEB SITES

Code of Massachusetts Regulations   *www.lawlib.state.ma.us/cmrindex.html*

Division of Professional Licensure of the Massachusetts Board of Registration of Real Estate Brokers and Salespersons—Application for Complaint *www.mass.gov/dpl/consumer/complaint.htm*

Massachusetts Board of Registration of Real Estate Brokers and Salespersons *www.mass.gov/dpl/boards/re/index.htm*

Massachusetts General Laws   *www.mass.gov/legis/laws/mgl/*

Massachusetts Office of Consumer Affairs Fact Sheet on Home Inspections *www.mass.gov/dpl/consumer/fspagehi.htm*

QUESTIONS

1. The Board of Registration of Real Estate Brokers and Salespersons was created to
   a. make new laws.
   b. make recommendations to the legislature.
   c. administer the license laws.
   d. raise money for the state.

2. Applicants for a salesperson's license MUST
   a. be at least 18 years old and have completed a 12-hour exam prep course.
   b. have completed 24 classroom hours of instruction in real estate subjects.
   c. have been actively engaged in real estate activities for at least six months.
   d. submit recommendations from three persons, two of whom are Massachusetts residents.

3. Which of these is NOT exempt from the license law?
   a. A salesperson employed by a broker
   b. A receiver acting under a court order
   c. A loan officer in a credit union
   d. A licensed auctioneer

4. In the event of the death of a sole proprietor of a real estate brokerage firm, a temporary license is issued. The license
   a. is good for one year and is not renewable.
   b. may be renewed if necessary.
   c. becomes a permanent license after one year.
   d. is given automatically.

5. A corporation may have a broker license if
   a. all its officers are personally licensed as real estate brokers.
   b. one officer is licensed as a broker and designated to perform all real estate duties.
   c. the corporation applies for a license.
   d. the corporation already has a salesperson's license.

6. Lenny holds a Massachusetts real estate broker's license. His brother took, and passed, the Massachusetts exam for Lenny because Lenny's car wouldn't start that day. Lenny lives in Massachusetts, but his only office is in Borderton, New Hampshire, which is only five minutes from the Massachusetts border. In his office, Lenny keeps his license locked safely in a file cabinet in the basement. Lenny recently sold a house to the Feldspars, although he neglected to mention to them that he was the owner of the house. Lenny deposited the Feldspars' earnest money in his wife's checking account for safekeeping. After closing the sale, Lenny visited neighboring homeowners to give them his card and to mention that the Feldspars were poor immigrants from Iceland who practiced a strange Viking religion, whose presence in the neighborhood would be likely to depress everyone else's property values. How many violations of the Massachusetts license law has Lenny committed?
   a. Two
   b. Four
   c. Six
   d. Zero—because his office is in New Hampshire

7. Which of the following, if true, would NOT be grounds for revoking the broker's or salesperson's license?
   a. Paying a commission to an unlicensed person who acted as a real estate salesperson
   b. Inducing a seller to break a contract so the broker can present a higher offer
   c. Affirmatively soliciting residential properties for sale
   d. Accepting a disclosed, voluntary, net listing from a prospective seller

8. When a complaint has been filed with the board against a licensee, the
   a. licensee must cease acting as a salesperson.
   b. licensee's license is immediately revoked.
   c. accused is tried in superior court.
   d. board may conduct an investigation to determine if the complaint is justified.

9. All deposits or payments of money received by a broker or salesperson must be

   a. kept in a designated location in the broker's office.

   b. placed in the salesperson's savings account.

   c. deposited in a special bank account maintained by the broker for such deposits.

   d. immediately turned over to the seller.

10. When a licensed broker changes his or her place of business

   a. a new license will be issued by the board immediately.

   b. his or her license may be revoked if the board is not notified.

   c. a new license will be issued for a full term.

   d. the new address must be approved by the board.

11. Broker Edna has received three offers on a property within an hour. The property is listed for $210,000. Offer A is for $209,500; Offer B is for $190,000; Offer C is for $175,000. What should she do?

   a. Ignore Offer C because it is ridiculously low

   b. Find out if the makers of Offer A and Offer B want to raise their offers under the circumstances

   c. Present all offers immediately

   d. Present the highest offer only

12. The Board of Registration is informed that a broker was guilty of discrimination on June 20 of this year. The broker had been found guilty of a similar charge on June 5 of the previous year. The board will suspend the broker's license for how many days?

   a. 50

   b. 60

   c. 45

   d. 90

CHAPTER

11

Real Estate Financing: Principles and Practice

■ MORTGAGE LAW

Massachusetts is a *title theory* state, meaning that the mortgage "splits" title to the property—the mortgagee takes legal title, while equitable title is retained by the mortgagor. The granting of the property to the mortgagee by the mortgagor is done with an instrument that is similar to a warranty deed, except that the document contains provisions permitting the mortgagor to get the property back if he or she fulfills certain conditions. Generally, these conditions are that they

- pay back the sum of money with interest as provided in a separate promissory note;
- keep the property insured for the benefit of the mortgagee;
- promptly pay the taxes assessed against the property;
- keep the property in good repair (do not allow the property to be "wasted"); and
- do not remove any buildings or improvements from the property.

■ FINANCING TECHNIQUES

Massachusetts banks are permitted to make, purchase, participate in, or service a wide variety of statutorily approved real estate mortgage loans, including certain loans in excess of 95 percent of value, open-end mortgages, and reverse mortgage loans.

In Massachusetts, several state agencies provide financing and loan programs for homeowners and renters. The Massachusetts Housing Finance Agency is the state's affordable housing bank. It lends money at rates below the conventional market to support rental and homeownership opportunities for low-income and moderate-income residents of the state. It also has loans for such programs as "Get the Lead Out" and "Septic Repair."

The Massachusetts Housing Partnership Fund is a self-supporting state agency that promotes more stable and diverse neighborhoods in cities and towns across the state through the development and preservation of affordable housing.

The Massachusetts Department of Housing and Community Development provides state and federal funds and technical assistance to strengthen communities and to help them plan new developments, encourage economic development, revitalize older areas, improve local government management, build and manage public housing, stimulate affordable housing through the private sector, and respond to the needs of low-income residents. It also administers the state's public housing programs, coordinates its antipoverty efforts, allocates federal community development programs, and provides a variety of services to local government officials.

■ PREDATORY LENDING

In August 2004 Massachusetts enacted a strong antipredatory lending law. The Predatory Home Loan Practices Act (MGL Chapter 183C Sec. 1-19) applies to all mortgage applications taken on or after November 7, 2004. Predatory lending is a term used to describe a wide range of unfair financial practices. Following are examples of predatory lending:

- Using false appraisals to sell properties for much more than they are worth
- Encouraging borrowers to lie about their income, expenses, or cash available for down payments to get a loan
- Knowingly lend more money than a borrower can afford to repay
- Charging high interest rates to borrowers based not on their credit history but on their race or national origin
- Charging fees for unnecessary or nonexistent products and services
- Pressuring borrowers to accept higher-risk loans such as balloon loans, interest only payments, and steep prepayment penalties
- Targeting vulnerable borrowers when they know borrowers are in need of cash due to medical, unemployment or debt problems
- Convincing homeowners to refinance again and again when there is no benefit to the borrower and thereby "stripping" homeowners' equity from their homes
- Using high-pressure sales tactics to sell home improvements and then financing them at high interest rates

A violation of Chapter 183 constitutes a violation of Chapter 93A.

■ AMORTIZED LOANS

In Massachusetts, amortized mortgage loans are referred to as *direct reduction loans*.

■ DEFAULT

Default occurs when any condition of the mortgage is not satisfied by the mortgagor. The mortgagee will make use of an *acceleration clause* that causes the entire debt to be due immediately. In most Massachusetts mortgages, the mortgagee will have included a *power-of-sale clause* giving it the right to immediately possess the property, to advertise the property as having been foreclosed, and, after a stated period, to sell the property and apply the proceeds to the unpaid balance of the loan.

The advertising period for a foreclosure is once a week for three weeks prior to the foreclosure, with the announcements appearing in a general circulation newspaper published in the county in which the property is located.

If the mortgage does not include a *power-of-sale clause*, the mortgagee must institute specific proceedings prior to selling the property. In either case, any proceeds obtained from the sale of the property in excess of the amount of the loan, interest, and court costs belong to the mortgagor.

A lender may want to prevent a future purchaser of the property from assuming the mortgage loan. For this purpose, the lender would include an *alienation clause* in the note. A defaulting borrower may cure all defaults before the foreclosure sale. This is called equitable redemption. The borrower may also refinance the loan with another lender to pay off the defaulted mortgage debt or to obtain sufficient funds to bid for the property at the foreclosure sale. No redemption is allowed after a mortgage foreclosure sale is complete. In a foreclosure sale, there may not be enough cash to pay the loan balance in full after deducting expenses and accrued unpaid interest. In this situation, the mortgagee may be entitled to a personal judgment against the borrower for the unpaid balance. Such a judgment is called a "deficiency judgment."

■ RELATED WEB SITES

Loan programs:
    Fannie Mae Loans   *www.fanniemae.com*
    FHA Loans   *www.hud.gov*
    Freddie Mac Loans (conventional loan products)   *www.freddiemac.com*
    Massachusetts Loans   *www.mass.gov*
    Veterans Affairs Loans   *www.va.gov*

Massachusetts Department of Housing and Community Development
www.mass.gov/dhcd/

Massachusetts General Laws, Chapter 183
www.mass.gov/legis/laws/mgl/183c-1.htm

Massachusetts Housing Finance Agency   *www.mhfa.com*

Massachusetts Housing Partnership Fund   *www.masshousing.com/portal/server.pt*

QUESTIONS

1. Massachusetts is a(n)
   a. lien theory state.
   b. intermediate theory state.
   c. title theory state.
   d. warranty deed state.

2. The granting of property to a mortgagee by the mortgagor is accomplished through a document similar to a
   a. quitclaim deed.
   b. warranty deed.
   c. defeasance clause.
   d. title registration.

3. In Massachusetts, an amortized mortgage loan is referred to as a
   a. straight loan.
   b. traditional mortgage.
   c. direct reduction mortgage.
   d. direct reduction loan.

4. The usual period during which Massachusetts lenders advertise a property that is in foreclosure proceedings prior to sale is how many weeks?
   a. One
   b. Two
   c. Three
   d. Four

5. A foreclosure on property must be advertised in a(n)
   a. official foreclosure newsletter distributed in the mortgagee's county of residence.
   b. newspaper published in the mortgagee's county of residence.
   c. newspaper published in the county in which the property is located.
   d. official publication circulated in the county in which the property is located.

6. How long is the defaulted borrower's redemption period after a foreclosure sale is complete?
   a. One year
   b. Six months
   c. Three years
   d. Zero—no redemption period

7. After a mortgage foreclosure sale, the money in excess of the loan, interest, and court costs belongs to the
   a. devisee.
   b. mortgagee.
   c. grantor.
   d. mortgagor.

8. The provision in a mortgage that permits the mortgagee to demand the full amount of the loan in the event the borrower defaults is called a(n)
   a. direct reduction clause.
   b. redemption clause.
   c. immediate possession clause.
   d. acceleration clause.

Leases

■ LEASING REAL ESTATE

In Massachusetts, leases for more than one year must be in writing to satisfy the statute of frauds. Leases for seven years or more must be written, acknowledged, and recorded, or their validity will be restricted to the original landlord.

Breach of Lease

If a tenant fails to pay the rent on time, a landlord can begin a statutory eviction proceeding. Massachusetts law provides specific procedures that must be followed to evict a tenant. For instance, a landlord cannot simply seize the property as soon as the rent payment deadline passes. The landlord must give two weeks' written notice to the tenant, who may prevent eviction by paying all overdue rent, plus the landlord's expenses, at any time during the two-week period.

In a tenancy at will, the law requires that the landlord give the tenant as much time to stay in the property as one rental period after the landlord provides a notice to quit the property. The minimum period of notice is 30 days (7 days in the case of rooming houses in which rent is due weekly), and the maximum is three months. Generally, the notice is effective at the beginning of the next rental period. A landlord may include in the notice an offer to allow the tenant to stay under terms different from the existing agreement.

■ STANDARD LEASE PROVISIONS

Certain lease provisions are legally void and unenforceable in Massachusetts. A lessor may not include a provision in the lease permitting him or her to enter the premises for any reason other than to make repairs or to show it to a prospective lessee. A lease may not require the tenant to waive the landlord's responsibility to keep the premises habitable, or to waive the landlord's liability for failing to provide heat, light, power, or other utilities or services required by the lease. (An example of a Standard Residential Lease form appears in Figure 12.1.)

No lease may contain a provision permitting the landlord to terminate it in the event the tenant should have children.

Prior to March 2005, landlords were responsible for providing and paying for water and sewer services in rental units. On March 16, 2005 M.G.L. c. 186, §22, became effective granting landlords of residential property the right to separately charge tenants for actual water and sewer costs providing that all of the comprehensive requirements were met.

Landlords can now install meters in apartments and single-family homes they rent to separately charge tenants for actual water usage. Landlords must certify in writing to the local Board of Health that the dwelling/unit is in compliance with the requirements as set forth in the law and have a written rental agreement with tenants that clearly provides for the separate charge. (See Figure 12.2.) The landlord must provide a copy of the approved water and sewer certification from the local Board of Health to the tenant.

Existing tenants are not subject to the law, however, and could not be made to pay separately for water due to grandfathering provisions in the law. Public housing tenants are exempt from the law as well.

Licensees, when representing a landlord, need to make sure landlords are aware of this ruling because many landlords unknowingly require tenants to pay for water and sewer services without separate meters and/or certification forms.

A landlord may not interfere with a tenant's right of *quiet enjoyment* of the premises, that is, the right to uninterrupted use of the property during the term of the lease. Prohibited interference includes failing to repair or maintain the premises, as well as active interference, such as efforts to regain possession of the property. A landlord who interferes with a tenant's right of quiet enjoyment may be subject to a fine and imprisonment as well as damages of up to three months' rent. A landlord can also be held liable for intentionally or willfully failing to furnish water, hot water, heat, light, power, gas, elevator service, telephone service, janitor service, or refrigeration service as is customary for a building. If a landlord transfers responsibility of payment for the utilities to the tenant without the tenant's knowledge or consent, the landlord can also be held liable.

F I G U R E   12.1

Sample Residential Lease Form

STANDARD RESIDENTIAL LEASE
(Fixed Term)

1. <u>**Parties.**</u> SAMPLE _____ , the "LANDLORD",
whose address and telephone number are
_____ , _____ , agrees to rent to
_____ , the "TENANT", whose current
home address and telephone number are _____
_____ , _____ the premises described in paragraph 2, below.

2. <u>**Description Of Premises.**</u> The premises (the "Premises") are described as *[insert street address and apartment no.]* _____
_____ and include
_____ , but exclude _____
_____ . *[insert references to yard, attic/basement storage, refrigerator, washer, dryer, dishwasher etc., as appropriate]*

3. <u>**Lease Term.**</u> The lease shall begin on _____ , _____ and shall end on
_____ , _____ . Delivery of keys to the LANDLORD or acceptance thereof shall not
constitute agreement of the LANDLORD to terminate.

4. <u>**Rent.**</u> The total rent for the Premises for the Lease Term is _____
_____ dollars ($ _____) , payable in monthly installments
of _____ dollars ($ _____)
which are **due in advance on the** _____ **day** of each calendar month. Rent shall be paid to
_____ . If a payment for
a particular month is made more than thirty (30) days after due date, a late fee of $ _____
shall be due. **A security deposit of $ _____ was received and a copy of receipt is attached.**

5. <u>**Time.**</u> TIME IS OF THE ESSENCE as to each provision of the Lease.

6. <u>**Utilities / Heating Fuel.**</u> The LANDLORD shall pay all charges for water and shall reasonably supply hot
water and heat (except to the extent that fuel for heat is separately metered to the Premises) during heating
season, as required by applicable law or code. The TENANT agrees to act reasonably to avoid wasting of water,
heating fuel or other utilities for which LANDLORD has agreed to pay.
Payment for the utilities listed shall be made by:

Fuel For Heat	Landlord ☐	Tenant ☐	*[check applicable box]*
Fuel For Hot Water	Landlord ☐	Tenant ☐	*[check applicable box]*
Electricity	Landlord ☐	Tenant ☐	*[check applicable box]*
Gas	Landlord ☐	Tenant ☐	*[check applicable box]*

[Note: fuel, electricity, gas and other utilities may be billed to TENANT only where separately metered]

7. <u>**Delivery Of Premises.**</u> On the date the Lease begins the LANDLORD shall deliver full possession of the
Premises to the TENANT, free of all occupants and of all personal property, except property included in the
Lease. If despite reasonable efforts the LANDLORD is unable to deliver full possession of the Premises on the
date the Lease begins, the LANDLORD shall not be liable to TENANT for any loss or damage nor shall this
Lease be void or voidable, but the rent for the Lease Term shall be proportionally reduced and the TENANT
shall not be liable for any rent until possession is delivered. Either party may terminate this Lease by written
notice if possession is not delivered within thirty (30) days after the beginning date of the Lease Term. Upon

#401/6.6.02/214655

F I G U R E   12.1 (Continued)

Sample Residential Lease Form

delivery of such notice all payments made by the TENANT pursuant to this Lease shall be immediately returned and all obligations of the TENANT and LANDLORD shall terminate and this Lease shall automatically become void and neither the TENANT nor LANDLORD shall have further recourse or remedy against the other. The TENANT authorizes the LANDLORD to commence any necessary proceedings in the name of the TENANT to recover possession.

8. **Occupancy / Use / Assignment / Subletting.** The Premises shall be used solely for residential purposes for occupancy of _____ persons of whom _____ are under six years of age, but shall not exceed limits established by law, regulation or ordinance. Should the TENANT desire or anticipate a change in occupancy of the Premises due to adoption, birth of a child or otherwise, the TENANT shall notify the LANDLORD at least sixty (60) days in advance. The TENANT shall not assign TENANT'S rights under this Lease and shall not sublet all or part of the Premises without prior written permission of the LANDLORD. Occupancy of any part of the Premises by any person, including a guest of TENANT, for a period of ten (10) or more consecutive days or for more than a total of fifteen (15) days in any sixty (60) day period shall require written permission of the LANDLORD. If the Premises are part of a condominium, apartment building or other multiple dwelling, the TENANT agrees to abide by all rules and regulations governing such dwelling. The TENANT agrees not to use or permit the Premises to be used for any improper or unlawful purpose and agrees to limit use of the Premises so that it does not disturb or interfere with comfort, safety or enjoyment of any person living nearby, including any occupant of the condominium, apartment building or multiple dwelling.

9. **Cleanliness / Alterations / Repairs.** The TENANT shall at all times maintain the Premises in a clean and sanitary condition and in the same condition as they were at the start of the tenancy, reasonable use and wear excepted. For other maintenance or repair of the Premises, the TENANT shall notify LANDLORD or

_____

[insert name, address, phone number] If the TENANT fails to maintain, as agreed, the LANDLORD shall have the option to make such repairs, whereupon the TENANT shall reimburse the LANDLORD upon demand. The TENANT shall not paint or wallpaper any part of the Premises without LANDLORD'S written permission nor shall the TENANT make any interior or exterior alteration or change in the Premises nor shall TENANT change any lock or re-key any lock without the written permission of the LANDLORD. Should a new lock be installed or an existing lock be altered or re-keyed, the TENANT shall immediately deliver a duplicate key to the LANDLORD at TENANT'S sole expense. The TENANT shall not install any washing machine, dryer, air conditioner, space heater, waterbed or fixture without written permission of the LANDLORD. Unless otherwise agreed, any lock or fixture installed in the Premises with permission of the LANDLORD shall become the property of the LANDLORD upon termination of the Lease. No object shall be thrown from any porch, balcony or window nor kept on any railing, fire escape or windowsill. The TENANT shall not place or store any property in any common area. The TENANT shall be liable for any misuse of any plumbing fixture or equipment, including disposal of rubbish or garbage that damages any fixture or clogs any pipe. The TENANT shall maintain any surrounding grounds for which TENANT is given exclusive use, including any trees and shrubbery, keeping same free of rubbish and weeds. At the termination of the Lease the TENANT shall surrender the Premises with all keys to LANDLORD in the same condition as they now are, reasonable use and wear excepted. Should the TENANT fail to turn over all keys at the end of the Lease, the LANDLORD shall be permitted to replace the locks and keys immediately at TENANT'S sole cost and expense. The TENANT shall be responsible for all damage or loss caused to the Premises during the Lease, whether by TENANT or by any invitee or guest of TENANT, excluding acts of God or any injury or loss caused by the LANDLORD or for which the LANDLORD is statutorily liable.

F I G U R E   12.1 (Continued)

Sample Residential Lease Form

10. **Parking.** The TENANT shall not be permitted to park or store any vehicle on the Premises or on any other property of LANDLORD. If LANDLORD expressly authorizes parking, it shall be at TENANT'S sole risk and expense.

11. **Fire / Casualty.** If the Premises or any common area providing a necessary means of egress/access to the Premises are damaged by fire or other casualty which materially interferes with the TENANT'S use of or access to the Premises, the LANDLORD may terminate the Lease by giving the TENANT written notice to become effective at the end of the then current month. If the LANDLORD has not exercised the option to terminate, the rent shall be reduced to the fair rental value of the Premises until the Premises is restored to its former condition. If the LANDLORD has not restored the Premises or egress/access within thirty (30) days, the TENANT may give notice of termination of the Lease to become effective at the end of the then current month.

12. **Government Regulations / Eminent Domain.** The LANDLORD shall not be liable for any loss, injury or damage caused by the LANDLORD'S inability to satisfy LANDLORD'S obligations or delay in satisfying LANDLORD'S obligations under the Lease resulting from any governmental order, law, code, rule or regulation, including any taking by eminent domain. Should all or part of the Premises or any necessary access/egress be taken by eminent domain or be subject to an order of condemnation which materially impairs TENANT'S access to or use of the Premises, then either party may notify the other of termination of the Lease to take effect on the effective date of taking, by thirty (30) days' written notice. Failure of TENANT to give notice of termination within thirty (30) days after the effective date of taking shall constitute a waiver. Should all or part of the Premises be taken by eminent domain, the TENANT shall have no right to any part of a *pro tanto* or other payment and hereby assigns all claims to LANDLORD.

13. **Insurance.** The TENANT shall have the obligation to procure and maintain any insurance covering personal property of TENANT from fire or other casualty. If the Premises is in a multi-unit residential dwelling, the LANDLORD will provide insurance coverage of up to $750 to cover the actual cost of relocation if the TENANT is displaced by fire or fire damage, pursuant to applicable law.

14. **Animals / Pets.** The Tenant shall not bring any live animal, bird, reptile or pet into the Premises nor permit any to remain at the Premises without written permission of Landlord, except as permitted by state or federal anti-discrimination laws.

15. **Lead Paint.** For premises built before 1978 TENANT acknowledges receipt of the "Tenant Lead Law Notification" regarding Massachusetts and federal lead laws and regulations, including notice of lead hazards and the possible presence of dangerous levels of lead. The TENANT further acknowledges that neither the LANDLORD nor any representative of LANDLORD has made any representation, express or implied, regarding the absence of lead paint or compliance with any lead law, except as set forth in writing.

16. **Entry And Inspection.** The LANDLORD or his agents or designees shall be permitted to enter the Premises at reasonable times and upon reasonable notice to TENANT for the purpose of inspecting the Premises; for the purpose of maintaining or repairing the Premises; to ensure compliance with any statute, code or regulation; or for the purpose of showing the Premises to any real estate agent, appraiser, mortgagee, prospective buyer or prospective tenant or inspector/contractor for prospective buyer/tenant.

17. **Indemnification.** The TENANT agrees to indemnify, defend and hold the LANDLORD harmless from any injury, loss or damage suffered by TENANT or by any person or property that occurs at the Premises or in any

F I G U R E   12.1 (Continued)

Sample Residential Lease Form

common area during the Lease, except for any injury, loss or damage caused by the negligence or unlawful act of the LANDLORD or for which the LANDLORD is statutorily liable.

18. **Breach / Abandonment.** If the TENANT breaches the Lease by failure to pay rent when due, the LANDLORD may terminate the Lease by giving the TENANT a fourteen (14) day Notice To Quit for nonpayment of rent, pursuant to applicable law. If the TENANT breaches any other term or provision of the Lease or made a misstatement in any rental application or is declared bankrupt or the Premises reasonably appear to have been abandoned, the LANDLORD may terminate the Lease by giving the TENANT a seven (7) day notice to vacate, upon the expiration of which the Lease shall terminate. Entry by the LANDLORD shall not be required before termination. Issuance of a notice pursuant to this paragraph shall be without waiver or prejudice to any other right or remedy of LANDLORD. In the event of such termination the TENANT shall be obligated to pay the LANDLORD a sum equal to the balance of the rent due under the remainder of the Lease until the date of commencement of the tenancy of a new tenant for the Premises together with: a) all costs and expenses reasonably incurred by LANDLORD to restore the Premises to the same condition as they were at the beginning of the Lease, including cleaning and painting; b) moving and storage charges for any personal property of TENANT either required by law to be moved and stored or in the discretion of the LANDLORD to be moved and stored; c) any costs reasonably incurred to advertise and locate a new tenant, including broker's fees; and d) any other damages permitted to be recovered; and e) interest at the legal rate from the date of breach, costs and attorneys' fees. Delay or failure of LANDLORD to commence legal proceedings shall not constitute a waiver of any right or remedy.

19. **Attorneys' Fees.** In the event that the LANDLORD reasonably requires services of an attorney to enforce the terms of the Lease or to seek to recover possession or damages, the TENANT shall pay the LANDLORD the reasonable attorneys' fee incurred and all costs, whether or not a summary process action or other civil action is commenced or judgment is obtained.

20. **Notices.** All notices required or permitted to be made under this Lease, including any notice of violation of law or the need for care maintenance or repair, shall be in writing and may be delivered in hand, sent by certified mail, return receipt requested or sent by United States Postal Service overnight Express Mail or other overnight delivery service, addressed to the LANDLORD or TENANT or their authorized representative at the address set forth in this paragraph or to the TENANT at the Premises during the term of the Lease. Such notice shall be deemed to have been given upon delivery or, if sent by certified mail on the date of delivery set forth in the receipt or in the absence of a receipt three business days after deposited or, if sent by Express Mail or other overnight mail or delivery, the next business day after deposited with the overnight mail or delivery service, whether or not a signature is required or received. Acceptance of any notice, whether by delivery or mail, shall be sufficient if accepted or signed by a person having express or implied authority to receive same. Notice shall also be deemed adequate if given in any other form permitted by law.

LANDLORD   TENANT
[print name] _____   [print name] _____
                _____   _____
[address]   _____   [address]   _____
[telephone] _____   [telephone] _____

21. **Counterparts / Facsimiles / Construction Of Agreement.** This Lease may be executed in counterparts. A signature transmitted by facsimile shall have the effect of an original. The TENANT warrants under the penalty of perjury that TENANT is at least 18 years of age. If two or more persons sign as TENANT their obligations are

MassForms®
Statewide Standard Real Estate Forms   ©1999, 2002 MASSACHUSETTS ASSOCIATION OF REALTORS®

Produced with ZipForm™ by RE FormsNet, LLC 18025 Fifteen Mile Road, Clinton Township, Michigan 48035   www.zipform.com   d.zfx joint and several. If any term or provision in the Lease is declared invalid, the remainder of the Lease shall not be affected. If the LANDLORD is a trust, corporation, limited liability company or entity whose representative executes this Lease in a representative or fiduciary capacity, only the principal or the trust or estate represented shall be bound, and neither the trustee, officer, shareholder or beneficiary shall be personally liable for any obligation, express or implied. This Lease shall be construed as a Massachusetts contract; is to take effect as a sealed instrument; sets forth the entire agreement between the parties; and may be canceled, modified or amended only by a writing signed by both the LANDLORD and the TENANT. Within thirty (30) days after the Lease has been signed by LANDLORD and TENANT the LANDLORD shall deliver a copy to TENANT.

22. **Additional Provisions.** _____

_____

_____

_____

UPON SIGNING, THIS DOCUMENT WILL BECOME A LEGALLY BINDING AGREEMENT. IF NOT UNDERSTOOD, SEEK ADVICE FROM AN ATTORNEY.

_____   _____   _____   _____
TENANT   Date   LANDLORD or authorized agent   Date

_____
Social Security Number

_____   _____
TENANT   Date

_____
Social Security Number

_____   _____
TENANT   Date

_____
Social Security Number

GUARANTEE

In consideration of the sum of one dollar ($1.00) and other good and valuable consideration, the sufficiency and receipt of which is hereby acknowledged, the undersigned guarantor ("Guarantor") hereby guarantees all obligations of TENANT in the Lease. All suretyship defenses and notice of default and demand are each waived.

WITNESS   GUARANTOR

_____   _____
                                                                    Date
                                             Print Name _____
                                             Address _____

                                             Telephone _____
                                             Social Security Number ____

F I G U R E   12.2

Massachusetts Department of Public Health Submetering of Water and Sewer Certification Form

MASSACHUSETTS DEPARTMENT OF PUBLIC HEALTH
SUBMETERING OF WATER AND SEWER CERTIFICATION FORM

In accordance with M.G.L. c. 186, § 22 and 105 CMR 410.000: Minimum Standards of Fitness for Human Habitation (State Sanitary Code Chapter II), the following dwelling unit is eligible for the imposition on the tenants of a charge for water and/or sewer service.

PROPERTY INFORMATION

Address: Unit #   # Of units in bldg.

City/Town: MA   Zip Code:

EQUIPMENT INSTALLATION INFORMATION

105 CMR 410.000 requires the installation of water conservation devices prior to a dwelling unit becoming eligible for the imposition on tenants of a charge for water and/or sewer. The devices must meet the following specifications:

Showerheads with maximum flow rate not to exceed $2\frac{1}{2}$ gallons per minute (2.5 gpm)
Faucets with maximum flow rate not to exceed $2\frac{2}{10}$ gallons per minute (2.2 gpm)
Ultra low flush water closets (toilets) not to exceed $1\frac{6}{10}$ gallons per flush (1.6 gpf)

The submetering equipment used to measure the quantity of water used for each dwelling unit and common area must meet the standards of accuracy and testing of the American Water Works Association or similar accredited association. A licensed plumber must install the water closets and submetering equipment.

Submetering equipment information: _____

Manufacturer   Model #

Licensed Plumber Certification

Print Name of Plumber   License #   Date

I certify that I have installed the submetering equipment listed above in accordance with accepted plumbing standards. I also certify that I have (check one): ☐ installed one or more water closets not exceeding 1.6 gallons per flush, or
☐ determined that all existing water closets do not exceed 1.6 gallons per flush. The required plumbing permit issued by the city/town is attached.

Signed under the pains and penalties of perjury,

Signature of Licensed Plumber

Property Owner Certification

I certify that: (1) This dwelling unit is eligible for the imposition on the tenants of a charge for water and/or sewer usage in accordance with the water submetering law (MGL c. 186, §22); (2) All showerheads, faucets, and water closets in this dwelling unit are water conservation devices that meet the standards specified above; (3) The water submeter measuring the use of water in the dwelling unit was installed by a licensed plumber and is in compliance with the standards specified above. I will provide to the tenants of this dwelling unit, prior to occupancy, a written rental agreement that clearly provides for the separate charging of water and/or sewer service, and a copy of this certificate form. I certify that all information included on this certification is true and accurate to the best of my knowledge.

Signed under the pains and penalties of perjury,

Print Name of Owner   Signature of Owner   Date

Received by Board of Health/Health Department _____

Name   Date

MDPH/CSP Submetering Certification Form 3/05

■ **FOR EXAMPLE**

I

The smoke detectors in Larry Landlord's property malfunctioned and sounded loud alarms for three days until the batteries finally died. The tenant sued, and Larry was held liable for three months' rent.

II

Tenants in Lucy Lessor's building were without hot water for three weeks. The tenants were not entitled to three months' rent, however, because Lucy had immediately hired a work crew to correct the problem as quickly as possible.

The landlord may enter the property without violating the tenant's right of quiet enjoyment

- in accordance with a court order;
- to make necessary repairs;
- to show the property to a prospective tenant; or
- if it appears that the tenant has abandoned the property, or if the tenant has given notice that he or she is leaving and is within the last 30 days of the rental so that a damage inspection is appropriate.

IN PRACTICE

In a 2002 Massachusetts Superior Court case, the court found that where a lessee and a proposed sublessee never agreed to the terms of a sublease or mutually executed a sublease, there was no sublease for the landlord to approve and therefore the landlord did not breach the lease by refusing to consent to a sublease. The court also found that the landlord's attempt to negotiate directly with the proposed sublessee at a higher rental value was not prohibited by the parties' lease. The landlord's offer to accept a termination fee in an amount that was less than the remaining amount due under the lease to cover some of the landlord's damages did not constitute an unfair and deceptive trade practice. *WHTR Real Estate Limited Partnership v. Venture Distributors* (2002, Super. Ct.) 16 Mass. L. Rep. 471.

Security Deposit

A lessor may require a prospective tenant to pay a security deposit prior to the beginning of the lease term. However, for leases of 100 days or less that are for vacation or recreational purposes, these security deposit rules do not apply. At the time a lease commences, no tenant may be required to pay an amount in excess of

- the first month's rent; and
- the last month's rent calculated at the same rate as the first month; and
- a security deposit equal to the first month's rent and the tenant is given a statement of condition; and
- the purchase and installation cost for a key and lock.

If a security deposit is required, the landlord must provide the tenant with a separate written statement of the property's condition at the time it is leased. Both the tenant and the landlord (or the landlord's agent) must sign the statement.

In addition, if a landlord requires a security deposit (SD) or last month's rent (LMR), the landlord must provide the tenant with a written receipt that includes specific information, namely the following:

- Amount of money received (SD and LMR)
- Date the money was received (SD and LMR)
- Intended use of the money (SD and LMR)
- Name of person receiving money (SD and LMR)
- Name of landlord, if different from person receiving the money (SD and LMR)
- A statement that the tenant is entitled to the interest on the deposit (SD and LMR)
- Address and apartment number (SD and LMR)
- Location and name of the bank where the money is deposited (SD only)
- Account number of the fund in which the money is deposited (SD only)
- A statement indicating that the tenant provide the landlord a forwarding address so when the tenant moves the landlord knows where to send the interest (LMR only)

The security deposit does not belong to the landlord. It remains the tenant's property, and the landlord must deposit it in a separate bank account within Massachusetts. It may not be commingled with the landlord's own assets, and it is not subject to claims of any creditor of the lessor. The tenant is entitled to the return of the security deposit within 30 days of the termination date of the lease. The landlord must pay interest on the security deposit and last month's rent at the rate of 5 percent per year or other such lesser amount of interest as has been received from the bank where the deposit has been held payable in accordance with the provisions of the Massachusetts General Laws. Interest does not accrue for the last month for which rent is paid in advance.

At the end of each year of the tenancy, landlords are required to send a notice restating where the interest is being held and to offer to the tenant any interest accrued on the security deposit and, if applicable, the last month's rent. The tenant may elect to deduct the amount of the interest from the next month's rent, request the interest be paid directly to him or her, or let it remain in the account.

The landlord is entitled to withhold the following three deductions from the security deposit:

1. Any unpaid rent
2. Any unpaid increase in real estate taxes for which the tenant is liable under the lease
3. The reasonable cost of repairing damage caused by the tenant, excluding normal wear and tear

If the cost of repairing damage is withheld from the security deposit, the landlord has 30 days in which to provide the tenant with a detailed, itemized list of the damages and repair costs, supported by such evidence as bills or receipts.

In the event that the lessor transfers the property, the account containing the tenant's security deposit is also transferred to the new owner. If the lessor fails to transfer the account, the tenant is entitled to stay on in the premises past the termination date of the lease for a period equivalent to the rental value of the security deposit.

The landlord forfeits his or her right to retain any part of the security deposit if he or she

- fails to deposit the funds in an independent interest-bearing account;
- fails to furnish the tenant with an itemized list of damages within 30 days after termination;
- fails to transfer the deposit to a new owner;
- includes and attempts to enforce an invalid provision in the lease, such as one waiving the tenant's rights;
- fails to return the balance of the security deposit together with any interest thereon to the tenant within 30 days of the termination of the lease; or
- fails to provide the bank name and account number where the security deposit is kept.

If a landlord fails to deposit funds in an independent interest-bearing account, fails to transfer a deposit to a new owner, or fails to return the deposit balance and any interest, the tenant may be awarded damages in an amount equal to three times the amount of the security deposit plus interest, court costs, and reasonable attorney's fees.

Protenant Legislation

The rights and obligations of landlords and tenants in Massachusetts are regulated under the Massachusetts Consumer Protection Act (MCPA), discussed in Chapter 1.

IN PRACTICE

Note that according to Massachusetts case law, the MCPA does not apply to the rental of a dwelling unit in an owner-occupied two-family house where the landlord owns no other rental property. Also, in the absence of a rent control statute, it is not inherently bad or evil, nor unfair or deceptive, to charge market rent.

In addition to those already discussed, some of the prohibited actions by landlords include

- renting property that contains a condition dangerous to the health, safety, or well-being of the occupants, or failing to repair such conditions;
- failing to keep promises made to the tenant at the time of renting;
- failing to reimburse the tenant for repairs the tenant made after being authorized by the landlord;
- failing to comply with state or local housing codes;
- demanding an increase in rent to pay higher taxes on the property unless a written lease obligates the tenant to do so;
- failing to make the written rental agreement clear and simple;
- depriving the tenant access to his or her dwelling without a proper court order or beginning court proceedings without following the statutory time limits;
- imposing interest on any payment until it is more than 30 days overdue; and
- failing to state in the lease that interest will be imposed on any payment after 30 days overdue and the amount of the penalty.

A tenant is entitled to enforce his or her rights, either through legal action or by informing an appropriate authority of the landlord's failure to comply either with the terms of the lease or with housing laws or building codes. Landlords are prohibited from retaliating, or threatening retribution, against the tenant. Landlords are also prohibited from having any provisions in their leases in which the effect is to indemnify the landlord, hold the landlord harmless, or preclude or exonerate the landlord from liability to the tenant for any injury, loss, damage, or liability arising from the landlord's misconduct on or about the leased premises or common areas.

Fair Housing

Discrimination in renting or leasing is prohibited under Massachusetts law and is discussed in detail in Chapter 15.

■ RELATED WEB SITES

Massachusetts General Laws   *www.mass.gov/legis/laws/mgl/*
www.mass.gov/legis/law/mgl/gl-186-toc.htm

QUESTIONS

1. In order to satisfy the statute of frauds, a 14-month lease must be
   a. written, acknowledged, and recorded.
   b. written and recorded.
   c. written.
   d. recorded.

2. A lease that runs for seven years or longer will be restricted to the original landlord unless it is
   a. written, acknowledged, and recorded.
   b. written and recorded.
   c. written.
   d. recorded.

3. A landlord who wants to begin statutory eviction proceedings CANNOT
   a. seize the property for nonpayment of rent.
   b. bring a writ in the court for eviction.
   c. bring a separate writ for the unpaid rent.
   d. give the tenant notice to quit the property.

4. John and Sally are tenants at will. Their rent is due the first of the month. The landlord has given them a notice to quit the property the day before the rent is due. How many days do they have before they must vacate the property?
   a. 14
   b. 30
   c. 10
   d. 90

5. A tenant's right of quiet enjoyment is the right to
   a. be free from noise.
   b. uninterrupted use of the premises.
   c. limited use of the premises.
   d. remain on the premises after breaching the lease.

6. The violation of the right of quiet enjoyment may result in
   a. immediate eviction.
   b. imprisonment but no civil damages.
   c. imprisonment, a fine, and damages of up to three months' rent.
   d. eviction after 30 days' notice.

7. The landlord may not ask for
   a. the last month's rent.
   b. a lock and key deposit.
   c. two months' security deposit.
   d. one month's security deposit.

8. The security deposit must be kept in
   a. a Massachusetts bank account.
   b. the landlord's possession.
   c. the landlord's bank account.
   d. a trust fund established for the tenant.

9. The owner of rented space is called the
   a. lessor.
   b. vendor.
   c. REALTOR®.
   d. mortgagee.

10. After the lease terminates, the tenant is entitled to the return of his or her security deposit
    a. within 30 days, including interest.
    b. within three weeks, including interest.
    c. unless the property has been transferred to a new owner.
    d. with no deductions withheld.

11. The rights and obligations of landlords and tenants are regulated by the
    a. Massachusetts Tenant's Rights Act.
    b. Massachusetts Antidiscrimination Act.
    c. Massachusetts Consumer Protection Act.
    d. Massachusetts Landlord/Tenant Act.

12. Which of the following is NOT a prohibited landlord action?
    a. Renting dangerous property
    b. Failing to comply with housing codes
    c. Failing to reimburse a tenant for authorized repairs
    d. Requiring an amount equal to three months' rent at the time the lease commences

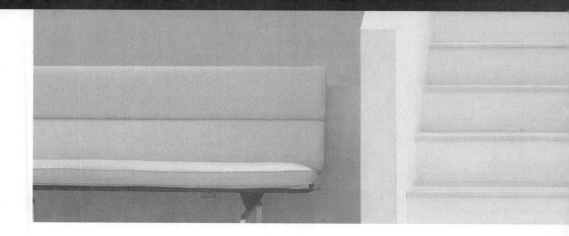

CHAPTER

13

Real Estate Appraisal

■ APPRAISING

Regulation of Appraisal Activities

In Massachusetts, real estate appraisal, like real estate brokerage, is a regulated profession. Appraisers are required to be certified or licensed by the state to appraise property for compensation in all but nonfederally related transactions. The licensing or certification requirement for appraisers does not, however, prevent a real estate broker or salesperson from giving his or her *opinion* of a property's value in the ordinary course of business, as long as he or she does not refer to the opinion as an "appraisal."

There are four classes of real estate appraisers recognized in Massachusetts:

1. State-certified general real estate appraiser
   - ■ To be a state-certified appraiser, an individual must meet the requirements of the Appraisal Foundation's Appraisal Qualifications Board and pass a state-administered examination.
   - ■ Appraisers must also meet the guidelines established in the Uniform Standards of Professional Appraisal.
   - ■ State-certified general appraisers may appraise all types of real property.
   - ■ The appraisal certificate is renewable every three years from its first date of issuance, provided that the appraiser complies with continuing education requirements.

2. State-certified residential real estate appraiser
    ■ To be a state-certified appraiser, an individual must meet the requirements of the Appraisal Foundation's Appraisal Qualifications Board and pass a state-administered examination.
    ■ Appraisers must also meet the guidelines established in the Uniform Standards of Professional Appraisal.
    ■ State-certified residential real estate appraisers are limited to the appraisal of certain residential property.
    ■ Certificates are renewable every three years from its first date of issuance, provided that the appraiser complies with continuing education requirements.
3. State-licensed real estate appraiser
    ■ An appraiser may be state-licensed if he or she meets the requirements of the Federal Financial Institutions Examination Council or its Federal Appraisal Subcommittee and passes a state-administered exam.
    ■ Appraisers must also meet the guidelines established in the Uniform Standards of Professional Appraisal.
    ■ State-licensed real estate appraisers are limited to the appraisal of certain residential property.
    ■ Licensed appraisers must meet the minimum requirements of Title XI.
    ■ A license is renewable every three years from its first date of issuance, provided that the appraiser complies with continuing education requirements.
4. Real estate appraisal trainee
    ■ No examination is required for trainees.
    ■ Trainees' activities are limited to assisting certified and licensed appraisers in the performance of appraisal assignments.
    ■ An appraisal trainee may renew his or her trainee license only once.

To be licensed or certified, an appraiser must demonstrate (on a written examination) several areas of expertise. A licensed or certified appraiser must demonstrate knowledge of the technical terminology of real estate appraisal, appraisal report writing, and real estate economics. He or she must have an understanding of the principles of land economics and real estate appraisal processes, as well as the challenges of gathering, interpreting, and processing data.

An appraiser must have an understanding of the standards for developing and communicating appraisals and a basic comprehension of the theories of depreciation, cost estimating, methods of capitalization, and appraisal mathematics.

Finally, an appraiser must have a basic understanding of real estate law and must be aware of the types of misconduct for which disciplinary proceedings may be instituted. Some of the acts or omissions that may form the basis for revoking or suspending an appraiser's license or certificate are

■ procuring or attempting to procure a certificate or license by providing false or incomplete information;
■ procuring or attempting to procure a certificate or license by means of bribery, misrepresentation, or fraud;
■ conviction of a crime substantially related to real estate appraisal;

- entry of a civil judgment against the appraiser based on an allegation of fraud, misrepresentation, or deceit;
- conviction of any felony;
- any act or omission involving dishonesty, fraud, or misrepresentation with the intent to either benefit the appraiser or injure another person;
- violating the confidentiality of government records; and
- negligence, incompetence, or failure to exercise reasonable diligence in developing an appraisal, preparing an appraisal report, or communicating an appraisal.

An appraiser may not accept any appraisal assignment contingent on the appraiser's reporting a predetermined estimate, analysis, or opinion, or where the fee is contingent on the appraiser reporting a particular valuation.

A certificate or license is renewable every three years from its first date of issuance, provided that the appraiser complies with continuing education requirements. An appraisal trainee may renew his or her trainee license only once.

■ RELATED WEB SITE

Massachusetts Board of Registration of Real Estate Appraisers
www.mass.gov/dpl/boards/ra/

QUESTIONS

1. Real estate appraisers must comply with state licensing regulations unless
   a. they are licensed real estate brokers.
   b. the transaction is not federally related.
   c. they have already taken a written examination.
   d. the property's value has been previously agreed upon.

2. The four categories of real estate appraisers recognized in Massachusetts are
   a. certified general; certified residential; licensed; trainee.
   b. licensed general; licensed residential; licensed trainee; certified.
   c. qualified general; Appraisal Foundation licensed; Federal Appraisal certified; trainee.
   d. prelicense appraiser; precertification appraiser; appraiser; appraiser-trainee.

3. Real estate brokers and salespersons may
   a. not estimate a property's value unless they are certified or licensed appraisers.
   b. appraise a property if they disclose that they are not professional appraisers.
   c. offer a seller an "appraisal opinion" of the value of the seller's property.
   d. offer their opinion of the value of a property but may not call it an appraisal.

4. A state-certified appraiser may
   a. appraise only residential property.
   b. appraise any real property.
   c. only assist a state-licensed appraiser.
   d. list and sell real estate for a commission.

5. The real estate appraiser examination
   a. must be taken every three years.
   b. includes real estate law.
   c. must be taken only by candidates for licensed residential real estate appraiser.
   d. includes depreciation and capitalization but not economics.

6. Laverne is a licensed real estate appraiser. She is convicted of fraudulently reporting a low appraised value on certain property so that the loan would be denied and her friend Shirley could step in and buy the property for less money. She is also convicted of robbing a bank. Laverne's license will
   a. not be revoked if she takes and passes the licensing examination.
   b. be revoked because of the fraud conviction but not because of the robbery.
   c. be revoked because of both the fraud and robbery convictions.
   d. not be revoked because Shirley did not personally benefit from the fraud, and bank robbery is not substantially related to appraisal.

CHAPTER

Land-Use Controls and Property Development

■ PUBLIC LAND-USE CONTROLS

Zoning Regulations

Through power conferred by state enabling acts, each city and town in Massachusetts develops its own city plan and zoning ordinances or bylaws. The *Zoning Act*, Chapter 40A of the Massachusetts General Laws, is the source of zoning authority for all communities in the state except Boston. It sets forth procedural rules for establishing zoning ordinances.

The *Zoning Act* specifically exempts land and buildings that did not conform to the prescribed use for the location at the time the zoning code was passed. The statute indicates that *nonconforming* (or *grandfathered*) *uses* may not continue forever and prescribes that if the use is abandoned and not used for a period of two years or more, the current zoning code must be followed. The statute also states that pre-existing nonconforming structures or uses may be extended or altered so long as the permit granting authority finds that the extension or alteration is not substantially more detrimental to the neighborhood than the existing nonconforming use.

Application for a Variance

Objections to the zoning of particular pieces of land may be taken to the Zoning Board of Appeals. Applicants for zoning variations must demonstrate that the desired variance will be in the public interest and that it will remain within the spirit of the ordinance. The applicant also must show that the change is necessary because of the hardship caused by the existing requirement and that the variance would affect only his or her property and not the general district. Decisions of the Zoning Board of Appeals may be appealed to the Massachusetts Superior Court.

IN PRACTICE

Zoning regulations do not affect the marketability of title to real estate. However, buyers should protect themselves in purchase agreements by including a contingency clause for securing the necessary permits and approvals from local zoning authorities before the buyers take title.

Planning Boards

In addition to local zoning boards, Massachusetts law provides for the creation of local and regional planning boards in all parts of the state. Planning boards have two major functions: planning and subdivision control. Subdivision control consumes most of a board's time, especially in growing suburban and rural areas.

Subdivision Control Law. Subdivisions are defined in Massachusetts as land divided into two or more lots that do not front on a public or approved road. The *Subdivision Control Law* is also in effect in every city, except for Boston, and in every town in Massachusetts that develops its own plan and zoning regulations. The basic purposes of subdivision control law include

- protecting the health, safety, convenience, and welfare of inhabitants;
- providing adequate access by roads that are safe and convenient for travel;
- lessening congestion on subdivision roads and adjacent public roads;
- reducing motor vehicle accidents;
- securing safety in case of fire, flood, panic, and other emergencies;
- ensuring compliance with applicable zoning ordinances and bylaws;
- securing adequate provision for water, sewer, drainage, underground utility services, fire, police, other municipal equipment, street lighting, and other requirements where necessary in a subdivision; and
- coordinating the ways in a subdivision with each other, with the public ways in the city or town where it is located, and with the ways in neighboring subdivisions.

The *Subdivision Control Law* may be used to encourage the use of solar energy and protect access to direct sunlight of solar energy systems.

To fulfill these objectives, planning boards must ensure not only that subdivision plans conform to local zoning bylaws, but also that developers provide adequately designed and constructed streets, installation of necessary utilities, and installation of drainage facilities.

To ensure compliance, planning boards may draft rules and regulations requiring environmental impact statements, compliance with board of health restrictions, strict and well-defined road and drainage standards, and specifications and performance bonds to ensure completion of roads and drainage systems.

When a subdivision plan is submitted, the board must give public notice and hold a public hearing. In addition, county officials may require a subdivision survey and plot plan to be recorded with each subdivision contingent on the local planning board's approval of the plan.

Uniform Building Code. The *Uniform Building Code* regulates residential, commercial, and industrial construction in Massachusetts. It supersedes local building codes.

"Antisnob" zoning.   In response to selective zoning practices in many cities and towns in the Commonwealth, the Massachusetts Legislature enacted an "anti-snob" zoning law in 1969 known as the *Massachusetts Comprehensive Permit Law.* In an effort to increase the supply and improve the regional distribution of low-income and moderate-income housing, the law allows certain public agencies and any nonprofit or limited dividend organization to construct low-income and moderate-income housing despite local zoning bylaws.

Prior to applying for a comprehensive permit, a proposal to build affordable housing must receive preliminary approval (normally a Project Eligibility or Site Approval letter) under a state or federal subsidy program. The application, including the eligibility letter and development plans, is then filed with the local zoning board of appeals. The board then seeks recommendations from other local boards.

The local zoning board of appeals holds a public hearing within 30 days of receiving an application to address any local concerns. Such concerns include health, safety, environmental, design, open space, and any other concerns raised by town officials or residents. The board must make a decision within 40 days after the public hearing has ended. In making its decision, the board acts on behalf of all other town boards and officials, but only with regard to matters where local restrictions are more stringent than state regulations. The board can issue a single comprehensive permit that classifies into a comprehensive category all local permits and approval normally required by local boards. It can also issue a comprehensive permit with conditions, or deny the permit. If a comprehensive permit is granted, the applicant, prior to construction, must normally present final development plans to the building inspector (or a similar official) to ensure that plans are consistent with the comprehensive permit and state requirements.

If an application for a comprehensive permit is denied or granted with conditions that would make construction uneconomic, the applicant may appeal the board's decision to the Housing Appeals Committee. An appeal must be taken within 20 days of the notice of the decision. A decision of the Housing Appeals Committee may be appealed to the Superior Court.

The general principle governing hearings before the local board and the Housing Appeals Committee is that all local restrictions, as applied to the proposed affordable housing, be "consistent with local needs." Massachusetts General Laws, Chapter 40B, Section 20 defines "consistency with local needs" as being reasonable in view of the regional need for low-income and moderate-income housing balanced against health, safety, environmental, design, open space, and other concerns.

IN   PRACTICE

If *less than 10 percent* of a municipality's total housing units are subsidized low-income and moderate-income housing units, there is a presumption that there is a substantial housing need that outweighs local concerns. Also, it is prevalent practice in Massachusetts to require 25 percent of certain developments to be affordable housing.

■ PRIVATE LAND-USE CONTROL FOR SUBDIVISIONS

Subdividers usually place restrictions on the use of subdivision lots to benefit all lot owners. To be valid, a parcel of adjacent land must benefit from the restriction. A subdivider may establish restrictions through a covenant in a deed or by a separate recorded declaration.

Much of the old common law governing restrictions has been changed by state statutes. In Massachusetts, restrictions may be created to exist for any length of time, but unless the creating document includes a definite time limit, they become void after 30 years.

Courts will refuse to enforce a restriction if

- changes in the neighborhood have frustrated the purpose of the restriction;
- the parties who have the right to enforce the restriction have acted in such a way as to make enforcement unfair;
- the general plan first contemplated by the subdivider has been abandoned or no longer exists;
- the highest and best use of the land is impeded by the restriction; or
- enforcement of the restriction is inequitable.

Persons who seek to have the restriction removed must demonstrate that the restriction is unenforceable for one or more of these reasons.

Environmental Protection Legislation

Control of environmental issues at the state level is exercised by the Department of Environmental Management. Environmental regulations are addressed in Chapter 16.

■ RELATED WEB SITE

Massachusetts General Laws   *www.mass.gov/legis/laws/mgl*

QUESTIONS

1. Zoning ordinances are developed by
   a. the Zoning Act.
   b. each city and town.
   c. each county.
   d. the local building inspector.

2. The Smiths' store does not conform to a particular town's current zoning ordinances, passed after they had been in business for several years. After the store is partially destroyed by fire, the Smiths want to go back into business. If the newly restored building still does not conform to current zoning, what will they be required to do if they wish to continue their old business?
   a. Rebuild an exact replica of the old store
   b. Abide by the current zoning ordinances
   c. Apply for a variance
   d. Get a permit for a new building

3. The owners of Blasto Concrete feel that their property has been improperly zoned for residential use. Their objection may be taken directly to the
   a. Massachusetts Superior Court.
   b. Zoning Board of Appeals.
   c. Department of Environmental Management.
   d. Zoning Board.

4. The two major functions of local and regional planning boards are planning and
   a. building code enforcement.
   b. "antisnob" zoning control.
   c. establishing uniform zoning ordinances.
   d. subdivision control.

5. A subdivision is land that does not have frontage on a public or approved road and is divided into how many lots?
   a. 2 or more
   b. 50
   c. 5
   d. 25 or more

6. Which of the following is NOT a purpose of subdivision control?
   a. Reducing motor vehicle accidents
   b. Ensuring the highest and best use of land
   c. Protecting health, safety, convenience, and welfare
   d. Securing safety in case of emergencies

7. Residential, commercial, and industrial construction in Massachusetts is regulated by the
   a. Uniform Building Code.
   b. local planning boards.
   c. Massachusetts Comprehensive Permit Law.
   d. local zoning ordinances.

8. The purpose of Massachusetts' "antisnob" law is to
   a. ensure that local zoning ordinances do not bar low-income and moderate-income housing.
   b. secure adequate provision of services to low-income and moderate-income residents.
   c. establish construction standards for low-income and moderate-income housing.
   d. enforce a uniform zoning law that creates mandatory low-income and moderate-income housing projects in higher-income areas.

9. If a subdivider's restriction on the use of subdivision lots does not contain a specific time limit, it will automatically become void after how many years?
   a. 10
   b. 25
   c. 30
   d. 40

10. Which of the following arguments is LEAST likely to persuade a Massachusetts court to refuse to enforce the subdivision restriction?
    a. The creating document contained no time limit and was written in 1964.
    b. The surrounding neighborhood has changed considerably.
    c. The restriction is not popular with the property owners.
    d. The restriction interferes with the highest and best use of the land.

Fair Housing and Ethical Practices

■ MASSACHUSETTS LAWS AGAINST DISCRIMINATION

Federal fair housing laws prohibit discrimination on the basis of race, color, religion, national origin, sex, familial status, and disability. The Massachusetts General Laws, Chapter 151B, Section 4, state that it is the policy of the Commonwealth to provide for fair housing to all its citizens. All discriminatory and unlawful practices in housing transactions are prohibited.

Protected Classes

The Massachusetts Fair Housing Law prohibits discrimination in housing and real estate activities on the basis of

- race,
- color,
- religion,
- sex,
- sexual orientation—which shall not include persons whose sexual orientation involves minor children as the sex object,
- children,
- national origin,
- genetic information,
- ancestry,
- veteran or member of the armed forces,
- age, or
- handicap.

While discrimination against persons who have children is prohibited, the prohibition does not apply to any situation in which the state sanitary code regarding the number of persons who may safely occupy the premises would be violated.

The provisions of Massachusetts law regarding fair housing practices regulate the activities of *all persons* who have an ownership interest of any kind in real property and not just real estate licensees. The broad prohibitions include discrimination in

- offering residential and commercial property for sale or lease;
- granting mortgage loans;
- appraising residential real estate; and
- offering membership or participation in multiple-listing or other brokers' organizations.

Applicable Real Estate

Massachusetts' antidiscrimination laws apply to the following types of real estate:

- Multiple dwellings (three or more independent family units) or continuously located housing accommodations, including publicly assisted housing
- Single-family residences that are directly *or through an agent* offered to the public for sale, lease, or rental by advertising in a newspaper or otherwise, by signs and notices located on the premises or elsewhere, by listing with a broker, or by other means of public offering
- Commercial space

Prohibited Activities

The following activities are specifically outlawed:

- Refusing to rent, lease, sell, or negotiate the sale of any property, or deny or withhold from any person or group of persons such accommodations because of the person's protected class
- Discriminating against any person or group in the terms, conditions, or privileges involved with the possession or acquisition of property, or in the furnishings of facilities and services in connection therewith, or because a person possesses a trained guide dog as a result of blindness or hearing impairment
- Making any inquiry or record regarding the race, creed, color, national origin, sex, sexual orientation, age, ancestry, or marital status of a person seeking to rent, lease, or buy property, or concerning the fact that the person is a veteran or a member of the armed forces, is blind or hearing impaired, or has any other handicap
- Making false representations regarding the availability of suitable housing, including failing to show all properties listed for sale or rent that are within the requested price range

Discrimination is illegal if its purpose is to relieve the owner of the responsibility for removing or covering lead paint. See Chapter 16 for information regarding environmental issues.

Exceptions

While there are some limited exceptions to the general rules barring discrimination, real estate professionals should regard all discrimination as suspect, and they should not rely on a possible exception as a means to commit a discriminatory act. Also, in Massachusetts, there are no exceptions for race or welfare recipiency. It should be noted that the exceptions under state law may not be permitted under federal antidiscrimination laws.

In Massachusetts, it is permissible to inquire into an applicant's age for the purpose of determining his or her creditworthiness, as long as no negative weight is given to applicants over age 62. The offering of credit life insurance or credit disability insurance in conjunction with any mortgage loan to a limited age group is not an unlawful practice. It is also not unlawful to refuse a mortgage or other credit to a minor, or to a person whose life expectancy, as determined by the most recent Individual Annuity Mortality Table, is shorter than the duration of the mortgage.

It is legal for a residential community to designate certain structures as housing for persons over age 55 or 62 on one or more contiguous parcels totaling more than five acres. State-assisted or federally assisted housing developments for the elderly are also legal.

As a rule, the term *age discrimination* does not apply to minors. Property owners and managers, landlords, lenders, and real estate agents may lawfully discriminate against minors *as clients*. This should be distinguished from discrimination against families with children, which is illegal.

Sexual orientation does not include persons whose orientation involves minor children as sex objects.

Two-family, owner-occupied residences are exempt from Massachusetts antidiscrimination laws (except with regard to persons receiving public or rental assistance).

In order for a property owner to use any of the exemptions stated in the statute, the property owner may not use a real estate agent and may not use discriminatory advertising.

While an owner is generally required to bear the reasonable expense of modifying structures to make them accessible to handicapped persons (including those with mobility, hearing, or sight impairments), he or she is not required to pay for unreasonable modifications. A modification or accommodation is considered unreasonable if it imposes an undue hardship on the owner, based on such factors as the

- cost and extent of the modification or accommodation;
- modification's effect on altering the marketability of the housing;
- type and size of the property; and
- availability of federal tax deductions.

Reasonable modifications in making housing accessible for persons impaired in mobility, hearing, and sight include but are not limited to

- installing raised numbers;
- installing a doorbell that flashes a light;

- lowering a cabinet;
- ramping a front entrance of five or fewer vertical steps;
- widening a doorway; and
- installing a grab bar.

No owner is required to bear the cost of modifying more than 10 percent of the units in his or her property to make them fully accessible to a person using a wheelchair. However, no additional rent or other charge for handicapped-accessible housing may be imposed.

Blockbusting

The practice of **blockbusting** is prohibited by Massachusetts law. *Blockbusting* is the act of encouraging people to sell or rent their homes by claiming that the entry of a protected class of people into the area will have some sort of negative impact on property values.

Redlining

Massachusetts law prohibits the practice of **redlining.** *Redlining* is the practice of refusing to make mortgage loans or issue insurance policies in specific areas for reasons other than the economic qualifications of the applicants.

Steering

Massachusetts law prohibits the practice of **steering.** *Steering* is the channeling of homeseekers to particular neighborhoods. It also includes discouraging potential buyers from considering certain areas.

Notices

Chapter 151B requires that a notice stating that the agency or office complies with the provisions of Massachusetts laws against discrimination must be conspicuously displayed in every real estate agency and rental office. The display also may include a summary of unlawful activities.

Any real estate agency or rental office that fails to comply with this requirement is subject to a fine of up to $100.

IN PRACTICE

In advertisements over a certain size, the fair housing logo must appear in the advertisement.

Enforcement

Because many of the provisions of the Massachusetts laws against discrimination are similar to those of the Federal Fair Housing Act of 1968, the Massachusetts regulations have been ruled "substantially equivalent to the federal law." For this reason, all fair housing complaints in Massachusetts are referred to and investigated by the Massachusetts Commission Against Discrimination, an agency that reports directly to the governor's office.

Complaints brought under the laws against discrimination must be filed with the commission within six months after the alleged discriminatory actions occur. The commission investigates all complaints and notifies the board of its findings. On finding probable cause for a complaint, the commission sends the accused violator a conciliation agreement ordering him or her to comply with the law, make some specific restitution, or take other affirmative actions.

The commission may award up to $2,000 in damages to persons against whom the accused has discriminated, and the board may suspend the real estate agent's license. The suspension for a first-time violation is 60 days. A 90-day suspension may be issued if the violation occurs within two years of a prior violation.

Any person who refuses to comply with the commission's orders may appeal to the Massachusetts Superior Court.

■ RELATED WEB SITES

HUD's Fair Housing and Equal Opportunity in Massachusetts
www.hud.gov/local/index.cfm?state=ma&topic=offices

HUD's Fair Housing Resources in Massachusetts
www.hud.gov/local/ index.cfm?state=ma

Massachusetts Commission Against Discrimination   *www.mass.gov/mcad*

Massachusetts General Laws   *www.mass.gov/legis/laws/mgl*

QUESTIONS

1. Which of the following is NOT included under the fair housing laws of Massachusetts?
   a. Veteran's status
   b. Marital status
   c. Bankruptcy status
   d. Public assistance status

2. Barbara Broker has four prospective clients: Joe refuses to sell to Roman Catholics; Kim refuses to sell to people of Welsh descent; Lee refuses to sell to people who own foreign cars; and Mike refuses to sell to "rich white guys." Which of Barbara's prospective clients is engaging in unlawful discrimination?
   a. Joe, Kim, and Lee only
   b. Lee and Mike only
   c. Joe, Kim, and Mike only
   d. Joe, Kim, Lee, and Mike

3. Mr. Smith is moving to Washington and has given Broker Bob the listing for renting his house. He gave Bob instructions that the property was not to be shown to people with children. Bob should
   a. inform the Fair Housing Authority.
   b. inform the Board of Registration.
   c. accept the listing.
   d. refuse the listing.

4. Massachusetts' antidiscrimination laws do NOT apply to which of the following types of real estate?
   a. Single-family residences sold by the owner
   b. Two-unit, owner-occupied residential dwellings
   c. Residential dwellings of three or more units
   d. Commercial buildings in commercially zoned areas

5. Two people come into Broker Betty's office: Yang is a blind woman in a wheelchair, and Zack is a homosexual man. By refusing to show them any properties, Betty has committed unlawful discrimination against
   a. Yang only.
   b. Zack only.
   c. both Yang and Zack.

   d. neither Yang nor Zack.

6. Two people applied for 30-year mortgages with Mighty Mortgage Company: Rob, a 14-year-old boy; and Sam, a 98-year-old man. Both were asked their ages. If Rob and Sam are turned down, Mighty Mortgage has unlawfully discriminated against
   a. neither Rob nor Sam.
   b. Rob only.
   c. Sam only.
   d. both Rob and Sam.

7. Larry Landlord owns a 30-unit apartment building. What is the maximum number of units he can be required to bear the cost of modifying to comply with Massachusetts law regarding the accommodation of a person using a wheelchair?
   a. All ground-level units
   b. Three
   c. Five
   d. Ten

8. All fair housing complaints in Massachusetts are referred to and investigated by the
   a. Massachusetts Commission Against Discrimination.
   b. governor's office.
   c. federal Fair Housing Commission.
   d. Massachusetts Superior Court.

9. License suspensions for a real estate agent found to have violated the antidiscrimination laws are how many days for a first violation and a second violation within two years?
   a. 30 and 60
   b. 60 and 90
   c. 60 and 120
   d. 90 and 120

CHAPTER 16

Environmental Issues and the Real Estate Transaction

■ ENVIRONMENTAL ISSUES

Massachusetts, along with most other states, has recognized the need to balance the legitimate commercial and residential use of land with the necessity of preserving vital resources and ensuring the quality of the air, water, and soil. Preservation of the state's natural environment enhances both the quality of life and property values. The prevention and cleanup of pollutants and toxic wastes not only revitalizes the land but creates greater opportunities for responsible development.

Massachusetts Law

The attorney general of Massachusetts is authorized to prevent or remedy damage to the environment. *Damage to the environment* means the destruction, damage, or impairment of any of Massachusetts' natural resources.

The statutory definition includes air and water pollution, improper sewage disposal, use of toxic pesticides, and excessive noise. Improper operation of dumping grounds; impairment of rivers, streams, floodplains, lakes, ponds, and other surface or subsurface water resources; and destruction of seashores, dunes, marine resources, underwater archeological resources, wetlands, open spaces, natural areas, parks, and historic districts or sites are all addressed by statute.

Hazardous Waste

The Massachusetts Oil and Hazardous Material Release Prevention and Response Act is the state-level implementation of the federal Comprehensive Environmental Response, Compensation, and Liability Act (CERCLA). If any toxic chemicals or petroleum products are on or under the soil of a property, the information should be given to a prospective buyer. If the owner suspects the presence of any hazardous waste, he or she should have an expert examine the site. In Massachusetts, the site inspection for toxic substances is called a "21E" site inspection. If toxins are present, arrangements will be made for their removal by the proper state authority. This environmental cleanup law is sometimes referred to as *Superfund*.

The law provides that the manager, transporter, or generator of hazardous wastes is responsible for cleaning up these wastes if they are spilled or improperly disposed of. If the responsible party cannot be found, then the site owner or landowner is held responsible for cleaning up the site. The state will move ahead and do the work, then record a claim (lien) at the Registry of Deeds for the cost. This lien takes priority over all other recorded liens, except when the greater part of the property is used for single-family or multifamily housing, in which case the lien follows other encumbrances. The lien remains on the property until the state files a release.

Generally, property may not be sold or transferred once a hazardous waste has been discovered there. If it is necessary for the state to clean up the pollution, a lien will exist against the property for the value of the cleaning costs. Owners may occasionally escape liability if they can establish that they are innocent landowners who took reasonable steps to determine the presence of hazardous waste when they purchased the property in question.

Because an automatic lien against the tainted land takes precedence over mortgages, most banks will demand that the property be inspected before they commit to a loan. The broker will have to negotiate the costs of the inspection between the seller and the buyer.

Wetlands

Land in Massachusetts that is in a wetland or bordering a wetland is legally protected property. Under the Wetlands Restriction Act, the Department of Environmental Protection may draw "nonencroachment lines" around any waterway in order to restrict harmful or destructive activities such as dredging, filling, or polluting. The Coastal Zone Management Act *and* Ocean Sanctuaries Act both restrict the use and development of the state's coastline out to the three-mile territorial limit. The Scenic Rivers Act, the Clean Waters Act, and a wide array of air, water, and land pollution regulations work together to protect Massachusetts' fragile wetland areas from the detrimental effects of land development.

Scenic Roads

Massachusetts' rural roads are protected by a law enacted in 1973 that recognizes that trees and stone walls that border local roads have scenic, aesthetic, and historic value. Any repair, maintenance, reconstruction, or paving work that involves destruction of trees or stone walls within the right-of-way of a rural road may not be undertaken until the planning board has held a public hearing and granted written permission for the work to commence.

■ HAZARDOUS SUBSTANCES

Lead-Based Paint

Massachusetts enacted one of the nation's first state lead poisoning prevention laws in 1971. The original law embodied the principle of primary prevention, which remains central to the current law. Since 1971, Massachusetts property owners have been required to permanently control specified lead-based paint hazards in any housing unit in which a child under the age of six resides.

The law was revised in 1987 in three ways. First, the amendments sought to improve the quality and safety of lead abatement work by requiring use of trained and licensed contractors, relocation of housing occupants during abatement, and daily and final cleanup in units undergoing abatement. Second, the amendments sought to increase the number of units brought into compliance by providing financial assistance (a $1,000 state income tax credit and a grant/loan program) and by mandating that prospective purchasers of residential premises receive notice about the lead law and have the opportunity to get an inspection. Third, the amendments embraced universal blood lead screening, mandating that physicians screen children and that health insurers cover those costs.

In 1993, the law was amended again. Compliance costs were lowered by allowing owners to use interim controls for up to two years before permanently containing or abating lead-based paint hazards. Other cost-reducing provisions allowed for the use of encapsulants and eased safety precautions when children would not be endangered. Owners were given a larger $1,500-per-unit state income tax credit, and a new fund was set up to provide funds for lead hazard control. Finally, owners who obtain certification from a licensed inspector that interim controls or abatement have been performed are no longer held strictly liable, and insurers are required to provide coverage for any negligence claims (short of gross or willful negligence) that may be brought against such owners.

Massachusetts' lead-law requirements apply to residential properties constructed before 1978 that are offered for sale or rental. (The required Tenant Lead Law Notification and Tenant Certification form is seen in Figure 16.1.) Adult rooming houses are exempt. Short-term vacation rental properties leased for fewer than 31 days are also exempt from the requirements as long as (1) the owner or owner's agent has performed a visual inspection at least annually, (2) the rental unit has no chipping or peeling paint, and (3) the tenant has received the Short-Term Vacation/Recreational or Rental Exemption Notification form (seen in Figure 16.2). This form must be provided to the tenant by the owner prior to entering into a tenancy agreement.

To bring a property into compliance lead paint must be removed or covered (that is, *encapsulated*) if found on window sills, stair risers, woodwork, doors, interior wall corners, stair risers, and railings up to a height of five feet. Any chipped or cracked plaster or paint must be removed. Flat wall surfaces do not normally have to be "de-leaded." In short, the de-leading requirement applies to all "mouthable" surfaces accessible to a child under the age of six.

FIGURE 16.1

Tenant Lead Law Notification Information and Tenant Certification Form

Tenant Lead Law Notification

What lead paint forms must owners of rental homes give to new tenants?

Before renting a home built before 1978, the property owner and the new tenant must sign two copies of this Tenant Lead Law Notification and Tenant Certification Form, and the property owner must give the tenant one of the signed copies to keep. If any of the following forms exist for the unit, tenants must also be given a copy of them: lead inspection or risk assessment report, Letter of Compliance, or Letter of Interim Control. This form is for compliance with both **Massachusetts and federal lead notification requirements.**

What is lead poisoning and who is at risk of becoming lead poisoned?

Lead poisoning is a disease. It is most dangerous for children under six years old. It can cause permanent harm to young children's brain, kidneys, nervous system and red blood cells. Even at low levels, lead in children's bodies can slow growth and cause learning and behavior problems. Young children are more easily and more seriously poisoned than others, but older children and adults can become lead poisoned too. Lead in the body of a pregnant woman can hurt her baby before birth and cause problems with the pregnancy. Adults who become lead poisoned can have problems having children, and can have high blood pressure, stomach problems, nerve problems, memory problems and muscle and joint pain.

How do children and adults become lead poisoned?

Lead is often found in paint on the inside and outside of homes built before 1978. The lead paint in these homes causes almost all lead poisoning in young children. The main way children get lead poisoning is from swallowing lead paint dust and chips. Lead is so harmful that even a small amount can poison a child. Lead paint under layers of nonleaded paint can still poison children, especially when it is disturbed, such as through normal wear and tear and home repair work.

Lead paint dust and chips in the home most often come from peeling or chipping lead painted surfaces; lead paint on moving parts of windows or on window parts that are rubbed by moving parts; lead paint on surfaces that get bumped or walked on, such as floors, porches, stairs, and woodwork; and lead paint on surfaces that stick out which a child may be able to mouth such as window sills.

Most lead poisoning is caused by children's normal behavior of putting their hands or other things in their mouths. If their hands or these objects have touched lead dust, this may add lead to their bodies. A child can also get lead from other sources, such as soil and water, but these rarely cause lead poisoning by themselves. Lead can be found in soil near old, lead-painted homes. If children play in bare, leaded soil, or eat vegetables or fruits grown in such soil, or if leaded soil is tracked into the home from outside and gets on children's hands or toys, lead may enter their bodies. Most adult lead poisoning is caused by adults breathing in or swallowing lead dust at work, or, if they live in older homes with lead paint, through home repairs.

How can you find out if someone is lead poisoned?

Most people who are lead poisoned do not have any special symptoms. The only way to find out if a child or adult is lead poisoned is to have his or her blood tested. Children in Massachusetts must be tested at least once a year from the time they are between nine months and one year old until they are four years old. Your doctor, other health care provider or Board of Health can do this. A lead poisoned child will need medical care. A home with lead paint must be deleaded for a lead poisoned child to get well.

What kind of homes are more likely to have lead paint?

In 1978, the United States government banned lead from house paint. Lead paint can be found in all types of homes built before 1978: single-family and multi-family; homes in cities, suburbs or the countryside; private housing or state or federal public housing. The older the home, the more likely it is to have lead paint. The older the paint, the higher its lead content is likely to be.

#CL95-17

MASSFORMS™
Statewide Standard Real Estate Forms
Massachusetts Association of REALTORS 256 Second Ave., Waltham MA 02451
Phone: 7818903700   Fax: 7818904919   Brian Doherty

©1999 MASSACHUSETTS ASSOCIATION OF REALTORS®

d.zfx

Produced with ZipForm™ by RE FormsNet, LLC 18025 Fifteen Mile Road, Clinton Township, Michigan 48035 www.zipform.com

F I G U R E   16.1 (Continued)

Tenant Lead Law Notification Information and Tenant Certification Form

Can regular home repairs cause lead poisoning?

There is a danger of lead poisoning any time painted surfaces inside or outside the home are scraped for repainting, or woodwork is stripped or removed, or windows or walls are removed. This is because lead paint is found in almost all Massachusetts homes built before 1978, and so many of Massachusetts' homes are old. Special care must be taken whenever home repair work is done. No one should use power sanders, open flame torches, or heat guns to remove lead paint, since these methods create a lot of lead dust and fumes. Ask the owner of your home if a lead inspection has been done. The inspection report will tell you which surfaces have lead paint and need extra care in setting up for repair work, doing the repairs, and cleaning up afterwards. Temporarily move your family (especially children and pregnant women) out of the home while home repair work is being done and cleaned up. If this is not possible, tape up plastic sheets to completely seal off the area where the work is going on. No one should do repair work in older homes without learning about safe ways to do the work to reduce the danger of lead dust. Hundreds of cases of childhood and adult lead poisoning happen each year from home repair work.

What can you do to prevent lead poisoning?

- Talk to your child's doctor about lead.
- Have your child tested for lead at least once a year until he/she is four years old.
- Ask the owner if your home has been deleaded or call the state Childhood Lead Poisoning Prevention Program (CLPPP) at 1-800-532-9571, or your local Board of Health.
- Tell the owner if you have a new baby, or if a new child under six years old lives with you.
- If your home was deleaded, but has peeling paint, tell and write the owner. If he/she does not respond, call CLPPP or your local Board of Health.
- Make sure only safe methods are used to paint or make repairs to your home, and to clean up afterwards.
- If your home has not been deleaded, you can do some things to temporarily reduce the chances of your child becoming lead poisoned. You can clean your home regularly with paper towels and any household detergent and warm water to wipe up dust and loose paint chips. Rub hard to get rid of more lead. When you are done, put the dirty paper towels in a plastic bag and throw them out. The areas to clean most often are window wells, sills, and floors. Wash your child's hands often (especially before eating or sleeping) and wash your child's toys, bottles and pacifiers often. Make sure your child eats foods with lots of calcium and iron, and avoid foods and snacks that are high in fat. If you think your soil may have lead in it, have it tested. Use a door mat to help prevent dirt from getting into your home. Cover bare leaded dirt by planting grass or bushes, and use mats, bark mulch or other ground covers under swings and slides. Plant gardens away from old homes, or in pots using new soil. Remember, the only way to permanently lower the risk of your child getting lead poisoned is to have your home deleaded if it contains lead paint.

How do you find out where lead paint hazards may be in a home?

The only way to know for sure is to have a lead inspection or risk assessment done. The lead inspector will test the surfaces of your home and give the landlord and you a written report that tells you where there is lead in amounts that are a hazard by state law. For interim control, a temporary way to have your home made safe from lead hazards, a risk assessor does a lead inspection plus a risk assessment. During a risk assessment, the home is checked for the most serious lead hazards, which must be fixed right away. The risk assessor would give the landlord and you a written report of the areas with too much lead and the serious lead hazards. Lead inspectors and risk assessors have been trained, licensed by the Department of Public Health, and have experience using the state-approved methods for testing for lead paint. These methods are use of a sodium sulfide solution, a portable X-ray fluorescence machine or lab tests of paint samples. You can get a list of licensed lead inspectors and risk assessors from CLPPP.

In Massachusetts, what must the owner of a home built before 1978 do if a child under six years old lives there?

An owner of a home in Massachusetts built before 1978 must have the home inspected for lead if a child under six years old lives there. If lead hazards are found, the home must be deleaded or brought under interim control. Only a licensed

F I G U R E   16.1 (Continued)

Tenant Lead Law Notification Information and Tenant Certification Form

deleader may do high-risk deleading work, such as removing lead paint or repairing chipping and peeling lead paint. You can get a list of licensed deleaders from the state Department of Labor and Workforce Development. Deleaders are trained to use safe methods to prepare to work, do the deleading, and clean up. Either a deleader, the owner or someone who works for the owner who is not a licensed deleader can do certain other deleading and interim control work. Owners and workers must have special training to perform the deleading tasks they may do. After the work is done, the lead inspector or risk assessor checks the home. He or she may take dust samples to test for lead, to make sure the home has been properly cleaned up. If everything is fine, he or she gives the owner a Letter of Compliance or Letter of Interim Control. After getting one of these letters, the owner must take care of the home and make sure there is no peeling paint.

What is a Letter of Compliance?

It is a legal letter under state law that says either that there are no lead paint hazards or that the home has been deleaded. The letter is signed and dated by a licensed lead inspector.

What is a Letter of Interim Control?

It is a legal letter under state law that says work necessary to make the home temporarily safe from serious lead hazards has been done. The letter is signed and dated by a licensed risk assessor. It is good for one year, but can be renewed for another year. The owner must fully delead the home and get a Letter of Compliance before the end of the second year.

Where can I learn more about lead poisoning?

Massachusetts Department of Public Health Childhood Lead Poisoning Prevention Program (CLPPP) (For more copies of this form, as well as a full range of information on lead poisoning prevention, tenants' rights and responsibilities under the MA Lead Law, how to clean lead dust and chips, healthy foods to protect your children, financial help for owners, safe deleading and renovation work, and soil testing.) 617-753-8400, 1-800-532-9571

Massachusetts Department of Labor and Workforce Development
(List of licensed deleaders)
617-969-7177, 1-800-425-0004

Your local lead poisoning prevention program or your local Board of Health

U.S. Consumer Product Safety Commission
(Information about lead in consumer products)
1-800-638-2772

U.S. Environmental Protection Agency, Region I
(Information about federal laws on lead)
617-565-3420

National Lead Information Center
(General lead poisoning information)
1-800-LEAD-FYI

Tenant Lead Law Notification Information and Tenant Certification Form

Tenant Certification Form

Required Federal Lead Warning Statement

Housing built before 1978 may contain lead-based paint. Lead from paint, paint chips, and dust can pose health hazards if not managed properly. Lead exposure is especially harmful to young children and pregnant women. Before renting pre-1978 housing, lessors must disclose the presence of known lead-based paint and/or lead-based paint hazards in the dwelling. Lessees must also receive a federally approved pamphlet on lead poisoning prevention. The **Massachusetts Tenant Lead Law Notification** and **Certification Form** is for compliance with state and federal lead notification requirements.

Owner's Disclosure

(a) Presence of lead-based paint and/or lead-based paint hazards (check **(i)** or **(ii)** below):

   (i) _____ Known lead-based paint and/or lead-based paint hazards are present in the housing (explain).

   _____

   (ii) _____ Owner/Lessor has no knowledge of lead-based paint and/or lead-based paint hazards in the housing.

(b) Records and reports available to the owner/lessor (Check **(i)** or **(ii)** below):

   (i) _____ Owner/Lessor has provided the tenant with all available records and reports pertaining to lead-based paint and/or lead-based paint hazards in the housing (check documents below):

   ☐ Lead Inspection Report;   ☐ Risk Assessment Report;   ☐ Letter of Interim Control;   ☐ Letter of Compliance

   (ii) _____ Owner/Lessor has no reports or records pertaining to lead-based paint and/or lead-based paint hazards in the housing.

Tenant's Acknowledgment (initial)

(c) _____ Tenant has received copies of all documents checked above.   (d) _____ Tenant has received no documents listed above.

(e) _____ Tenant has received the Massachusetts Tenant Lead Law Notification.

Agent's Acknowledgment (initial)

(f) _____ Agent has informed the owner/lessor of the owner's/lessor's obligations under federal and state law for lead-based paint disclosure and notification and is aware of his/her responsibility to ensure compliance.

Certification of Accuracy

The following parties have reviewed the information above and certify, to the best of their knowledge, that the information they have provided is true and accurate.

Owner/Lessor	Date	Owner/Lessor	Date
Tenant	Date	Tenant	Date
Agent	Date	Agent	Date

Owner/Managing Agent Information for Tenant (Please Print):

_____
Name   Street   Apt.

_____
City/Town   Zip   Telephone

_____ I (owner/managing agent) certify that I provided the Tenant Lead Law Notification/Tenant Certification Form and any existing Lead Law documents to the tenant, but the tenant refused to sign this certification.
The tenant gave the following reason: _____
The Massachusetts Lead Law prohibits rental discrimination, including refusing to rent to families with children or evicting families with children because of lead paint.

Contact the Childhood Lead Poisoning Prevention Program for information on the availability of this form in other languages.

Tenant and owner must each keep a completed and signed copy of this form.

Address of Property/Unit _____

c:\wp50\lead1995\forms\clp95-17.wp/Rev.5/98

MASSFORMS®   ©1999 MASSACHUSETTS ASSOCIATION OF REALTORS®
Statewide Standard Real Estate Forms

FIGURE 16.2

Short-Term Vacation/Recreational or Rental Exemption Notification Form

The Commonwealth of Massachusetts
Executive Office of Health and Human Services
Department of Public Health
Childhood Lead Poisoning Prevention Program
470 Atlantic Avenue, Second Floor
Boston, MA 02210-2208
(617) 753-8400/800-532-9571

ARGEO PAUL CELLUCCI
GOVERNOR
JANE SWIFT
LIEUTENANT GOVERNOR
WILLIAM D. O'LEARY
SECRETARY
HOWARD K. KOH, MD, MPH
COMMISSIONER

SHORT-TERM VACATION OR RENTAL EXEMPTION NOTIFICATION

Under the Massachusetts Lead Law (M.G.L.c.111, s.199B) and Regulations (105 CMR 460.100(D)), the owner of the property located at:

_____
          (street)   (apt.)   (city)

MA _____ that is being rented or occupied for vacation purposes, certifies that all paint in the dwelling
     (zip)
unit is intact including on the exterior parts of the windows and qualifies for an exemption from the Lead Law which requires the owner to abate or contain lead paint if a child under six years of age is in residence.

The Department of Public Health advises parents of young children under six years of age who are tenants or occupants under this exemption for a period not to exceed a total of thirty-one days, that occupying a dwelling unit for a short period of time where lead paint is intact does not present a health hazard for children under six years of age. Should you be concerned about peeling paint that you have found in the dwelling unit, contact:

_____   _____
   Name of Owner or Agent Authorized   Telephone Number
          To Make Repairs

Date of Visual inspection when all paint or other coating was intact on relevant surface: _____

_____   _____
    Signature of Owner or Agent Performing   Date
          Visual Inspection

Number of Days Rented or Occupied (Not to Exceed 31 Days)

_____   _____
     Signature of Tenant or Occupant   Signature of Owner or Agent
     with Child Under Six Years of Age   Presenting Notification to Tenant

_____   _____
          Date   Date

If peeling paint is present in the dwelling unit, the owner is not exempt from the obligations of the Lead Law.

THIS FORM MUST BE COMPLETED FOR A VALID EXEMPTION

©1999 MASSACHUSETTS ASSOCIATION OF REALTORS®

#706

MASSFORMS™
Statewide Standard Real Estate Forms
Massachusetts Association of REALTORS 256 Second Ave., Waltham MA 02451
Phone: 7818903700   Fax: 7818904919   Brian Doherty

d.zfx

Produced with ZipForm™ by RE FormsNet, LLC 18025 Fifteen Mile Road, Clinton Township, Michigan 48035 www.zipform.com

Owners or brokers of pre-1978 properties may not discriminate against potential buyers or tenants who have children who would force lead abatement repairs to be done.

While there is no requirement that a lead inspection be undertaken prior to selling or purchasing a home, brokers and owners are required to notify prospective purchasers if lead paint is present and that licensed inspectors are available who can determine the levels of lead content. Sellers must inform purchasers of actual or possible lead hazards whether or not a real estate broker is involved in the sale.

If property was constructed prior to 1978, the state-approved lead disclosure form, entitled Property Transfer Notification Certification (seen in Figure 16.3), signed by the seller *must* then be signed by the prospective buyer or tenant, whether or not lead paint is present. The form certifies that the buyer has been informed of the existence of a lead paint hazard. Owners must declare on the form whether they have knowledge of the presence of lead paint. The buyer must also indicate whether the ten-day period for a lead inspection is being selected or waived. The listing and selling agents must sign the disclosure indicating they have informed the buyer and seller of the possible presence of lead.

The disclosure must be accompanied by the Childhood Lead Poisoning Prevention Program (CLPPP) packet—published by the Department of Public Health—that presents information on lead-based paint, childhood lead poisoning, and the legal requirements of the lead law in a question-and-answer format. (See Figure 16.4.) In addition, real estate agents must verbally inform purchasers of the lead law's abatement requirement and of their right to have a lead inspection of the property, and, when requested, provide a list of those who have been licensed to perform lead paint inspections and abatement.

If the purchaser wants to have an inspection performed, the seller must allow the potential purchaser a ten-day opportunity to conduct lead-paint and risk assessment inspections before the purchaser becomes obligated under a contract to purchase. The purchase-and-sale agreement may or may not be contingent on the property passing the inspection tests. If no test is performed on a pre-1978 property prior to closing, the purchaser has 90 days after closing to have the property inspected. A purchaser is required to abate a lead hazard within 90 days of securing title to the property if a child under six will live in it.

Asbestos

Massachusetts law requires that every property owner must maintain all asbestos material in good repair and free from any defects including, but not limited to, holes, cracks, tears, or any looseness that may allow the release of asbestos dust, or any powdered, crumbled, or pulverized asbestos material. Anyone who handles asbestos-containing material must do so in a manner that does not cause or contribute to air pollution.

F I G U R E   16.3

Property Transfer Notification Certification Form

PROPERTY TRANSFER NOTIFICATION CERTIFICATION

This form is to be signed by the prospective purchaser before signing a purchase and sale agreement or a memorandum of agreement, or by the lessee-prospective purchaser before signing a lease with an option to purchase for residential property built before 1978, for compliance with federal and Massachusetts lead-based paint disclosure requirements.

Required Federal Lead Warning Statement:
Every purchaser of any interest in residential property on which a residential dwelling was built prior to 1978 is notified that such property may present exposure to lead from lead-based paint that may place young children at risk of developing lead poisoning. Lead poisoning in young children may produce permanent neurological damage, including learning disabilities, reduced intelligence quotient, behavioral problems and impaired memory. Lead poisoning also poses a particular risk to pregnant women. The seller of any interest in residential real property is required to provide the buyer with any information on lead-based paint hazards from risk assessments or inspections in the seller's possession and notify the buyer of any known lead-based paint hazards. A risk assessment or inspection for possible lead-based paint hazards is recommended prior to purchase.

Seller's Disclosure
(a) Presence of lead-based paint and/or lead-based paint hazards (check (i) or (ii) below):
    (i) _____ Known lead-based paint and/or lead-based paint hazards are present in the housing (explain).

_____
    (ii) _____ Seller has no knowledge of lead-based paint and/or lead-based paint hazards in the housing.
(b) Records and reports available to the seller (check (i) or (ii) below):
    (i) _____ Seller has provided the purchaser with all available records and reports pertaining to lead-based paint and/or lead-based paint hazards in the housing (check documents below).
    ☐ Lead Inspection Report;   ☐ Risk Assessment Report;   ☐ Letter of Interim Control;   ☐ Letter of Compliance
    (ii) _____ Seller has no reports or records pertaining to lead-based paint and/or lead-based paint hazards in the housing.

Purchaser's or Lessee Purchaser's Acknowledgment (initial)
(c) _____ Purchaser or lessee purchaser has received copies of all documents checked above.
(d) _____ Purchaser or lessee purchaser has received no documents.
(e) _____ Purchaser or lessee purchaser has received the Property Transfer Lead Paint Notification.
(f) _____ Purchaser or lessee purchaser has (check (i) or (ii) below):
    (i) _____ received a 10-day opportunity (or mutually agreed upon period) to conduct a risk assessment or inspection for the presence of lead-based paint and/or lead-based paint hazards; or
    (ii) _____ waived the opportunity to conduct a risk assessment or inspection for the presence of lead-based paint and/or lead-based paint hazards.

Agent's Acknowledgment (initial)
(g) _____ Agent has informed the seller of the seller's obligations under federal and state law for lead-based paint disclosure and notification, and is aware of his/her responsibility to ensure compliance.
(h) _____ Agent has verbally informed purchaser or lessee-purchaser of the possible presence of dangerous levels of lead in paint, plaster, putty or other structural materials and his or her obligations to bring a property into compliance with the Massachusetts Lead Law - either through full deleading or interim control - if it was built before 1978 and a child under six years old resides or will reside in the property.

Certification of Accuracy
The following parties have reviewed the information above and certify, to the best of their knowledge, that the information they have provided is true and accurate.

_____	_____	_____	_____
Seller	Date	Seller	Date
_____	_____	_____	_____
Purchaser	Date	Purchaser	Date
_____	_____	_____	_____
Agent	Date	Agent	Date

Address of Property / Unit _____

CLPPP Form 94-3, 6/30/94, Rev. 5/95

MassForms™
Statewide Standard Real Estate Forms   ©1995 MASSACHUSETTS ASSOCIATION OF REALTORS®

Produced with ZipForm™ by RE FormsNet, LLC 18025 Fifteen Mile Road, Clinton Township, Michigan 48035   www.zipform.com   dis.zfx

F I G U R E   16.4

Sample Childhood Lead Poisoning Prevention Program (CLPPP) Packet

MASSACHUSETTS ASSOCIATION OF REALTORS®
256 Second Ave. • Waltham, MA 02451

The Commonwealth of Massachusetts
Executive Office of Health and Human Services
Department of Public Health
Childhood Lead Poisoning Prevention Program
470 Atlantic Avenue, Second Floor
Boston, MA 02210-2224
(617) 753-8400 / (800) 532-9571

MITT ROMNEY
GOVERNOR

KERRY HEALEY
LIEUTENANT GOVERNOR

RONALD PRESTON
SECRETARY

CHRISTINE C. FERGUSON
COMMISSIONER

CHILDHOOD LEAD POISONING PREVENTION PROGRAM (CLPPP)
PROPERTY TRANSFER LEAD PAINT NOTIFICATION

Under Massachusetts and federal law, this notification package must be given to buyers and tenants with an option to buy homes built before 1978. This package must be given in full to meet state and federal requirements. It may be copied, as long as the type size is not made smaller. Every seller and any real estate agent involved in the sale must give this package before the signing of a purchase and sale agreement, a lease with an option to purchase, or, under state law, a memorandum of agreement used in foreclosure sales. Sellers and agents must also tell the buyer or tenant with an option to buy any information they know about lead in the home. They must also give a copy of any lead inspection report, risk assessment report, Letter of Compliance or Letter of Interim Control. **This package is for compliance with both state and federal lead notification requirements.**

Real estate agents must also tell buyers and tenants with an option to buy that under the state Lead Law, a new owner of a home built before 1978 in which a child under six will live or continue to live must have it either deleaded or brought under interim control within 90 days of taking title. This package includes a check list to certify that the buyer or tenant with an option to buy has been fully notified by the real estate agent. This certification should be filled out and signed by the buyer or tenant with an option to buy before the signing of a purchase and sale agreement, a lease with an option to purchase or a memorandum of agreement used in a foreclosure sale. It should be kept in the real estate agent's files. After getting notice, the buyer or tenant with an option to buy has at least 10 days, or longer if agreed to by the seller and buyer, to have a lead inspection or risk assessment if he or she chooses to have one, except in cases of foreclosure sales. There is no requirement for a lead inspection or risk assessment before a sale. A list of private lead inspectors and risk assessors licensed by the Department of Public Health is attached.

Sellers and real estate agents who do not meet these requirements can face a civil penalty of up to $1,000 under state law; a civil penalty of up to $10,000 and possible criminal sanctions under federal law, as well as liability for resulting damages. In addition, a real estate agent who fails to meet these requirements may be liable under the Massachusetts Consumer Protection Act.

The property transfer notification program began in 1988 and has been very successful. It provides information you need to protect your child, or your tenants' child from lead poisoning. Massachusetts has a tax credit of up to $1,500 for each unit deleaded. There are also a number of grants and no-interest or low-interest loans available for deleading. It's up to you to do your part toward ending lead poisoning.

PLEASE TAKE THE TIME TO READ THIS DOCUMENT. LEAD POISONING IS THE NATION'S NUMBER ONE ENVIRONMENTAL DISEASE AFFECTING CHILDREN. DON'T GAMBLE WITH YOUR CHILD'S FUTURE.

CLPPP Form 94-2, 6/30/94, Rev. 5/98

MASSFORMS™
Statewide Standard Real Estate Forms
Massachusetts Association of REALTORS 256 Second Ave. Waltham MA 02451
Phone: 7818903700   Fax: 7818904919   Brian Doherty

©1999 MASSACHUSETTS ASSOCIATION OF REALTORS®

EQUAL HOUSING OPPORTUNITY

dis.zfx

Produced with ZipForm™ by RE FormsNet, LLC 18025 Fifteen Mile Road, Clinton Township, Michigan 48035   www.zipform.com

F I G U R E   16.4 (Continued)

Sample Childhood Lead Poisoning Prevention Program (CLPPP) Packet

MASSACHUSETTS ASSOCIATION OF REALTORS®
256 Second Ave. • Waltham, MA 02451

What is lead poisoning? How do children become lead-poisoned?

Lead poisoning is a disease. It is most dangerous for children under six years old. In young children, too much lead in the body can cause permanent harm to the brain, kidneys, nervous system and red blood cells. Even at low levels, lead in children's bodies can slow growth and cause learning and behavioral problems. The main way children get lead poisoned is by swallowing lead paint dust. They do not have to chew on leaded surfaces or eat paint chips to become poisoned. Most childhood lead poisoning is caused by children's normal behavior of putting their hands or other things, such as toys, in their mouths. If their hands or these objects have touched lead dust, this may add lead to their bodies. Children can also be exposed to lead from such other sources as lead-contaminated soil or water, but these sources alone rarely cause lead poisoning. Lead can be found in soil near old, lead-painted houses. If children play in bare, leaded soil, or eat vegetables or fruit grown in such soil, or if leaded soil is tracked into the home and gets on children's hands or toys, lead may enter their bodies.

What are the symptoms of lead poisoning? How is it detected?

Most lead poisoned children have no special symptoms. The only way to find out if a child is lead poisoned is to have his or her blood tested. The Massachusetts Lead Law requires all children between 9 months and 4 years old to be screened annually for lead. If your child has been exposed to lead, or if you do not know if your child under age six has been screened for lead, ask your child's doctor, other health care provider or your local board of health for a simple screening test of your child.

What is the treatment for lead poisoning?

Treatment of a lead poisoned child starts with finding and removing the lead hazards to which the child is exposed. This will include a lead inspection of the child's home, and if lead hazards are identified, deleading of the home. Medical treatment depends on the child's blood lead level and the child's response to the removal of the lead source. Parents will be taught about protecting their child from lead exposure. They will need to watch the child's progress through frequent blood tests. If necessary, the child may receive special drugs to help rid his body of excess lead. With this treatment, drugs are given daily for as long as several weeks. Sometimes this must be done more than once. A child who has been lead poisoned will need a lot of blood tests for a year or more. He or she should be tested for learning problems before starting school.

Are children under six years old the only ones at risk of lead poisoning?

No. Young children are usually more easily and seriously poisoned than older children or adults, but lead is harmful to everyone. Lead in the body of a pregnant woman can hurt her baby before birth. Older children and adults who live in older housing with lead paint hazards may become exposed to lead and could potentially develop lead poisoning through home renovation. Most lead poisoning in adults is caused by work-related exposure or home renovation. Even hobby supplies, such as stained glass, bullets and fishing sinkers, can expose people to lead. Lead poisoning in adults can cause high blood pressure, problems having children for both men and women, digestive problems, nerve disorders, memory loss and problems concentrating, and muscle and joint pain. Adults who have any of these symptoms and who have been exposed to lead should consider being screened for lead. Those who are regularly exposed to lead through their work are required by law to have their blood tested once a year for lead.

F I G U R E   16.4 (Continued)

Sample Childhood Lead Poisoning Prevention Program (CLPPP) Packet

MASSACHUSETTS ASSOCIATION OF REALTORS®
256 Second Ave. • Waltham, MA 02451

What are the dangers of lead paint in homes, and when was it used?

Lead paint in homes causes almost all childhood lead poisoning. Lead is so harmful that even a small amount of fine lead dust that cannot be seen, can poison a child. Lead paint covered by layers of nonleaded paint can still poison children, especially when it is disturbed, such as through normal wear and tear, or home repair work. When such lead paint is on moving surfaces, such as windows, fine lead dust is released through normal use. This dust settles, where it can be easily picked up on children's toys and fingers. Household paint with poisonous (now illegal) levels of lead was in use in Massachusetts from the 1690s until 1978. In 1978, the U.S. government banned lead from house paint. Lead can be found in all types of pre-1978 homes, homes in cities, suburbs or the countryside; private housing and state or federal public housing; single-family and multi-family homes. The older the house, the more likely it is to contain lead paint. The older the paint, the higher the likely lead content.

Can routine home repairs cause lead poisoning?

There can be a danger of lead poisoning whenever painted surfaces inside or outside the home are scraped for repainting, or woodwork is stripped or removed, or windows or walls are removed. This is because lead paint is found in almost all Massachusetts homes built before 1978, and so many of Massachusetts' homes are old. Do not use power sanders, propane torches or heat guns to remove leaded paint, as these methods create a lot of lead dust and fumes. Temporarily move your family (especially children and pregnant women) out of the home while the work is being done and cleaned up, or at a minimum, tape up plastic sheets to completely seal off the work area. Get a lead inspection done, so that you will know which surfaces have lead paint and need extra care when preparing for and doing home repair work, and during cleanup afterwards. Do not do repairs in older homes without learning about safe ways to do the work to reduce the danger of lead dust. Hundreds of cases of childhood and adult lead poisoning result each year from do-it-yourself home projects.

How does the owner of a home built before 1978 in which a child under six years old lives meet the requirements of the Massachusetts Lead Law?

The first step is to have a lead inspection or risk assessment done. A licensed lead inspector will test the surfaces of the home for lead and give the owner a written report that states where there is lead in amounts considered a violation by state law, and record any lead hazards that must be corrected. A risk assessor, who is a specially licensed lead inspector, will do a lead inspection plus a risk assessment, during which he or she checks the home for the most serious lead hazards that must be fixed for interim control. (See question about interim control, below.) Only a licensed deleader may do high-risk work, such as removing lead paint or repairing chipping and peeling lead paint. Either a deleader, the owner or someone who works for the owner (an agent) can do certain other deleading and interim control tasks. (See next question.) An owner or agent must get special training to perform the deleading tasks they may do. After the work is done, the lead inspector or risk assessor returns to check the home. He or she may take dust samples to test for lead and makes sure the home has been properly cleaned up. If everything is fine, he or she gives the owner a Letter of Compliance or a Letter of Interim Control. After getting one of these letters, the owner must take reasonable care of the property, mainly by making sure there is no peeling lead paint.

Can I do some of the deleading myself?

In Massachusetts, the owner or someone who works for the owner (an agent) can do certain deleading activities. These include covering surfaces with certain materials; removing certain building parts; capping baseboards; installing vinyl siding on the exterior, and applying encapsulants. Encapsulants are special liquid coatings made to be long-lasting barriers over lead paint. Before any of these deleading tasks are done, the owner must first have a lead inspection done and whoever is going to do the work must get special training. Contact CLPPP for information about this training. In addition, owners or their agents can perform structural repairs and lead dust cleaning for interim control. Before doing this work, owners and agents should get and read CLPPP's interim control booklet.

MASSFORMS
Statewide Standard Real Estate Forms

©1999 MASSACHUSETTS ASSOCIATION OF REALTORS®

F I G U R E   16.4 (Continued)

Sample Childhood Lead Poisoning Prevention Program (CLPPP) Packet

MASSACHUSETTS ASSOCIATION OF REALTORS®
256 Second Ave. • Waltham, MA 02451

Is there financial help for deleading?

There is a state income tax credit of up to $1,500 per unit for full deleading. A credit of up to $500 per unit is available for interim control work that also contributes to full deleading. There are also grants and no-interest, deferred loans, or low-interest loans available to eligible property owners. These funds are available through the U.S. Department of Housing and Urban Development, the Massachusetts Executive Office of Communities and Development, the Massachusetts Housing Finance Authority, local city and town community development planning departments, and banks.

Does deleading improve the value of my property?

Many homeowners have found that the benefits of deleading are not unlike the benefits of other home improvement projects. Replacement windows and doors can save the homeowner money because they are more energy efficient. Having a legally deleaded home, whether it is a single-family or multi-family, owner-occupied or rental unit, can make it easier to sell or rent, often at a better price.

What surfaces must be deleaded for full compliance with the Massachusetts Lead Law?

Owners of homes built before 1978 where children under six years of age live must have the following lead hazards corrected to get a Letter of Compliance:
* any peeling, chipping or flaking lead paint, plaster or putty;
* intact lead paint, other coating or putty on moveable parts of windows with sills five feet or less from the floor or ground and those surfaces that come in contact with moveable parts;
* intact lead paint or other coating on "accessible mouthable surfaces." These surfaces generally include woodwork, such as doors, door jambs, stairs and stair rails, and window casings.

What is interim control?

Interim control is a set of temporary measures that property owners can take to correct urgent lead hazards, especially peeling or chipping lead paint and lead dust. These steps protect residents from lead poisoning until the home is fully deleaded. Homes in good condition may need little or no work to get interim control status. Owners then have up to two years before they have to fully delead the home. For that period, they are free from strict liability under the state Lead Law should a child become lead poisoned in the home. In addition to the repair of peeling and chipping lead paint and the cleaning of lead dust, other work may be necessary for interim control. This includes fixing water leaks or other damage that makes lead paint peel and chip; making window wells smooth and easy to clean; making windows work properly and deleading any badly chipping and peeling lead-painted surfaces.

Property owners interested in interim control must hire a licensed risk assessor. He or she will then decide what work, if any, needs to be done to get a Letter of Interim Control. The original Letter of Interim Control is good for one year. The property owner can have the home reinspected before the end of that year, and if all conditions are met, the home can be recertified for another year. By the end of the second year, the home must be deleaded, if a child under six still lives there, for the owner to remain free of strict liability.

F I G U R E   16.4 (Continued)

Sample Childhood Lead Poisoning Prevention Program (CLPPP) Packet

MASSACHUSETTS ASSOCIATION OF REALTORS®
256 Second Ave. • Waltham, MA 02451

Does my family have to be out of the house during deleading or interim control work?

Residents must be out of the house for the entire time that a deleader is doing deleading work inside a home, and for some of the deleading work by owners and their agents. Residents may stay at home, but out of the work area, while a deleader, property owner or owner's agent without a deleader's license does certain other deleading tasks, or such interim control work as structural repairs or lead dust cleaning. Residents who have been out of the house may not return until the deleading work that made it necessary for them to leave is complete, the home is cleaned up, and a lead inspector or risk assessor has checked and found this work has been properly done. For complete details, contact CLPPP.

Are there any exemptions to the Massachusetts Lead Law?

The Lead Law applies only to homes built before 1978 in which a child under six lives. Any home or apartment having fewer than 250 square feet of living space, or which is in a rooming house, is exempt, as long as no child under age six is living there. Finally, homes rented for 31 days or less for vacation or recreational purposes are also exempt, as long as there is no chipping or peeling lead paint in the home and the renter has received the Short-Term Vacation Rental Notification.

What are the requirements of the state Lead Law if there is a lease with option to buy?

When there is a lease with an option to buy a home built before 1978 in effect, the owner of the property must have it deleaded or brought under interim control if a child under six lives there. If the tenant with an option to buy such a home proceeds to purchase it, he or she becomes responsible for meeting the requirements of the Lead Law if a child under six lives there after the purchase.

How can I find out about how lead inspections, risk assessments and deleading should be done?

All lead inspections, risk assessments and deleading must be done according to the Regulations for Lead Poisoning Prevention and Control, 105 Code of Massachusetts Regulations 460.000 and the Deleading Regulations, 454 CMR 22.00. For full information, homeowners may get these regulations at the State House Book Store, State House, Boston, MA 02133. The phone number is (617) 727-2834.

Lead inspectors and risk assessors licensed by the Department of Public Health have been trained and are experienced in using the state-approved methods for testing for lead paint. These methods are the following: use of a solution of sodium sulfide, a portable x-ray fluorescence machine or lab tests of paint samples removed from the home. Deleaders licensed by the Department of Labor and Workforce Development have been trained to use safe methods to prepare for and do deleading work, and clean up afterwards. They may delead using any of the following methods: removing paint, removing building parts, covering and encapsulating. When removing paint, they cannot use certain very dangerous methods, such as open flame burning, dry abrasive blasting or power sanding without a special vacuum attachment.

F I G U R E   16.4 (Continued)

Sample Childhood Lead Poisoning Prevention Program (CLPPP) Packet

MASSACHUSETTS ASSOCIATION OF REALTORS®
256 Second Ave. • Waltham, MA 02451

How do I get a lead inspection or risk assessment?

Included as part of this notification package is a listing of private licensed lead inspectors organized alphabetically, and private licensed risk assessors, similarly organized. Ask to see the inspector or risk assessor's license, to make sure it is current. You should arrange for the inspection or risk assessment as quickly as possible after deciding you want one. If you do have an inspection or risk assessment, you must give the seller a copy of the report.

What is the best time to delead or undertake interim control?

The best time to delead a home or bring it under interim control is when the home is vacant, so that residents will not be exposed to lead and household furnishings will not be contaminated with lead. In addition, it often is efficient, and reduces costs, to combine deleading with other repair work being done to a vacant home.

What is a Letter of Compliance and a Letter of Interim Control?

Under the state Lead Law, a Letter of Compliance is a legal letter that says either that there are no lead paint hazards or that the home has been deleaded. The letter is signed and dated by a licensed lead inspector. A Letter of Interim Control is a legal letter that says work necessary to make a home temporarily safe from lead hazards has been done. It is signed and dated by a licensed risk assessor. A Letter of Interim Control is good for one year, but can be renewed for one more year. The owner must fully delead the home and get a Letter of Compliance by the end of the second year if a child under six still lives there. The Lead Law does not require the removal of all lead paint from a home. An owner who gets a Letter of Compliance or Letter of Interim Control must take reasonable care to keep up the home, mainly by making sure there is no chipping or peeling lead paint. If an owner fails to take reasonable steps to maintain the home, he or she may become liable for damages to a child lead poisoned as a result of the owner's breach of that duty of reasonable care.

RENTAL PROPERTY INFORMATION

What liability do rental property owners have if they don't comply with the state Lead Law?

If a property owner of a home built before 1978 in which a child under six lives fails to delead or bring the home under interim control, and a child is lead poisoned as a result, the property owner is strictly liable for all damages. An owner is not strictly liable for lead poisoning if a Letter of Compliance or Letter of Interim Control is in effect. Strict liability means owners may be liable even if they did not know lead paint was in the home. Since harm to the kidneys and blood cells, delays in growth, learning disabilities and emotional and behavioral disturbances resulting from lead poisoning can have life-long effects, monetary damages awarded against an owner responsible for a child's lead poisoning can be substantial. Failing to delead or bring under interim control a home to which the Lead Law applies is also an emergency public health matter, and can carry criminal penalties. An owner who is notified by a public agency of Lead Law violation in a property he or she owns, and who willfully fails to correct the dangerous conditions, is also subject to punitive damages, which are three times the actual damages found. These provisions are in addition to any other legal rights the lead-poisoned child may have.

MASSFORMS®   ©1999 MASSACHUSETTS ASSOCIATION OF REALTORS®
Statewide Standard Real Estate Forms
Produced with ZipForm™ by RE FormsNet, LLC 18025 Fifteen Mile Road, Clinton Township, Michigan 48035   www.zipform.com   dis.zfx

F I G U R E   16.4 (Continued)

Sample Childhood Lead Poisoning Prevention Program (CLPPP) Packet

MASSACHUSETTS ASSOCIATION OF REALTORS®
256 Second Ave. • Waltham, MA 02451

Can I avoid state Lead Law requirements by not renting to a family with children under six?

The Massachusetts Lead Law makes it illegal to refuse to rent to families with children under six, or evicting or refusing to renew the lease of families with children under six, because of lead paint. Discrimination against families with young children is also a violation of the U.S. Fair Housing Act and the Massachusetts anti-discrimination statute. Parents cannot waive the rights of their children to live in lead-safe housing or agree to assume to risks of lead exposure. Owners who violate these laws face heavy penalties. The Massachusetts Commission Against Discrimination investigates and prosecutes cases of discrimination against families with children because of lead paint.

It is also illegal for lenders to deny financing because a home has lead paint, or because financing could trigger future duties under the Lead Law. This does not restrict the right of a lender to process or deny a mortgage application in accordance with accepted underwriting practices and criteria.

If I am considering buying a pre-1978 house to rent out, and a child under six lives in one of the apartments, should I have at least that unit and common area inspected for lead now?

Yes. If there are children under six living in such an apartment and the apartment does not have a Letter of Compliance or Letter of Interim Control, buyers should find out whether or not the apartment has lead hazards and will have to be brought into compliance with the state Lead Law. This information will be important in deciding whether to buy the property and at what price. As noted above, new owners have 90 days from the date of taking title to have such an apartment deleaded or brought under interim control. Therefore, they should arrange deleading or interim control work to begin as soon as possible after taking title, to be sure the work is done within 90 days.

Can a landlord delay a tenancy to bring a home into compliance with the state Lead Law?

A landlord who will be deleading a home or bringing it under interim control may delay the start of the tenancy up to 30 days. This can be done as long as a lease between the landlord and the new tenant does not exist. During this delay period, the new tenants are responsible for their living expenses. If there is a signed lease, however, the landlord is responsible for temporary housing during relocation necessary for deleading work.

Must a landlord arrange temporary housing for a tenant while a rental home is being deleaded?

Under the state Lead Law, tenants have to be relocated for the time that certain deleading work is taking place inside the home. They may not return until that work is done, the home is cleaned up, and a licensed lead inspector or risk assessor checks and finds it is fine for residents to move back in.

The landlord and tenant are responsible for working out an acceptable plan for alternative housing if it is necessary. The landlord may move the tenant to another place to live, which may be another house, apartment, motel or hotel. The landlord is responsible for paying the tenant's reasonable moving costs and any temporary housing costs over and above the rent of the home being deleaded. During the time the home is being deleaded, the tenant remains responsible for paying the normal rent they would pay for this period as their share of the cost of temporary housing. The Lead Law states the temporary housing must not cause undue economic or personal hardship to the tenant.

MASSFORMS™
Statewide Standard Real Estate Forms
©1999 MASSACHUSETTS ASSOCIATION OF REALTORS®

F I G U R E   16.4 (Continued)

Sample Childhood Lead Poisoning Prevention Program (CLPPP) Packet

MASSACHUSETTS ASSOCIATION OF REALTORS®
256 Second Ave. • Waltham, MA 02451

What is tenant notification?

The goal of the federal and state requirements for tenant notification is to help reduce lead poisoning by giving all tenants of homes built before 1978 information about lead in their home. The program also educates tenants and landlords about the dangers of lead poisoning, its prevention, and the Massachusetts Lead Law. Tenant notification applies to all tenants, whether or not they have a child under six living with them.

Before renting a home, landlords, managing agents or any real estate agent involved in the rental must give new tenants copies of any existing lead forms for the home. These include lead inspection reports, risk assessment reports, a Letter of Compliance (no matter how old) or a Letter of Interim Control. If the landlord or agent does not have any or all of these forms for the home, he or she simply does not give them. In addition, the landlord or agent must give new tenants the Tenant Lead Law Notification. This form addresses lead poisoning, specific prevention tips for parents, the requirements of the Lead Law and an explanation of the lead forms. Attached to the Tenant Lead Law Notification is the Tenant Certification form. This is to be filled out and signed by both the tenant and the landlord or agent. Each party gets a copy to keep. **These forms have been approved to satisfy both state and federal lead notification requirements.** Landlords or agents may choose to include the Tenant Lead Law Notification/Tenant Certification form in a written lease, instead of using a separate form.

Landlords and agents who fail to carry out their tenant notification obligations are liable for all damages caused by their failure to do so , and are subject to a fine up to $1,000.

INSURANCE INFORMATION

How can an owner of rental housing in Massachusetts built before 1978 get insurance to cover potential lead liability?

The answer depends on the number of units that the property owner wishes to insure, and whether the property owner lives in the building for which insurance is sought. An owner-occupant who insures four or fewer units may be covered by homeowners insurance. Generally, the property owner who is not an owner-occupant will need to get commercial liability insurance, as will an owner-occupant who wishes to insure more than four units.

Homeowners insurance may be available from several different sources: the regular, "admitted" market, the FAIR Plan or the "surplus lines" market. The regular, "admitted" market is the usual market for insurance. The FAIR Plan offers homeowners insurance to property owners unable to find coverage in the regular market. The "surplus lines" market is a less regulated, and generally more expensive market. It provides insurance to those who cannot find coverage elsewhere.

Under state Division of Insurance regulations, if an insurer in the regular market decides to write homeowners insurance on rental housing for which a Letter of Compliance or Letter of Interim Control is in effect, the insurer must provide coverage of lead paint liability arising from those premises. **Neither the state Lead Law nor the insurance regulations require a regular market insurer to write liability insurance, including homeowners insurance, on a particular property.** If a Letter of Compliance or Letter of Interim Control is in effect for only part of a property, the coverage for lead liability will extend to only that part of the property. Such insurance will also apply to any common areas covered by the Letter of Compliance or Letter of Interim Control. It will not, however, extend to injuries resulting from gross or willful negligence. The FAIR Plan's coverage of lead liability is subject to the same regulations that apply to the regular market.

An insurer in the regular market, or the FAIR Plan, may ask the property owner to prove that there is a Letter of Compliance or a Letter of Interim Control for the home sought to be insured. Once the proof is provided, coverage for lead liability will apply as of the date of the Letter. If the Fair Plan determines that a given property is eligible for insurance, or if a regular market insurer elects to insure certain premises, either may exclude lead liability coverage on any part of the property it ensures to which no Letter of Compliance or Letter of Interim Control applies. If either the Fair Plan or a regular market insurer uses such an exclusion, it must offer the owner of the premises the chance to buy back the excluded coverage. There is an additional charge for the lead liability "buyback" coverage. The amount of this charge is regulated by the Division of Insurance.

MassForms™
Statewide Standard Real Estate Forms
8
©1999 MASSACHUSETTS ASSOCIATION OF REALTORS®

Produced with ZipForm™ by RE FormsNet, LLC 18025 Fifteen Mile Road, Clinton Township, Michigan 48035 www.zipform.com   dis.zfx

F I G U R E   16.4 (Continued)

Sample Childhood Lead Poisoning Prevention Program (CLPPP) Packet

MASSACHUSETTS ASSOCIATION OF REALTORS®
256 Second Ave. • Waltham, MA 02451

In the surplus lines market, there is no requirement to cover lead liability arising from premises to which a Letter of Compliance or Letter of Interim Control applies. Surplus lines insurers generally exclude coverage of lead liability, do not offer the buyback coverage, and charge higher prices then the regular market.

Since the FAIR Plan does not provide commercial liability insurance, property owners who need to get such coverage (as opposed to homeowners insurance) must get it from either the regular market or the surplus lines market. Commercial liability insurance from the surplus lines market, like homeowners insurance from that market, usually will exclude coverage of lead liability, will not include the buyback option, and will cost more than regular market coverage.

While a regular market insurer can decline to write commercial liability insurance on a given property, once such an insurer decides to write such coverage, it must then insure lead liability arising from any part of the property covered by a Letter of Compliance or Letter of Interim Control. If such an insurer chooses to insure a property, it may exclude coverage of lead liability on any part of the premises for which no Letter of Compliance or Letter of Interim Control is in effect. If such insurer applies such an exclusion, it must offer the property owner the opportunity to buy back the excluded coverage. The lead liability insurance regulations described above as applicable to regular market homeowners insurance also apply to commercial liability insurance from the regular market.

Owners of rental housing should try to get coverage for lead liability, whether they have met the requirements of the Lead Law or not, by seeking regular market coverage through insurance agents, or by contacting direct writing companies that are listed in the telephone directory, before resorting either to the FAIR Plan or the surplus lines market.

If I own and occupy a single-family house, does my homeowners insurance cover lead liability?

Under the state lead liability insurance regulations, coverage of lead liability cannot be excluded from regular market and FAIR Plan homeowners insurance policies on single-family owner-occupied homes. Instead, lead liability coverage is included in such policies. However, a family member covered by a homeowners policy cannot make a lead liability claim against another family member covered by the same policy. The requirements of the lead liability insurance regulations do not apply to homeowners coverage from the surplus lines market.

How are new owners affected by the lead liability insurance regulations?

If a buyer of rental housing built before 1978 meets the state Lead Law's requirements and gets a Letter of Compliance or Letter of Interim Control within 90 days after becoming the owner, then, under certain conditions, they will be able to get coverage for lead liability for the period they owned the property before they deleaded or brought it under interim control. This will happen if a regular market insurer chooses to provide liability coverage on the property. Such an insurer is required to provide lead liability coverage to a new owner who obtains a Letter of Compliance or Letter of Interim Control within 90 days after becoming the owner of the property. Such coverage will go back to the time that the new owner took title to the property, unless the liability insurance went into effect some time after the taking of title. In the latter case, the coverage of lead liability will extend back to the time that the liability insurance held by the new owner first went into effect on the premises. The rule for new owner lead liability insurance coverage for the FAIR Plan is the same as for the regular market. These special rules for lead liability insurance for new owners do not apply to insurance from the surplus lines market.

****

F I G U R E   16.4 (Continued)

Sample Childhood Lead Poisoning Prevention Program (CLPPP) Packet

MASSACHUSETTS ASSOCIATION OF REALTORS®
256 Second Ave. • Waltham, MA 02451

What happens next?

That's up to you! At this point, you should be well informed about lead poisoning, the effects of lead hazards in the home, and your responsibilities under the Massachusetts Lead Law. In the past, the Department of Public Health has had to devote its childhood lead poisoning resources to provide services to the thousands of Massachusetts children who were poisoned, as well as to providing services to children whose blood lead levels are elevated, to prevent them from becoming lead poisoned. Between the Department's work and the preventive deleading carried out by property owners, we have been successful at reducing the number of lead poisonings among young children in Massachusetts. All of us at the Department are hopeful that we will continue that partnership, in which the correction of lead hazards in the homes of young children *before* those children are lead poisoned is so important.

Where can I get more information on lead poisoning?

Massachusetts Department of Public Health
Childhood Lead Poisoning Prevention Program (CLPPP)
(For more copies of this form, and full range of information on owners' and tenants' rights and responsibilities under the state Lead Law, financial help for owners, safe renovation work, and soil testing)
617-753-8400, 1-800-532-9571

Massachusetts Department of Labor
and Workforce Development
(List of licensed deleaders)
617-727-7047, 1-800-425-0004

Massachusetts Housing Finance Agency
(Get the Lead Out loan program information)
617-854-1000

U.S. Environmental Protection Agency
Region 1 (New England)
(Information about federal laws on lead)
617-565-3420

National Lead Information Center
(General lead poisoning information)
1-800-LEAD-FYI

U.S. Consumer Product Safety
Commission
(Information about lead in consumer products)
1-800-638-2772

In general, when asbestos-containing material is being removed, Massachusetts law requires the following: adequately wet asbestos-containing material exposed during the removal operation; lower the material to the ground level so as to not cause airborne emissions of asbestos; and ensure no release of asbestos into the air by maintaining adequate wetness, sealing the work area, and using a local exhaust ventilation and collection system designed to capture asbestos particulate material. Then the material must be sealed in a leak-tight container that is adequately labeled. The container may be stored at an approved refuse transfer station facility or it may be disposed of at an approved sanitary landfill special waste site.

Fuel Storage

In Massachusetts, no person may construct, maintain, or use any tank or container of more than a 10,000-gallon capacity for the storage of any fluid other than water, unless it is located underground with a permit from the marshal. Storage tanks are inspected annually by the marshal at a fee. Notification of an inspection is to occur not less than 14 days prior to the inspection date. Note that in addition to inspections, the marshal, the head of the fire department, or their authorized personnel may enter at reasonable times any establishment or other place where an underground storage tank is located. They may inspect and obtain samples of substances contained in the tank and may conduct monitoring or testing of the tanks, equipment, contents, or surrounding soils, air, surface water, or ground water. Such an inspection is to be commenced and completed with reasonable promptness.

Any tank that has been used for storing flammable or combustible fluids cannot be removed or relocated unless a permit has been obtained from the state fire marshal or the official designated by him. Abandoned underground residential tanks—used exclusively for heating or for the heating of domestic water on the premises where it is stored—must be drained, cleaned properly, and filled with clean sand, pea gravel, or a concrete slurry, or removed from the ground as directed by the head of the fire department. Notice of the abandonment of a tank must be reported to the board of health for the city or town in which the tank is located.

Every owner of an underground tank first put into operation on or after January 1, 1991, must, within 30 days after the tank is put into operation, notify the local department of public health of the tank, specifying the age, size, type, location, and uses of the tank. However, this does not apply to a farm or residential tank of 1,100 gallons or less capacity used for storing motor fuel for noncommercial purposes or to a tank used for storing heating oil for consumptive purposes where it is stored.

Owners of underground storage tanks may be required to maintain a leak detection system, along with records and reporting of leaks and corrective actions.

Anyone in violation of the above regulations is presumed to have engaged in irreparable harm to the public health, safety, welfare, and environment. The presumption may be rebutted by competent evidence. Note that each day a violation occurs or continues is deemed a separate offense.

IN PRACTICE

Most cities and towns require property owners whose heating systems have been converted from oil heat to gas heat, and who still have an unused oil tank in the basement, to remove the tank prior to the closing of the sale. Sellers or their agent should contact their local fire chief for instructions.

Old Industrial or Waste Sites

In 2002, the Brownfields Legislation became federal law. Under the law, states and localities receive funds to clean up polluted industrial sites. As of January 2004, Massachusetts has received over $30.5 million to assess and clean up properties that have been abandoned or underdeveloped because of contamination or the fear of contamination.

■ OTHER ENVIRONMENTAL ISSUES

Smoke Detectors

In Massachusetts, sellers are required to provide buyers with smoke detector compliance certificates before a property closing can occur. An appointment must be made with the local fire department for an inspection of the property and a fee must be paid. A fire official will examine the property to check that detectors are of the correct type, in the right location, and are working properly. A certificate will be signed by the official. The original certificate must be presented at the closing.

Carbon Monoxide Detectors

Effective March 31, 2006, the Commonwealth of Massachusetts enacted legislation requiring carbon monoxide detectors for all residential dwellings equipped with fossil-fuel burning equipment that produces carbon monoxide or which have enclosed parking attached to living areas. The law and regulations apply to all homes, not just property that is being transferred. Inspections for compliance are performed, prior to a closing, by the local fire department and can be done in conjunction with the smoke detector inspection. If the inspection is done simultaneously with the smoke detector inspection there is no additional charge. Maximum fees are defined in the law for inspections performed separately.

Fossil fuel burning equipment includes any natural gas, propane, or oil furnace, water heater, or fireplace; pellet stove or woodstove; and gas or propane ranges. At least one carbon monoxide (CO) detector must be placed on each finished level of a home. In addition, a CO detector must be placed within ten feet of the door to each bedroom.

The law also requires that landlords install, maintain, and test carbon monoxide detectors within their tenants' units and provides penalties for any person who tampers with these life safety devices.

Title 5: On-Site Sewage Disposal Systems

Few changes in real estate law have stirred as much controversy as Title 5 of the Massachusetts Environmental Code. Title 5 requires that all properties that have on-site sewage disposal systems are to have those systems inspected when a change in ownership of property is going to take place, or when an addition to the property is planned.

Homes that are not connected to a sewer system use cesspools or septic systems, both of which are regulated by the state Department of Environmental Protection (hereinafter *the department*) and local boards of health. A *cesspool* is a waste disposal system with a pipe that runs from a structure and empties waste into a single pit. A *septic system* is a disposal process that includes a septic tank, distribution box, and soil absorption system designed to filter waste and avoid waste concentrations in the soil. Cesspools and septic systems that are not functioning properly are a major cause of the pollution in Massachusetts' coastal waters, rivers, and water supplies.

In 1995, the state environmental code, Title 5, began requiring inspections of septic systems and cesspools prior to a home's being sold or enlarged. The results of an inspection must be reported to the local board of health within 30 days, and a copy of the inspection must be given to the buyer. In most cases, systems that fail inspection must be repaired within two years regardless of whether the house is actually sold or transferred. In 1996, an additional regulation requires that most septic system replacements or upgrades also need a soil evaluation test performed by a department-approved soil evaluator.

Systems that show signs of failure or that threaten the environment or public health must be upgraded. However, the department does not require all disposal systems to be in absolute compliance with the rules: *maximum feasible compliance* is the standard that must be met. Alternative technologies, such as sand filters and composting toilets, have been approved. A loan program through the Massachusetts Housing Finance Authority's Home Improvement Program is available to assist low-income and moderate-income homeowners who must upgrade their systems. In addition, starting in 1997, a Title 5 tax credit equal to 40 percent became available for eligible homeowners for the design and construction costs incurred in upgrading or repairing a septic system. The tax credit relief provides credits of up to $1,500 per year with a maximum credit of $6,000 over a four-year period.

Title 5 is a lengthy and complex regulation. However, it is important for real estate salespersons and brokers to become familiar with the general requirements of Title 5 for inspection and lending purposes. For example, many mortgage lenders require septic system or cesspool repairs or upgrades to be completed before a closing or that funds for such a repair or upgrade be placed in an escrow before a closing.

Cesspool and septic system inspections are required

- within two years before the sale of a home or transfer of title or six months after the sale if weather conditions preclude prior inspection;
- in certain inheritance situations;
- in certain insolvency proceedings;
- when the use of the home is changed;
- when the home is expanded and a building, or occupancy permit, is required; or
- when the footprint of the house is enlarged.

Inspections are not required

- when a mortgage is refinanced;
- when title to the house is transferred from one spouse to another or placed in a particular family trust;
- when the system was inspected within three years before the sale of the house and the owners have records showing that their system was pumped annually since the inspection;
- when the local board of health has issued a certificate of compliance within two years before the time of transfer of title;
- when the homeowner has entered into an enforceable agreement that is binding on subsequent buyers, with the board of health requiring a system upgrade or connection to the municipal sewer system within two years of transfer or sale; or
- when the community has adopted a plan approved by the department requiring periodic inspections, and the system was inspected at the most recent time as required by the plan.

Some homeowners choose to voluntarily have their septic system or cesspool inspected as a way of assessing the system's condition. These inspection results are not reported to the local board of health or the department.

IN PRACTICE

In a 1996 Massachusetts court case, a real estate broker was found to have violated the *Massachusetts Consumer Protection Act* when she mistakenly believed that the house she was selling had no sewage problems, had a Title 5 system, and negligently convinced the buyer not to have a septic system inspection. *Vanderwiel v. Jones*, 1996 Mass. App. Div. 184 (1996).

The Title 5 Addendum is illustrated in Figure 16.5.

Mold

Mold is a growing concern in all parts of the country. Mold can be found almost anywhere and can grow on almost any organic substance as long as moisture and oxygen are present. Few states have enacted legislation concerning mold. Currently, Massachusetts has no legislation on mold. Not only is it a serious health concern in new building construction, mold is also an area of increasing litigation.

Radon

While there are no Massachusetts state regulations regarding radon, the Environmental Protection Agency has issued recommended guidelines. The Massachusetts Department of Health's Radiation Control Program can advise property owners on how to get their homes tested for radon and assist them in interpreting the results. Also, the Radiation Control Program has a booklet describing methods of reducing high concentrations of radon.

Radon is a naturally occurring radioactive gas produced in the ground through the normal decay of uranium and radium. As it decays, radon produces new radioactive elements or decay products called *radon daughters* that cannot be detected by human senses because they are colorless, odorless, and tasteless.

FIGURE 16.5

Sample of Title 5 Addendum

SAMPLE

TITLE 5 ADDENDUM

The Massachusetts Department of Environmental Protection ("DEP") has established regulations governing on-site, subsurface sewage disposal systems, including septic systems and cesspools, that apply at the time of sale or transfer of a property served by an on-site subsurface system. (Title 5 of the Massachusetts Environmental Code, 310 CMR 15.301 et seq.) The regulations require that septic systems and cesspools be inspected by a licensed inspector "at or within two years prior to the time of transfer of title" to the property to determine if the system complies with DEP requirements. An inspection performed up to three years prior to sale or transfer of title may be used if the inspection report is accompanied by system pumping records demonstrating that the system has been pumped at least once a year during that time. If weather conditions preclude an inspection at the time of transfer, the regulations permit the inspection may be conducted up to six months after sale or transfer. A copy of the inspection report shall be submitted to the buyer or other person acquiring title. The fact that a system passes an inspection is not a guarantee or warranty that the system will continue to operate satisfactorily in the future. If the system fails the inspection criteria established by the regulations, the system will need to be repaired, upgraded or replaced in accordance with Title 5. A state income tax credit may be available for forty percent of the cost of repair or replacement of a failed system serving one's primary residence up to a maximum credit of $6000.00 (where repair or replacement of a system costs $15,000 or more), subject to applicable law.

_____ _____
BUYER   Date

_____ _____
SELLER   Date

_____ _____
BUYER   Date

_____ _____
SELLER   Date

#508/10.31.99/140979

MASSFORMS™
Statewide Standard Real Estate Forms
Massachusetts Association of REALTORS 256 Second Ave, Waltham MA 02451
Phone: 7818903700   Fax: 7818904919   MAR

© 1999 MASSACHUSETTS ASSOCIATION OF REALTORS®

dsasd.zfx

Produced with ZipForm™ by RE FormsNet, LLC 18025 Fifteen Mile Road, Clinton Township, Michigan 48035 www.zipform.com

Radon gets into homes through small spaces in the soil and rock on which a house is built and can seep into a home through dirt floors, floor drains, sump pits, joints, or tiny cracks and pores in hollow-block walls. Radon concentrations tend to be greater in basements. Radon can also dissolve in well water and contribute to airborne radon in homes when released through running water.

The harmful effects of decaying radon include damage to lung tissue that increases the risk of developing lung cancer.

One remedy to reduce the exposure of radon is to increase home ventilation so the radon is allowed to escape. Another approach is to determine how the gas is entering a home and to then seal that area to prevent the gas from continuing to enter.

■ RELATED WEB SITES

Act relative to the installation of carbon monoxide alarms and smoke detectors in residential buildings   *www.mass.gov/legis/laws/seslaw05/sl050123.htm*

Massachusetts Department of the Environment   *www.mass.gov/envir/*

Massachusetts Department of Environmental Protection
www.mass.gov/dep/dephome.htm

Massachusetts Environmental Code   *www.mass.gov/dep/service/matrix.htm*

Massachusetts General Laws   *www.mass.gov/legis/laws/mgl*

Massachusetts General Laws, Chapter 148 Section 26F½ 527CMR 31:00
www.mass.gov/legis/laws/mgl/148-26f.htm

Massachusetts Wetlands Restoration Program   *www.mass.gov/czm/wrp/index.htm*

Title 5 Regulations in the Code of Massachusetts Regulations
www.lawlib.state.ma.us/title5.html

QUESTIONS

1. In Massachusetts, what is the name of the law that is similar to CERCLA or Superfund?
   a. Massachusetts Oil and Hazardous Material Release Prevention and Response Act
   b. Massachusetts Hazardous Substances Act
   c. Massachusetts Oil and Hazardous Materials Cleanup Act
   d. Massachusetts Toxins in the Environment Act

2. Harry, a landlord, owns property where young children (younger than age six) live. He is aware that the apartments have lead paint and has enacted interim controls from a licensed inspector. If Harry is sued by a tenant, how would the court find him?
   a. Strictly liable
   b. Negligent
   c. Grossly negligent
   d. None of the above

3. Under what circumstances must a lead disclosure form be signed by a prospective buyer or tenant?
   a. The home was built before 1978 and has lead paint.
   b. The home was built before 1978 and may or may not have lead paint.
   c. The home was built after 1978.
   d. The prospective buyer has an infant.

4. In what year did the Brownfield Legislation become law?
   a. 2003
   b. 2000
   c. 2001
   d. 2002

5. If a house sale occurs during the month of February and Massachusetts weather is so bad that a septic system inspection cannot be done, when must the inspection be done?
   a. Within 30 days
   b. Within 4 months
   c. Within 6 months
   d. Within 8 months

6. Pedro and Maria live in a rural area and have a septic system. They take advantage of the low interest rates and refinance their mortgage. Which of the following statements is *TRUE?*
   a. They don't need a septic system inspection.
   b. They need a septic system inspection within two years of the refinancing.
   c. They need a septic system inspection within 30 days of the refinancing.
   d. They need a septic system inspection at any time in the future.

Sources for Real Estate Information— Massachusetts

- Board of Registration of Real Estate Brokers and Salespersons
  239 Causeway Street, Suite 500
  Boston, MA 02114
  617-727-3074
  www.mass.gov/dpl/boards/re

- Massachusetts Association of REALTORS®
  256 Second Avenue
  Waltham, MA 02451
  781-890-3700
  www.marealtor.com

- Board of Registration of Home Inspectors
  239 Causeway Street, Suite 500
  Boston, MA 02114
  617-727-3074
  www.mass.gov/dpl/boards/hi/index.htm

- Massachusetts Commission Against Discrimination
  One Ashburton Place, Room 601
  Boston, MA 02108
  617-994-6000

- 436 Dwight Street, Room 220
  Springfield, MA 01103
  413-739-2145
  www.mass.gov/mcad

- Massachusetts Bar Association
  20 West Street
  Boston, MA 02111
  Boston Office 617-338-0500
  Springfield Office 413-731-5134
  www.massbar.org

- Massachusetts Department of Revenue
  www.dor.state.ma.us

- Massachusetts Executive Office of Environmental Affairs
  www.mass.gov/envir

- Massachusetts Department of Housing and Community Development
  www.mass.gov/dhcd

- Massachusetts General Laws
  www.mass.gov/legis/laws/mgl

- Code of Massachusetts Regulations
  www.lawlib.state.ma.us/cmrindex.html

Answer Key

The numbers in parentheses following each answer refer to the page in this Supplement on which the correct answer is explained.

CHAPTER 1

1. **d** (16) The statute of frauds applies to conveyances of property but not to employment agreements. Because a listing agreement is considered an employment agreement, the statute of frauds does not apply.

2. **a** (17) The Massachusetts Supreme court ruled in *Tristram's Landing v. Wait* that a broker is entitled to a commission if the broker produces a ready, willing, and able buyer who enters into a binding contract with the seller and the transaction is closed in accordance with the provisions of the agreement. A signed listing agreement is not necessary.

3. **c** (9) The Massachusetts Consumer Protection Act (MCPA) requires that a broker disclose any known material defects regarding a property to a buyer or prospective buyer. The fact that the buyer or prospective buyer did not ask the question does not relieve the broker of the responsibility to disclose the information.

4. **a** (9–10) Under the Massachusetts Consumer Protection Act, a broker can be held liable for any untrue claim or representation as well as for any omissions. If the seller requests that a broker not reveal a material defect in the property and the broker agrees, then the broker can be held liable for misrepresentation through omission. Brokers must reveal all known material defects regarding a property to a prospective buyer.

5. **a** (5) When a real estate agent agrees to represent a buyer, the agent is held to be a fiduciary. A fiduciary implies a position of trust and carries with it fiduciary duties.

6. **d** (2–3) The fiduciary duties owed by the agent to the principal are commonly referred to as OLDCAR: obedience, loyalty, disclosure, confidentiality, accountability, and reasonable care.

7. **b** (17) The Massachusetts Supreme court ruled in *Tristram's Landing v. Wait* that a broker is entitled to a commission if the broker produces a ready, willing, and able buyer who enters into a binding contract with the seller and the transaction is closed in accordance with the provisions of the agreement.

8. **a** (19) The buyer, after contacting Broker B to see the house, entered into an exclusive-right-to-represent agreement with Broker B. Broker B helped the buyer to obtain mortgage preapproval, showed several other houses for comparison and initiated a series of continuous and uninterrupted events that resulted in the agreement of the buyer and seller. Broker A may not be entitled to a commission.

9. **c** (16) An oral or implied agency relationship may be terminated at will; a written agency relationship, however, can be terminated only by agreement of both parties or by operation of the law.

10. **c** (2) As of July 1, 2005, the most common agency relationships practiced in Massachusetts are seller, buyer, disclosed dual, and designated agency.

CHAPTER 2

1. **a** (22) An agent is hired by a seller to represent him or her in the sale of his or her home using a listing agreement that defines the responsibilities and rights of the parties and that is considered an employment contract.

2. **b** (28) A net listing is illegal in Massachusetts: MGL CH 112 section 87AAA of the Massachusetts License Law states it is illegal for a licensee to accept a net listing from a prospective seller to sell real estate for a stated price that authorizes the broker to keep as commission any amount of money received from the sale in excess of the stated price.

3. **b** (23–24) An open-listing agreement allows the owner of the property to hire as many brokers as he or she wishes without exclusivity to any one, and it also allows the seller to retain the right to sell the property himself or herself. This type of agreement need not be in writing.

4. **b** (23) An exclusive-right-to-sell agreement is a written agreement appointing the broker the exclusive agent for the sale of property for a specified period of time. The listing broker is entitled to a commission if the property is sold by the owner, by the broker, or by anyone else.

5. **c** (28) Bill accepted a net listing, which is illegal in Massachusetts, and is therefore in violation of the Massachusetts License Law. (See the answer to question #2 above.)

6. **d** (28) In a cobroker agreement, the cooperating broker has no contractual relationship with the seller and therefore must look solely to the listing broker for commission.

7. **c** (29) CMA is an acronym for competitive market analysis.

8. **d** (29) The sales price of a home should always be determined by the seller of the property. A broker provides a seller with a competitive market analysis (CMA) to assist in determining a price range based on similar properties that have recently sold.

9. **b** (29) Massachusetts requires that all appraisers be certified or licensed by the state.

10. **c** (29) It is the seller's responsibility to set the selling price. A broker should avoid recommending or setting a specific price. Using the data from the competitive market analysis (CMA), the broker may advise the seller how the price the seller sets frequently determines how quickly a sale might occur.

CHAPTER 3

1. **c** (35) Unless stated otherwise, when a valid deed is delivered the law presumes that a fee simple estate has been conveyed.

2. **b** (35) Dower rights become effective at the death of a spouse.

3. **d** (36) In Massachusetts you may acquire a homestead right in one of two ways: (1) include in the deed of conveyance a "declaration" that the principal residence will held as a homestead or (2) record a signed declaration in the appropriate registry of deeds.

4. **d** (37) One of five factors used to establish an easement by prescription is that a benefited parcel of land, usually abutting or adjacent, must exist.

5. **a** (37–38) When Lorenzo sold the back half of his land to Mike and gave Mike the right to cross his land to reach Mike's property, an easement by necessity was created. Both Lorenzo's deed and Mike's deed should reference the easement.

6. **b** (38) A license is merely permission for a certain right of usage and not a grant of ownership.

7. **a** (38) Because a license is a personal right and not an interest in the land itself, it is the smallest right a person can have in real estate.

8. **d** (39) Littoral rights refer to rights along lakes, oceans, and other standing waters.

9. **d** (39) Remember that riparian refers to rivers and the word *riparian* literally means "riverbank"; so if a river is navigable, the adjacent landowner owns the land to the bank of the river.

10. **c** (36) The purpose of a homestead right is to protect the family against eviction by general creditors and to protect each spouse individually by requiring both to execute any deed conveying the homestead property.

11. **a** (39) An owner whose property is adjacent to a large pond (riparian = riverbank) owns the property only to the shore, and the owner's use of the water must be approved under the state environmental laws.

CHAPTER 4

1. **c** (41) Unless a specific form of ownership is specified, a deed conveying ownership to two or more people in Massachusetts is presumed to be held as an estate in common.

2. **d** (42) Because under tenants by the entirety both husband and wife own the "entire" property, the surviving spouse will be the sole owner.

3. **d** (42–43) A cooperative owner purchases shares in the corporation that holds title to the building. In return for stock in the corporation, the owner receives a proprietary lease, granting occupancy of a specific unit. Because she or he does not own the unit her or his interest is treated as personal property.

4. **a** (42) Tenants by the entirety is limited to two married persons who cannot convey or partition their interest without destroying the tenancy.

5. **d** (42) Because the deed specifically states that Burt and Carol intended their ownership to be as tenants by the entirety, they hold the property as tenants by the entirety.

6. **c** (41) Common property or community property is not recognized in Massachusetts. It is a system of property ownership based on the theory that each spouse has equal interest in the property acquired by the efforts of either spouse during the marriage.

7. **a** (43) A tenant residing in a building that is being converted to condominiums shall be given the chance to purchase the unit he or she occupied at terms equal to or better than those offered to the general public.

8. **c** (42–43) A cooperative owner purchases shares in the corporation that holds title to the building.

9. **b** (44) Time-share property is considered a single parcel for purposes of assessment and taxation.

10. **a** (43) Condominium ownerships combine mixed forms of ownership such as joint tenancy with an estate in common. Both forms of ownership, however, are fee simple estates.

11. **d** (43) In Massachusetts the procedure for offering a unit for sale to the tenants of a building being converted to condominiums requires the owner to provide a signed purchase and sales agreement to the tenant and give to the tenant 90 days to sign the agreement and accept the offer.

CHAPTER 5

1. **a** (47–48) In a deed, a street address alone is not considered a sufficient description of a parcel of land.

2. **a** (47) A metes-and-bounds description starts at a well-marked point of beginning, follows the boundaries of the land, and returns to the point of beginning so that the parcel of land is completely enclosed.

3. **c** (47–48) A licensed surveyor is the only one qualified to provide the data for a metes-and-bounds description.

4. **c** (49) Lot 12 with 150 feet has the greatest amount of frontage on Jasmine Lane.

5. **c** (49) Lots 1, 14, and 15 on Goodrich Boulevard and lot 15 on Jasmine street have utility easements.

6. **c** (49) As indicated by the arrow pointing north, both Carney and Goodrich Boulevard run north and south.

7. **d** (49) Block A lot 3 has only 30 feet of frontage on Jasmine.

8. **c** (49) Lots 1, 2, 3, and 15 on Block A are outlined using a metes-and-bounds description.

9. **c** (49) Lot 8, Block A has street exposure on Wolf Road, Carney Street, and Jasmine Lane

10. **b** (49) Based on the description given, the parcel of land described is one fourth of the total lot. The total lot size is 120 ft. × 90 ft. = 10,800 sq. ft., and 10,800 ÷ 4 = 2,700 sq. ft.

CHAPTER 6

1. **a** (51) Every town and city raises revenue through a property tax to fund their budgets. Each, therefore, is responsible for assessing property owners and collecting the taxes.

2. **c** (51) All property within a community is assessed at the same time at 100 percent of its full cash value or fair market value.

3. **d** (52) If no redemption is made within two years from the date of the tax sale, an owner can start action to obtain title to the land.

4. **c** (52) The new owner can bring an action in the land court to register the title and confirm ownership.

5. **a** (52) A municipal lean certificate is obtained from the local tax collector.

6. **a** (52) The owner has one year right of redemption from the date of the tax sale to redeem the property.

7. **d** (53) Contractors or subcontractors who provide services without a written contract can claim a mechanic's lien for up to 30 days' work during the 90 days preceding recording.

8. **c** (53) The contractor or subcontractor has 90 days after the recording of the Statement of Account.
9. **c** (52) The ability to file a mechanic's lien extends only to suppliers and laborers and not homeowners.
10. **b** (53) The value of the work protected by the lien is $500 × 22 days = $11,000.
11. **b** (54) the Condominium Super Lien law allows the condominium association to collect up to six months of fees after taxes and municipal debts have been paid but before any other mortgage obligations.

CHAPTER 7

1. **a** (56) The statute of frauds requires a contract for the sale of real estate be in writing to be enforceable.
2. **a** (56) In Massachusetts, a person becomes of age and can be held responsible for his or her contracts upon reaching 18 years of age.
3. **d** (56) A closing date is not required to be part of a written memorandum. A description of the premises, the identity of the parties and their signatures, and consideration are all required under the statute of frauds.
4. **d** (67) Once the contract is signed, Roberto has the right to become the owner or to have the title transferred.
5. **c** (57) Massachusetts License Law requires that all brokers deposit escrow monies immediately upon the pendency of a transaction. *Pendency* is the term used in license law as a way of helping the licensee understand that as soon as a property goes under agreement the monies must be deposited.
6. **d** (67) As stated in question #4 above: Once a contract is signed, the buyer has the right to become the owner or to have the title transferred.
7. **b** (67) A liquidated damages clause permits the seller to retain all or part of the earnest money deposit as liquidated damages in the event of the buyer's default.
8. **d** (57) Bob is required by law to deposit all monies received on behalf of a buyer or seller into an escrow account. By depositing the money into his personal account, he is in violation of the license law for commingling funds. Bob should have discussed with the parties whether they wanted the monies deposited into an interest-bearing account or noninterest-bearing account.
9. **b** (67) If the contract stipulated that in the event of a default by the buyer, the seller and broker may keep the earnest money deposit then they may do so. The house can be put back on the market, providing all parties are in agreement.
10. **c** (67–68) Installment contracts are seldom used in Massachusetts because this type of transaction carries a high level of risk.

CHAPTER 8

1. **d** (74) When a person dies without a will, they die intestate. The property of a person who dies without a will (intestate) passes to his or her heirs according to the laws of descent and distribution.
2. **a** (73) Although a witness does not have a right to read a will that they are witnessing, any devise or legacy given to a witness is void.

3. **c** (72–73) Transferring of a property by deed is considered voluntary because the grantor is electing to make the transfer.

4. **a** (72) A quitclaim deed transfers only whatever right, title, and interest the grantor has in the property and warrants that the premises are free of all encumbrances made by the grantor.

5. **d** (71) Recording is only mandatory in the case of registered land and is optional for nonregistered land.

6. **a** (72–73) To acquire land by adverse possession, the use must be without the permission of the owner.

7. **c** (73) The sales price of $203,500 ÷ $500 = 407 × $2.28 = $927.96.

8. **a** (73) $150,800 − $40,000 = $110,800 ÷ 500 = 221.6 or 222 × $2.28 = $506.16

9. **c** (72) Grantors (sellers) who warrant only against claims of persons by, through, or under themselves are transferring property by a quitclaim deed.

10. **c** (71) One of the requirements of a valid deed is that delivery be made to the grantee (buyer).

11. **b** (72) When property transfers by a quitclaim deed, the grantors warrant only against claims of persons by, through, or under themselves. Therefore Mary cannot be forced to pay any claim made against the property based on Ollie's previous ownership.

12. **c** (73–74) In Massachusetts, when a person dies without a will (intestate), the statutory distribution of the estate when a person is married with children is one-half goes to the surviving spouse and one-half is divided between the children or descendants of a deceased child.

13. **d** (73–74) In Massachusetts, if a person is not married, has no children, and dies without a will, the statutory distribution of the estate will be 100 percent to father or mother, brother or sisters, or other relatives. Therefore Doug's estate will go to his parents, and Darryl's will escheat to Massachusetts because he has no relatives.

CHAPTER 9

1. **b** (76) Whenever registered land is transferred, a new certificate of title is issued to the new owner.

2. **b** (78) In Massachusetts, the buyer customarily pays for a title search as part of his or her closing costs.

3. **a** (78) Once a "suit to quiet title" has been concluded and the rightful owner is determined from that day forward, the land court certificate provides evidence of title without the need for an additional search of public records.

4. **c** (78–79) Title insurance provides the policyholder with protection from losses that might arise based on defects in the title that might have occurred prior to the policy being issued.

5. **c** (77) All instruments in writing affecting any estate, right, title, or interest in land are usually recorded with the Registry of Deeds of the county in which the land is located.

CHAPTER 10

1. **c** (82) The Board of Registration of Real Estate Brokers and Salespersons was created to administer the license law.
2. **b** (82) Any person who applies for a salesperson's license must provide proof that he or she has completed 24 hours of classroom instruction in real estate subjects approved by the board.
3. **a** (85) Any salesperson who associates with a broker must have a valid, active salesperson's license.
4. **a** (85) Upon the death of a sole proprietor, the board will issue a temporary license good for one year from the broker's date of death.
5. **b** (84) When a license is issued to a corporation, at least one officer or partner must obtain a broker's license in his or her own name, and that officer is designated to perform all real estate activities.
6. **c** (86–87) Lenny has committed six violations of the Massachusetts License Law: (1) Lenny obtained his license fraudulently; (2) he does not maintain a usual place of business within the commonwealth because his only office is in New Hampshire; (3) he did not prominently display his license as required; (4) he did not disclose that he is the owner of the house as required; (5) he commingled the earnest money into his wife's checking account; (6) he committed blockbusting by soliciting listings based on the potential change in value of properties due to the Feldspars' ethnic and religious beliefs.
7. **c** (86) Soliciting residential properties for sale is a normal part of a licensees job.
8. **d** (86) Upon receipt of a verified, written complaint, the board will hold a hearing to review the facts. Should it be determined that the licensee has violated any part of the license law, the board may suspend, revoke, or refuse to renew their license.
9. **c** (88) All money received by the broker that belongs to another party must be deposited in a fiduciary bank account, called an *escrow account*, maintained by the broker as a depository for funds unless otherwise agreed to in writing.
10. **b** (85) A licensed broker must promptly notify the board of any changes in his or her place of business (30 days). Failure to do so is grounds for revocation of the broker's license.
11. **c** (89) All offers must be presented forthwith to the property owner. It is up to the owner to decide if an offer is too low.
12. **d** (86–87) The first time a broker is found guilty of discriminatory practices, he or she will receive a suspension of 60 days. If the violation occurs within two years of the previous violation, then the suspension shall be for a period of 90 days.

CHAPTER 11

1. **c** (94) When an person in Massachusetts purchases a property, the title is "split" between the mortgagee (bank), who takes legal title to the property, and the mortgagor (owner), who takes equitable title. This "splitting" of title makes Massachusetts a title theory state.

2. **b** (94) A mortgagor (owner) who grants property to a mortgagee (bank) uses a document similar to a warranty deed. This document contains provisions for the mortgagor (owner) to get the property back by fulfilling certain conditions, such as pay back the money borrowed with interest, keep the property insured, pay the taxes, keep the property in good repair, and so on.

3. **d** (96) An amortized mortgage loan in Massachusetts is referred to as a direct reduction loan. A fixed amount is paid on the principal each month while the amount that is applied to the interest varies.

4. **c** (96) In Massachusetts, prior to a foreclosure sale the property must be advertised once a week for three weeks.

5. **c** (96) The advertisement must be in the general circulation newspaper published in the county in which the property is located.

6. **d** (96) Prior to the foreclosure sale, the borrower can cure all faults; once a foreclosure sale has occurred, however, the borrower has no redemption period.

7. **d** (96) After a mortgage foreclosure sale has occurred and all debts relative to the mortgage have been paid (loan, interests, and court cost), the remaining monies, if any, will accrue to the mortgagor (owner).

8. **d** (96) The provision in a mortgage that permits the bank to demand that the borrower pay in full the amount of the loan in the event the borrower defaults is an *acceleration clause*. This provision must be stated in the mortgage; otherwise, the right does not exist.

CHAPTER 12

1. **c** (98) A lease for more than one year must be in writing in order to satisfy the statute of frauds.

2. **a** (98) Typically a lease follows the property from owner to owner; however, a lease that runs for seven years or more must be written, acknowledged, and recorded, or the validity will be restricted to the original landlord.

3. **a** (98) If rent is due and payable on the 1st of the month and the landlord has not received the rent, the landlord cannot simply seize the property. The landlord must give two weeks' written notice to the tenant, who can prevent eviction by paying all overdue rent, plus expenses, at any time during the two-week period.

4. **b** (98) John and Sally have one rental period or a minimum of 30 days after the landlord gives them the notice to quit.

5. **b** (99) The tenants right of quiet enjoyment entitles them to possess the property without interruption or interference from the landlord during the term of the lease.

6. **c** (99) A landlord who interferes with a tenants right of quiet enjoyment may be subject to a fine and imprisonment, as well as damages of up to three months' rent.

7. **c** (106–7) In Massachusetts a landlord cannot collect a security deposit that exceeds one month's rent.

8. **a** (107) The security deposit must be kept in a bank within the Commonwealth of Massachusetts.

9. **a** (98) The owner of rented space is called the *landlord* or *lessor*.

10. **a** (107) After the termination of a lease, the landlord has 30 days to return the security deposit, plus interest but minus any cost to repair damages made by the tenant, if any. If the landlord has deducted damages, the landlord must provide to the tenant a detailed, itemized list of the damages and repair cost supported by bills or receipts.
11. **c** (108) The Massachusetts Consumer Protection Act regulates the rights and obligations of landlords and tenants.
12. **d** (106) At the commencement of a lease, the landlord may collect first and last month's rent as well as a security deposit equal to one month's rent for a total of three months rent in advance.

CHAPTER 13

1. **b** (111) Appraisers are required to be certified or licensed by the state of Massachusetts unless the transaction is not federally related.
2. **a** (111) In Massachusetts an appraiser is required to be a certified general; certified residential; licensed; or trainee appraiser.
3. **d** (111) A licensed real estate broker or salesperson may provide to a prospective seller their "opinion of value" but may not call it an appraisal.
4. **b** (111–12) A state certified appraiser may appraise any type of property, while a state certified residential appraiser may appraise only residential property.
5. **b** (112) A real estate appraiser examination, which is taken only once, includes real estate law, theory of depreciation, methods of capitalization, and economics.
6. **c** (112–13) Both conviction of a felony and fraud are reasons for revocation of an appraiser license.

CHAPTER 14

1. **b** (115) In Massachusetts, each city and town develops its own city/town plan and zoning ordinances.
2. **c** (115) The Smiths must apply for a variance showing a hardship created by the existing requirement.
3. **b** (115) The Zoning Board of Appeals will hear objections from any residential property owner who feels their property has been improperly zoned.
4. **d** (116) Planning and subdivision controls are the two major functions of local and regional planning boards.
5. **a** (116) Subdivisions are defined as land divided into two or more lots that do not front on a public or approved road.
6. **b** (116) A subdivider looks for the highest and best use of the land. Subdivision controls have to do with safety and protection of the residents of the subdivision.
7. **a** (116) The Uniform Building Code is a national code that has been adopted by many states to regulate residential, commercial, and industrial construction. Massachusetts also has a state building code (780 CMR) that is consistent with the common code format of the national code. In addition most municipalities have their own local building codes. When a conflict exists, local codes are typically superseded by state and national codes.

8. **a** (117) The "antisnob" law, also known as the Massachusetts Comprehensive Permit Law, was created to increase the supply and improve the regional distribution of low-income and moderate-income housing despite local zoning bylaws.

9. **c** (118) Subdividers usually place restrictions on the use of subdivision lots to benefit all the lot owners. These restrictions will expire after 30 years unless a specific time frame is stated in the covenants of the deed or in a separate declaration.

10. **c** (118) A restriction that is not popular with the property owners is not in itself sufficient reason for a court to refuse to enforce a subdivision restriction. The party looking to have the restriction removed must demonstrate that the restriction is unenforceable for one or more reasons, such as the "restriction interferes with the highest and best use of the property"; "the changes in the neighborhood have frustrated the purpose of the restriction"; "the general plan not longer exists"; and so on.

CHAPTER 15

1. **c** (120) Veteran's status, marital status, and persons receiving public assistance are protected classes in Massachusetts. The act of filing bankruptcy is not a protected class.

2. **c** (120–21) Refusing to sell to someone simply because they own a foreign car is not a discriminatory act. However refusing to sell to someone based on their ethnicity (Welsh descent), their religious beliefs (Roman Catholic), or race (rich white guy) does violate the Massachusetts fair housing laws because each of theses groups is a protected class.

3. **d** (120–21) Bob should refuse the listing. If Bob were to accept the listing, he would be participating in an illegal act of discrimination and both Bob and Mr. Smith would be in violation of the Massachusetts Fair Housing Law.

4. **b** (122) Two-family, owner-occupied residences are exempt from Massachusetts antidiscrimination laws providing the owner does not use a real estate agent to rent the unit, does not use discriminatory advertising, and does not discriminate against persons who receive public or rental assistance.

5. **c** (120) Both handicap status and sexual orientation are protected classes under the Massachusetts antidiscrimination laws.

6. **a** (122) It is permissible to ask an applicant's age to determine creditworthiness providing that no negative weight is given to Sam's application based on his age. No person(s) can be refused a mortgage simply because they are over the age of 62.

7. **b** (122–23) Because an owner is not required to modify more than 10 percent of the units in his or her property, the maximum number of units Larry would be required to modify is three.

8. **a** (123) Because Massachusetts regulations are "substantially equivalent to the federal fair housing laws," all fair housing complaints are referred to and investigated by the Massachusetts Commission Against Discrimination.

9. **b** (124) Under Massachusetts License Laws, any licensees found in violation of Massachusetts Fair Housing Laws will have their licenses suspended for a period of 60 days for the first offense. If a second violation occurs within two years, their licenses will be suspended for 90 days.

CHAPTER **16**

1. **a** (126–27) The Massachusetts Oil and Hazardous Material Release Prevention and Response Act is the state-level implementation of the federal Comprehensive Environmental Response, Compensation, and Liability Act (CERCLA).

2. **d** (128) Harry has received a legal letter under state law that says the work necessary to make the home temporarily safe from serious lead hazards has been done. The courts would find that because Harry has taken the necessary steps to make the property comply with the lead laws, he would not be found liable.

3. **b** (128, 134) Real estate agents are required to present to a prospective buyer or tenant a lead disclosure form for all properties built prior to 1978 whether or not the property has lead paint. Both owner/landlord and buyer/tenant must sign the same form.

4. **d** (147) The Brownfield Legislation, a federal law that provides funds to states and localities to clean up polluted industrial sites, became effective in 2002.

5. **c** (148) The inspection can be done up to six months after the sale.

6. **a** (149) Title V does not require septic inspections when a home is refinanced.

Index